Project Zero Frameworks for Early Childhood Education
Volume 2

Project Spectrum:
Early Learning Activities

Project Zero Frameworks for Early Childhood Education
Volume 2

Howard Gardner
David Henry Feldman
Mara Krechevsky
General Editors

Project Spectrum:
Early Learning Activities

Jie-Qi Chen
Editor

Emily Isberg
Mara Krechevsky
Contributing Editors

Teachers College • Columbia University
New York and London

National Association for the Education of
Young Children • Washington, DC

Published by Teachers College Press, 1234 Amsterdam
Avenue, New York, NY 10027

NAEYC Order #720

Grateful acknowledgment is made for permission to reprint
the following selections:

"Sensory Scavenger Hunt" from *Let Nature Be the Teacher*, by
Lucille N. Gertz. Illustrations by Nancy N. Childs. © 1993 by
Lucille N. Gertz. Reprinted by permission of the author.

"Swing Song" from *The Little Hill: Poems and Pictures by Harry
Behn*. © 1949 by Harry Behn. © renewed 1977 by Alice L.
Behn. Reprinted by permission of Maria Reiner.

Excerpts from *Movement in Early Childhood and Primary
Education* by R. Pangrazi and V. Dauer. © 1981 by Allyn &
Bacon. Reprinted/adapted by permission of Allyn & Bacon.

Excerpt from *The Moral Child* by William Damon. © 1988 by
William Damon. Reprinted by permission of the author.

ISBN 0-8077-3767-4 (paper)

Printed on acid-free paper

Manufactured in the United States of America

05 04 03 02 01 00 99 98   8 7 6 5 4 3 2 1

CONTENTS

Acknowledgments vii
Jie-Qi Chen

Overview of Project Spectrum 1
Jie-Qi Chen, Emily Isberg, and Mara Krechevsky

Mechanics and Construction Activities 23
Jie-Qi Chen

Science Activities 49
Jie-Qi Chen

Music Activities 81
Roger Dempsey

Movement Activities 107
Julie Viens

Math Activities 137
Winnifred O'Toole, Jie-Qi Chen, and Miriam Raider-Roth

Social Understanding Activities 169
Winnifred O'Toole and Jie-Qi Chen

Language Activities 195
Julie Viens

Visual Arts Activities 225
Roger Dempsey

ACKNOWLEDGMENTS

This book is the product of 9 years of research, conducted by the members of Project Spectrum from 1984 to 1993. My colleagues and I are grateful to the Spencer Foundation, the William T. Grant Foundation, and the Rockefeller Brothers Fund for funding this work.

Many people deserve appreciation and acknowledgment for the role they played in helping develop, shape, and refine this guidebook. I would like to thank all the Spectrum staff members whose research on children's cognitive development laid the groundwork for *Project Spectrum: Early Learning Activities.* I also wish to thank those researchers who wrote the individual guides: Roger Dempsey, Miriam Raider-Roth, Winnifred O' Toole, and Julie Viens. These Spectrum staff members not only assumed responsibility for drafting individual guides or sections, but also helped one other by brainstorming ideas and offering valuable comments on the activities.

Some of the activities presented here are based on Project Spectrum preschool assessment activities, developed or inspired by Lyle Davidson, Tom Hatch, Laurie Liebowitz, Ulla Malkus, Valerie Ramos-Ford, Larry Scripp, Janet Stork, Joseph Walters, Carey Wexler-Sherman, and Dennis Palmer Wolf. I am grateful for their contributions, as well as those of their collaborators and advisors. Thanks also are due to the other individuals who contributed directly to this book, including Corinne Greene, who came up with the idea of take-home activities, wrote half of them, and also drafted the list of anticipated learning center problems and remedies; Miriam Raider-Roth, for writing the rest of the take-home activities and the mini-lessons on learning center management; and the authors or originators of individual activities. These include: Connie Henry (Math); Emily Isberg (Mechanics and Construction, Science, Social Understanding); Tammy Kerouac (Mechanics and Construction); Ilyse Robbins (Visual Arts); and Tammy Mulligan, who shared many ideas that enriched the Social Understanding, Science, and Mechanics and Construction guides.

In addition, Andrea Bosch, Jill Christiansen, Jim Gray, Elise Miller, and Ilyse Robbins Mohr helped during the early stages of the project by observing and critiquing the implementation of Spectrum activities in the classroom. Ann Benjamin and Lyn Fosoli commented on and critiqued early versions of each guide. Janet Stork, Deborah Freeman, Tammy Mulligan, and Julia Snyder also provided thoughtful suggestions. Ann Benjamin provided insight and guidance in compiling the list of instructional resources for teachers; Nancy Jo Cardillo, Meredith Eppel, Kimberly Johns, Cindy Kirby, Vanessa Trien, Ed Warburton, and others shared favorite titles. All of these contributions are sincerely appreciated.

Warmest thanks also go to the Somerville public school teachers Mary Ann DeAngelis, Pam Holmes, Jean McDonagh, and Marie Kropiwnicki, who field-tested the Spectrum activities and gave us their honest and valuable criticisms; to John Davis and Wayne LaGue, formerly superintendent of schools and director of curriculum in Somerville, who generously supported Spectrum research in their district; and to the Somerville first graders who participated in the Spectrum project and enthusiastically piloted our activities.

I am most grateful to Shirley Veenema for transforming the manuscript into the skillfully laid-out book you hold in your hands, for creating a design that is as useful as it is pleasing, and for shepherding the pages through the production process. Project Spectrum's own Roger Dempsey and Andy Winther of the University Publisher's Office created the irresistible illustrations—Roger by hand, and Andy by computer. Kathy Cannon contributed the graphics that grace the beginning of each guide, as well as several drawings in the Visual Arts guide. Karen Chalfen is responsible for the careful and thorough job of proofreading.

Warmest thanks go to the two contributing editors, Mara Krechevsky and Emily Isberg. I am most grateful to Mara, director of Project Spectrum, for her wise counsel, steadfast support, and encouraging voice throughout the project. Her leadership was essential to the success of this project, from the ideas she contributed to its planning, through her effective supervision of the field studies, to her insightful suggestions and comments on the completed manuscript.

I am indebted to Emily for her superb skills in coordinating the final stage of the book and for her dedication to the quality of the project. She carefully reviewed all sections of the book, from the introduction to the lists of instructional resources, with a critical mind and discerning eye. Her keen editing, questions, suggestions, and redrafting helped pull the individual guides together into a coherent whole.

Finally, I would like to express sincere gratitude to the principal investigators of Project Spectrum, David Feldman and Howard Gardner, for their intellectual inspiration, guidance, and support. Their ideas inform all aspects of this guidebook.

Jie-Qi Chen
Cambridge, MA

Spectrum at a Glance

Three months into the first grade, Donnie's teacher already had run out of ways to reach him. He could not recognize letters, solve simple addition problems, or perform readiness activities. Even though he spent much of the day getting remedial help, his teacher expected he would have to repeat the year.

His classmate Charlie* also performed poorly in all subject areas. Beyond that, he was bored. Faced with a task, he would stare blankly at the paper, lean back in his chair, and get into mischief.

Linda, on the other hand, showed promise at the beginning of the school year, progressing competently through the unit on simple addition. But she got lost when subtraction was introduced to the class, and struggled over worksheets that were riddled with her mistakes.

Donnie, Charlie, and Linda attended a public elementary in a working-class community in the greater Boston area. By most traditional measures, they were failing at school. Nor were they alone. Approximately one fourth of the students in the city's public school system spoke English as a second language, and 8 of the 10 elementary schools received federal funding to provide special services under the Chapter I program. Many of the children were beginning school without the skills needed to succeed in a standard curriculum emphasizing reading, writing, and math.

Yet they may have had strengths in other areas, such as music, movement, or visual arts, that also are intellectual endeavors and considered valuable in the world of work. What if these children were evaluated using different measures, designed to tap abilities not usually exercised in school or examined by pencil-and-paper tests?

During the 1989–1990 school year, Donnie, Charlie, Linda, and their classmates helped field-test a series of assessment activities for Project Spectrum, a research and development project codirected by David Feldman of Tufts University and Howard Gardner of Harvard Project Zero in collaboration with the Somerville, Massachusetts public schools. The goal was to determine whether relative strengths could be identified in a first-grade, "at-risk" population, and if so, whether nurturing these strengths could help children improve their academic performance. Here is what happened.

Donnie proved more capable than any of his classmates at taking apart and re-assembling a meat grinder. He also put back together an oil pump, a feat few of the other children could match. His teacher was so amazed by his ability and concentration on the task that she spent the next 3 nights designing an assembly area that would later be implemented in her classroom. She also made Donnie the classroom's "expert fixer," enabling him to experience, for the first time, a feeling of success and self-worth at school.

Charlie showed himself a gifted storyteller when asked to create a tale using a "storyboard," a felt-covered board outfitted with toy figures and other props. Although schools generally value language abilities, they tend to emphasize written expression; thus, Charlie's oral abilities had escaped notice. To build on this strength, Charlie's teacher asked him and his classmates to make their own storyboards, a project that captivated the usually-disinterested student.

Linda experienced a moment of insight while playing the Bus Game. In this game designed by Spectrum researchers, children must keep count as a toy bus makes its way

_____

* Names of the Spectrum students have been changed to protect their privacy.

around a game board, taking on and discharging cardboard passengers. As she used chips to symbolize passengers getting on and off the bus, Linda suddenly remarked, "Is this take-away?" Her subtraction worksheets improved afterward, showing that she did indeed "get it."

These experiences convinced us that the Spectrum approach could be used not only to identify children's strengths, but also to engage them in the school curriculum. In each case, the teacher used her newfound insight into the child's abilities or interests to modify her lesson plans to meet more fully the student's needs. For Donnie, that meant adding a new learning center to the classroom; for Charlie, including an oral element in language arts projects; and for Linda, illustrating key mathematical concepts with more manipulatives. Presumably, classmates with similar interests and learning styles also would reap the benefits as the teacher expanded her repertoire.

The Early Years

Project Spectrum was founded in 1984 to develop an innovative approach to assessment and curriculum for the preschool and early primary years. The work was based on the conviction that each child exhibits a distinctive profile of different abilities, or spectrum of intelligences. The power of these intelligences is not fixed, but can be enhanced by educational opportunity and an environment rich in stimulating materials and activities. Once a child's areas of strength have been identified, teachers can use the information to design an individualized educational program.

The approach grew from the theoretical work of David Feldman and Howard Gardner. In his 1983 book, *Frames of Mind: The Theory of Multiple Intelligences*, Gardner challenged the traditional psychological view of intelligence as a single capacity. He proposed that all individuals possess at least seven independent intelligences — linguistic, logical-mathematical, musical, spatial, bodily-kinesthetic, interpersonal, and intrapersonal — each with its own symbol system and methods of problem solving. *

Feldman's theory of nonuniversal development, presented in his 1980 book, *Beyond Universals in Cognitive Development*, challenged the view that intellectual development is virtually inevitable and will occur in all children regardless of background and experience. Instead, he proposed that cognitive structures must be built gradually and independently in each domain, a process that requires sustained work and favorable environmental conditions.

For the first 4 years, the goal of the project was to develop a new means of assessing the cognitive abilities of preschool children. With support from the Spencer Foundation, our Spectrum research team devised a set of activities (including the assembly, storyboard, and Bus Game exercises described above) that can be used to assess children as they play games and perform tasks using tools and materials appropriate to the discipline. These activities do not require children to use the written word. Thus they tap directly into a wider range of cognitive and stylistic strengths than are addressed by traditional assessment instruments. The activities are described in *Project Spectrum: Preschool Assessment Handbook*, published by in tandem with this volume by Teachers College Press.

In the 5th year, Project Spectrum received support from the William T. Grant Foundation to examine whether these assessment techniques were appropriate for older children (kindergarten and first-grade levels) who were at risk for school failure. Students were identified as at-risk on the basis of teacher observations of classroom behavior and performance, as well as students' scores on a battery of standardized reading, arithmetic, and

---

* Gardner has recently proposed the existence of an eighth intelligence, that of the naturalist (Gardner, 1998).

readiness tests. Our research team worked with Donnie's, Charlie's, and Linda's two classrooms in Somerville, Massachusetts, to develop an age-appropriate, streamlined battery of Spectrum assessment activities. After conducting a series of formal evaluations with this instrument, we found that relative strengths indeed could be identified among the target student group.

In 1990, Project Spectrum received funding from the Grant Foundation to work with four classrooms in different schools in the same community. The goal of the Learning Center Project was to find out if the Spectrum approach could be used in a public school setting to promote academic achievement and school adjustment. Using the assessment activities as a starting point, we collected and developed learning activities in each of eight disciplines — language, math, movement, music, general science, mechanics and construction, social understanding, and visual arts. In addition to revealing children's strengths, the activities were designed to introduce children to the tools and basic skills of the discipline, or domain, they represented (e.g., pitch discrimination in music, observational skill in science). The activities, revised on the basis of teacher feedback, are presented here in eight individual guides, one for each of the domains listed above.

During this project, the activities were conducted at learning centers—distinct areas, such as a naturalist's corner or woodworking area—where children could use stimulating materials to perform specified activities or independently explore the domain. Teachers operated one or more learning centers for at least 2 hours, twice a week, throughout the year. They carefully observed their students at work, took notes, and with the support of Spectrum researchers, tried to adapt their curriculum to the children's strengths and interests.

By the end of the program, we were able to identify areas of strength for 13 of the 15 students considered at risk for school failure, based on the competence and interest they exhibited at learning center tasks. Although one year was too short a time to effect long-lasting academic change, we did find that the children consistently enjoyed their Spectrum experiences and were highly motivated to participate. When working in their skill areas, these children showed an enthusiasm, self-confidence, and cooperative spirit their teachers had not observed before.

The teachers emphasized the benefits of learning more about their students' strengths. Armed with more and more positive information about the children most at risk, the teachers were better able to involve them in the academic program. Each teacher devised her own, creative ways to build bridges between children's identified areas of strength and other areas of learning.

In other efforts, we have expanded Spectrum's scope beyond school walls. With support from the Rockefeller Brothers Fund, we collaborated with a children's museum and a preschool to develop sets of classroom-based units and interactive museum exhibits that would reinforce each other, drawing on the unique features of both learning environments. We also established a mentorship program to give children opportunities to work with adults who shared an area of intellectual strength or interest. Ten mentors, including park rangers, urban planners, a musician, and a poet, visited the classroom once a week throughout the academic year, conducting hands-on activities that they devised with the support of Spectrum researchers.

During its 9-year history, Project Spectrum has proved to have a wide range of applications. Thus, we believe that Spectrum is best thought of not as a discrete program or set of activities, but as a theory-based approach that emphasizes the importance of recognizing and nurturing children's diverse cognitive abilities. This approach has been used to help to bring about important changes in teachers' teaching and students' learning.

Putting the Activities in Context

When we describe our research at workshops around the country, teachers generally ask us to share the learning center activities. At first we were reluctant to do so, for fear that practitioners would focus on the activities themselves instead of on the framework in which they are embedded, or that they would expect a full-fledged curriculum, which we do not offer. The activities are in no way intended to substitute for a systematic approach to basic skills or other facets of the kindergarten or first-grade curriculum. Instead, Spectrum can be considered as a program for building bridges: between the child's curiosity and the school curriculum; between the child's strengths and the intellectual demands of school; between classroom endeavors and the world outside. The activities are simply vehicles to help teachers and students travel along these roads.

Numerous requests, however, have convinced us that some teachers might find the activities compiled in this guide useful as examples of different ways to look at their students and address their needs. We hope teachers can use them to supplement their own curricula, expand into new territories they do not usually teach, or integrate instruction with assessment. The activities also can serve as catalysts, providing ideas to help teachers develop their own projects or find ways to reach children who are not responding to a more traditional, language-centered approach. We encourage classroom teachers to adapt these activities to their own situations, teaching styles, and class composition.

It is important to point out that whereas some of the activities described in this guide were created by Spectrum researchers (including the projects based on the original preschool assessment activities), others were adapted from existing curricular sources. We purposely built upon popular activities in the hope that teachers would see that they do not need to toss out their lessons and start anew; instead, they can take existing practices and add the Spectrum perspective, which we will explain in greater detail in the following pages. We hope to model ways that teachers can re-purpose familiar, tried-and-true activities so that they gain new insights into their students, and students gain more enthusiasm for, and pride in, their schoolwork.

The activities should not be considered in isolation, but in the context of a framework that encompasses four steps: (1) introducing children to a wide range of learning areas, (2) identifying children's areas of strength, (3) nurturing the strengths that are identified, and (4) bridging children's strengths to other subject areas and academic performances.

Introducing Children to a Wide Range of Learning Areas

According to the theory of multiple intelligences (MI theory), all individuals exhibit each of the intelligences, but they differ in the extent to which these intelligences are developed, presumably for both hereditary and environmental reasons. Rich educational experiences are essential for the development of each person's particular configuration of interests and abilities. Students who have trouble with some academic subjects, such as reading or math, are not necessarily inadequate in all areas. They may shine, as Donnie did, when asked to put together the pieces of an appliance, or to sing back a song the teacher has just performed. The Spectrum framework tries to provide these students with the same opportunities to demonstrate their strengths that are provided routinely to students who rely on their linguistic and logical-mathematical intelligences.

Interestingly enough, intelligences that are relatively neglected by the school curriculum, such as bodily-kinesthetic, spatial, and interpersonal, may be highly valued in the workplace.

Basketball players and other athletes are not the only professionals who use motor skills to solve problems (and bring home a paycheck); so do assembly workers and surgeons, actresses and carpenters, mechanics and sculptors, to name just a few. These individuals also need highly developed spatial skills, as do pilots, architects, and engineers. And while interpersonal skills may be key elements in some careers, including teaching and sales, the ability to understand, cooperate with, negotiate with, and persuade others is critical to success in almost any endeavor. It stands to reason that not only the individual child, but also society as a whole, will benefit from an educational approach that recognizes and cultivates the different intelligences.

In introducing children to a wide range of areas, Spectrum also tries to engage students in real-world tasks. The concept of *end state* was used to focus on skills and abilities needed for successful performance in adult roles, particularly in the world of work. To develop oral language skills, children might conduct an interview like a television journalist; to develop written language skills, they might write a letter or "publish" their poems in a class book. Math activities might include opportunities to make change at a pretend bakery, or to devise different ways of measuring ingredients for cookies. Thus, children can relate the skills they are learning in school to activities they perform, or wish to perform, in everyday life.

During the Learning Center Project, Spectrum systematically introduced children to the eight domains of knowledge mentioned earlier: language, mathematics, movement, music, science, mechanics and construction, social understanding, and visual arts. These eight domains were selected in an effort to translate Gardner's seven intelligences and Feldman's developmental domains into a format appropriate to children of early elementary age. The Spectrum learning areas were tailored to the school curricula to make it easier for teachers to incorporate the activities into their lesson plans.

The concepts of *intelligence* and *domain* are closely related but different. Intelligence is the ability to solve problems or fashion products valued by a particular culture or community. It is a biological potential that, to a great extent, is shaped by cultural and educational influences. A domain is a body of knowledge within a culture, such as mathematics, art, basketball, or medicine. Performance in a domain may require more than one intelligence; children playing handmade instruments during a music activity, for example, may draw on both musical and bodily-kinesthetic intelligences. By the same token, a single intelligence may be deployed in many domains. For example, children may use spatial intelligence for figuring out how to move an object using a lever (mechanics and construction) as well as for creating designs out of string (visual arts).

The learning centers were designed to give all the children a roughly equal opportunity to explore all the available materials in all eight domains. For some of the children, working directly with these materials offered a chance to demonstrate understandings not revealed by paper-and-pencil tasks, such as the ability to match a pitch or build a tall tower. For other children, who might not have coloring markers and building blocks at home, the materials offered a chance to discover new learning arenas in which they might be deeply curious or perhaps could even excel.

Some teachers have pointed out that their schools do not have sufficient funds to purchase the materials suggested in this guide. These teachers might take a highly selective approach, focusing on those activities and materials that "fill in the gaps" and give children a chance to explore domains they might not encounter otherwise. We urge them to ask parents to contribute materials, from no-longer-needed calculators to plastic containers, and to seek out other sources for supplies, such as recycling centers, children's museums, local businesses, and discount stores. This said, we must underline that the materials are not effective in and of themselves; what matters is the way in which teachers use the materials to observe and gain insight into their students when they are actively engaged in their work.

Other teachers have asked us about the differences between classrooms based on the Spectrum approach and other quality or developmentally appropriate early childhood classrooms. These two types of classroom share certain features, such as a variety of hands-on materials, different learning corners or centers, and the element of student choice. What distinguishes the Spectrum classroom is the variety of domains available and their systematic use for identifying and supporting children's areas of strength and interest. Guided by the Spectrum framework, the teachers are continually expanding their repertoire to reach an ever wider and more diverse range of learners.

Identifying Children's Areas of Strength

A child is constantly humming in class. One teacher thinks, "How annoying! Why can't Michael focus on his work and stop disrupting the class?" Another thinks, "Michael seems interested in music. Maybe I could try to set a counting game to music, or catch his attention by introducing a lesson with a song." Instead of focusing exclusively on her student's weaknesses or deficits, the second teacher is trying to identify and nurture his strengths, an important element of the Spectrum approach. It is our belief that every child has relative strengths, viewed either in the context of the class as a whole, or in the context of his or her individual intellectual profile.

Teachers can identify children's areas of strength both through formal assessments and informal observations such as the one above. Just as children's learning is an ongoing process, so should be assessment. When assessment is naturally embedded in the learning environment, it allows teachers to observe children's performances in various situations over time. Such observations make it possible to gain multiple samples of a child's ability, document the dynamics and variation of the child's performances within a domain and across domains, and thus more accurately portray the child's intellectual profile.

The Spectrum approach also weaves together instruction and assessment. Children come to school with different environmental and educational experiences; when teachers assess their ability to perform a specific task, they also are assessing their subjects' familiarity with the materials and their prior experience in the domain. For example, children who have little experience with art materials are less likely to demonstrate strengths in the art area. Therefore, when they first are introduced to a domain, children need time to explore and experiment freely with materials. The more structured activities that they attempt next can serve both instructional and assessment purposes; children become more skillful in their use of tools and materials, and teachers can observe them at work on an ongoing basis.

Many teachers gather information through informal observations, but they are not always clear about what they are looking for. As a result, their observations may have only limited use for planning learning experiences. Spectrum maintains that observations are most informative when they are domain specific. For example, rather than observing a child's fine-motor skills, the teacher might determine whether these skills differ when the child is writing or building a structure. Instead of examining whether or not the child plays with classmates, the teacher might take a close look at what kind of social role the child assumes (e.g., leader, caregiver, or friend) while engaging in group play.

To assist teachers in domain-specific observations, we developed a set of "key abilities" for each domain. We attempted to identify those abilities crucial to success in the domain, such as numerical reasoning and logical problem solving in math, or body control and sensitivity to rhythm in movement. The key abilities, listed in the front of each activities guide, were developed on the basis of empirical research, review of the literature, and consultation with experts in the field.

In the Learning Center Project, the teachers and Spectrum researchers identified children's strengths on the basis of their demonstrated interest and competence. Interest was assessed in terms of the frequency with which a child chose a particular learning center and the length of involvement in that learning center. Competence was evaluated in terms of the key abilities. These key abilities were specific enough to enable teachers to examine students' work and determine their level of competence in a particular domain. Using these lists as guides, teachers could jot down informal observations while children were working independently at the learning centers, and also evaluate the work itself when projects or units were completed.

The key abilities could also be used in other contexts, such as analyzing or reviewing children's portfolios for student reports or parent conferences. For example, instead of saying, "Look, Tom has made great progress in art during the year," a teacher could evaluate and describe the artwork in Tom's portfolio according to a range of artistic features, such as use of color, spatial orientation, and representational skills (see list of key abilities in the Visual Arts guide).

In addition to looking for children's strengths in the assessment process, we also examined their "working styles." Table 1 presents a working styles checklist developed by Spectrum for observing preschool children. We use the term *working style* to describe the way in which a child interacts with the materials of a subject area; the child, for example, may appear persistent, confident, or easily distracted. Working style refers to the process dimension of the child's work, rather than the product.

Our research has indicated that children's working styles may vary according to the task: A child with strength in the science area might exhibit surprising patience when conducting experiments, but become easily frustrated at a game of hopscotch. Analyzing whether a child's difficulty with a particular task is rooted in style or content might help a teacher individualize instruction. For example, the teacher might be able to identify situations or domains in which a child requires very specific directions in order to perform, takes the initiative and thus is able to work with minimal supervision, or is easily distracted and might benefit from activities that can be completed quickly.

Nurturing Children's Areas of Strength

Once a child's area of strength has been identified, teachers can provide the support needed to enhance and develop that strength. Many teachers committed to developmentally appropriate instruction recognize the individual differences of their students and set up their classrooms so that, to the extent possible, children can learn at their own pace. These teachers may build choice time into their daily schedules so that children can select activities based on their current interests. They may use open-ended assignments (such as writing and illustrating a story, or creating a structure out of toothpicks) that can be successfully performed by children of varying abilities. They may make available a range of materials, for example by putting books of varying difficulty in the reading area for children to select based on their reading skills.

The Spectrum approach encourages teachers to go a few steps further, helping them match their curriculum to the strengths and interests they have discovered in their class. The children, for example, may not only choose from available materials, but also influence what materials are made available. For example, if a child demonstrates a special interest and strength in the mechanical learning area, her teacher might try to provide more tools, machines, or building materials to encourage her to explore the area further. Using the key

TABLE 1: WORKING STYLES CHECKLIST

Child _____   Observer _____

Activity _____   Date   _____

Please mark which working styles are distinctive during your observation. Mark only when obvious; one from each pair need not be checked. Please include comments and anecdotes whenever possible and write a general, overall phrase that best describes how the child approaches the activity. Star (*) any outstanding working style.

Child is   Comments

    easily engaged in activity   _____

    reluctant to engage in activity   _____

    confident   _____

    tentative   _____

    playful   _____

    serious   _____

    focused   _____

    distractible   _____

    persistent   _____

    frustrated by activity   _____

    impulsive   _____

    reflective   _____

    apt to work slowly   _____

    apt to work quickly   _____

    conversational   _____

    quiet   _____

    responds to visual ___ auditory ___ kinesthetic ___ cues

    demonstrates planful approach   _____

    brings personal strength to activity _____

    finds humor in content area   _____

    uses materials in unexpected ways   _____

    shows pride in accomplishment   _____

    attends to detail; is observant   _____

    is curious about materials   _____

    shows concern over "correct" answer   _____

    focuses on interaction with adult   _____

abilities as a guide, the teacher might also can develop activities and projects to further develop the child's particular abilities, knowledge, and skills.

The teacher might try additional strategies that not only extend the child's skills, but also give her a feeling of success and recognition. One such strategy is inviting the child to act as a group leader in her area of strength. The child can lead classmates to the learning center or area, demonstrate an activity, serve as a resource, manage materials and cleanup, or help to train the next leader. As the child assumes additional responsibility, practices skills, and receives positive reinforcement, her area of strength is nurtured and developed.

Information about children's strengths also should be shared with parents. In the course of our research, we identified strengths in several children (in science, visual arts, music, and social understanding) that neither their teachers nor families had recognized previously. Once aware of these strengths, parents can provide positive reinforcement and enrichment, such as the opportunity to plant a garden, visit a museum, or perhaps even to take music lessons. Teachers also may be able to suggest to parents activities they can do with their children, including the take-home activities listed at the end of each guide in this book.

It is important to note that nurturing children's strengths does not mean "labeling" them or limiting their experience in other areas. A child known as a willing helper should not be expected to help all the time; a child with strong language skills should be encouraged to take risks and experiment in areas where she feels less comfortable. A wide range of learning experiences will enable children to manifest and develop fully their potentials and interests. Within this framework, recognizing and reinforcing children's strengths helps them develop self-confidence and self-esteem, as well as positive feelings about school.

Bridging Children's Strengths to Other Subject Areas

The fourth and final step in the Spectrum approach involves using the child's experiences in her areas of strength to lead her into a wider range of learning areas. We refer to this process as *bridging* (see also Feuerstein, 1980). We recognize the importance of mastering basic skills in the early elementary years. The elementary through high school curriculum is built on the assumption that children have mastered certain fundamentals, and those children who have not will experience increased frustration and feelings of failure as the years go by. However, we believe that there are multiple approaches to the mastery of basic skills. Some children might benefit from strategies that rely heavily on drill and practice to overcome deficits in reading or math. Other children might be more responsive to an alternative strategy, such as bridging, designed to increase their desire to master basic skills by embedding these skills in tasks that the children perceive as meaningful and interesting.

Bridging may occur in a number of ways. These include: (a) The child discovers an area of strength, enjoys exploring it, and feels good about herself. The experience of being successful gives the child the confidence needed to enter more challenging domains. (b) The learning style particular to the child's area of strength is used as a vehicle for engaging the child in an area of challenge. For example, a musical child may find a number game more appealing if it is set to music. (c) The content of a child's area of strength is used to engage the child in other areas, particularly those central to success in school. For example, a child with mechanical interests and abilities could be asked to read and write about machines. (d) Some structural component of an area of strength is assumed to be relevant to performance in another, remote area. For example, a child sensitive to the rhythmic aspect of music might respond to rhythmic aspects of language or movement.

We believe that bridging strategies can be geared not just to an individual child, but to a class as a whole. One class, for example, may include a number of children with an interest in cars, trucks, and tools, while another class may include a number of children who learn best when movement is involved. In the latter case, the teacher might encourage children to make letter shapes with their bodies, with playdough, with paint; to act out stories and poems they are reading; or to use the storyboard and other manipulatives to make up their own stories. She might build on the children's' interests by selecting stories about athletes or sports for reading assignments, or making these stories available at choice time. In other words, the teacher is using specific insights into the class to lead them into, and keep them engaged in, the curriculum she normally covers.

Students are motivated to learn new skills and stick with a challenging problem when they find the problem interesting and meaningful. For example, a child who wants to grow vegetables may be motivated to read the instructions on the seed package or measure distance between the rows. But adults must play an active role in this and other bridging processes. Our own experience and that of others (Cohen, 1990) has shown that engaging materials and problems invite children's participation, but do not automatically enable them to develop skills. Nor do children automatically bring their strengths from one area of learning to another. Teachers must model how tools and other materials can be used, ask questions to help children reflect on their work, offer guidance when children are perplexed, and use other pedagogical techniques to help children grasp the concepts and skills embedded in the activities or projects they devise. Bridging clearly requires additional time and effort on the teacher's part, but it can pay off in feelings of accomplishment for both adult and child.

How the Activities Guides Are Organized

As explained earlier, this book is composed of eight individual activities guides in the areas of language, math, movement, music, general science, mechanics and construction, social understanding, and visual arts. It is based on the activities we developed for a 1989–1990 research project devoted to improving the academic performance of at-risk first graders in a Boston-area public school. It does not attempt to provide a year-long curriculum or an in-depth, comprehensive study of the eight domains of knowledge. Instead, it offers a sample of the different types of activities that teachers can use to gain insight into, and build upon, their students' areas of strength.

Each guide includes 15 to 20 activities. These activities were selected because they: (a) reflect a range of intelligences, (b) highlight and exercise key abilities in a designated domain, (c) involve hands-on problem solving in a meaningful context, and (d) provide information that will help teachers adapt their curriculum for individual children.

In general, each activities guide includes a combination of free-play and structured activities. Some of the structured activities are skill related; that is, they are intended to challenge children with tasks at or slightly beyond their current level of ability in a given domain. Other structured activities integrate children's varied learning experiences with the goals of the first-grade curriculum. For example, children might be asked to describe their experience with an assembly activity in journal form, so that they practice writing skills.

All eight activities guides are presented in a similar format. There is a brief introduction to the domain, including suggestions for an orientation session with students. We then describe key abilities — those abilities crucial to success in the domain. There is a brief introduction to the domain and to the activities. Suggestions are included for an orientation session and for materials that students can use for free exploration as well as for the activities. We then describe key abilities—those abilities crucial to success in the domain. Some guides include a page describing materials specially made to conduct Spectrum activities, like the Bus Game or the pretend "TV." Next appear the activities themselves.

For each activity, we list the objective, core components (the key abilities stimulated by the activity), materials, and step-by-step procedures. We often include notes to teachers at the end of the activity, suggesting variations, modifications, and extensions. The activities are designed to support both instruction and assessment. As children work, teachers can use the lists of core components as the basis for observing and documenting children's interests and abilities in different domains. To help teachers track student development, activities within a domain are organized according to key abilities in all the guides except Science, which distinguishes short experiments from activities conducted over a period of weeks or months.

To help teachers balance the size of student groups and the amount of supervision needed to implement activities, we divided the activities into four categories:

- Child-directed small-group activity: Teacher gives a brief talk or demonstration; then four to six children perform the activity on their own or together.

- Teacher-directed small-group activity: Teacher stays with a small group of children to work on the project. The rest of the class might be involved in activities they can perform without assistance.

- Child-directed large-group activity: Teacher introduces the activity and then all or half the children in the class perform it, either individually or cooperatively. The teacher's presence may be important but not necessary to implement the activity.

• Teacher-directed large group activity: Teacher supervises as the whole classroom performs the activity. Teacher's presence is critical for students to complete the task.

Finally, at the end of each activities guide we provide several "take-home activities." These take-home activities are designed to involve parents in the process of discovering and nurturing their child's areas of strength. In many cases, they correspond to classroom activities, so that the designated skills and concepts can be reinforced and practiced both at school and at home. Take-home activities are presented in a format similar to that of the classroom activities, outlining the learning goals as well as the necessary materials and procedures. Most of the materials can be found around the house.

Different Ways to Implement the Spectrum Approach

Because the Spectrum approach is based on a theory about different forms of intelligence and the different ways in which children learn, it can be incorporated into a variety of instructional practices. Although we chose to set up learning centers where children could explore specific domains of knowledge, there are many other ways teachers can integrate Spectrum ideas and activities into their curriculum. In fact, one of the most exciting aspects of the Spectrum approach is that teachers and schools across the country have adapted it to meet their community's distinctive needs.

Teachers might get a feel for the Spectrum approach by "adding on" individual activities to enrich and supplement their curriculum. If they notice that children are having a difficult time grasping a particular concept, they might try to present the concept in a variety of ways, using activities that involve movement, art, music, or other domains. By carefully observing the responses of their students, they can determine which approaches are most effective for an individual child or the class as a whole.

Spectrum can also be modified to support theme-based instruction. It offers a framework to help teachers consciously address diverse abilities as they organize a thematic unit. For example, the What Makes Bread Rise? activity in the Science guide, suggested to us by first-grade teacher Tammy Mulligan of the Eliot-Pearson Children's School (who was inspired by Bernie Zubrowski's book *Messing Around with Baking Chemistry*), could serve as the starting point for a unit on bread. Children learn about the scientific method by designing experiments to test various hypotheses about which ingredients make bread rise. As they conduct experiments, they get to use their bodies, practice the reading and math skills involved in following instructions and recording results, and develop the social skills required by working with others. Social understanding also increases as they collect family recipes and learn about the types of bread that are eaten in different cultures. As a culminating project, they might hold a bake sale, make signs and other decorations, figure out how much to charge for each loaf, and make change for purchases. All of these activities help deepen children's understanding of the process by which bread is made, a process they perceive as meaningful to their lives.

The Hospital activity in the Social Understanding guide also can be used to launch a theme-based unit. Teachers can help children convert a dramatic play corner or other area of the classroom into a pretend hospital room. Using props donated by parents, children can make up and act out stories about going to the hospital; explore stethoscopes, gauze, and other materials with medical purposes; and invent contraptions that help the bedridden call the nurse or fetch a toy. They might explore careers by visiting a hospital and talking with staff members, or by inviting parents and friends who work in a hospital to visit their class. They might think about how it feels to be in the hospital by performing creative movement activities, visiting patients, or writing them letters. They might read books about hospitals, then create their own stories, drawings, books, or songs to reflect upon what they have learned.

We would like to emphasize that not every thematic unit must exercise all the intelligences or explore all eight domains of knowledge. The activities should each serve to deepen children's understanding of, or provide a new method of entry into, the subject matter at hand. If a domain cannot be explored meaningfully in one unit, the teacher can make every effort to include it in the next.

In part to assure that all domains received "equal time," at least at first, we chose the learning center approach. Learning centers also provided an efficient way of introducing children to the fundamental principles of a variety of domains. We believe that all the domains should be explored as bodies of knowledge in their own right, not just used as vehicles for presenting challenging subject matter. In the Spectrum classrooms, the teachers set up distinct areas—tables, counters, corners—to serve as learning centers. Teachers who do not have sufficient space might store learning center materials in boxes, which individuals or groups could use and put away when they are finished.

Teachers may have many other ways of implementing the Spectrum framework, and we would welcome hearing about them. Some teachers might even wish to combine the methods discussed above. For example, one teacher in our project used learning centers to support theme-based units. During a unit on astronomy, she set up storyboards in the language center that children could use to tell stories about outer space, and encouraged students to interview each other on various topics in space exploration—an activity adapted from the Class Census in the Social Understanding guide.

Learning Center Management

Although learning centers can be found in many preschool classrooms, they are quite foreign to some first grades. Elementary teachers introducing learning centers for the first time may find that they are overwhelmed with management issues, from maintaining discipline during independent work, to helping children transition from one activity to the next, to planning so many new activities at the same time (see Table 2). Indeed, we found that management issues consumed much time and energy when the Spectrum approach was first implemented in early elementary classrooms.

To make the implementation process easier for others, we would like to share some of the solutions that the Spectrum teachers and researchers worked out together to the problems they encountered most frequently. Please regard these as "helpful hints" rather than rules. Although they are specifically geared to learning centers, they might also be helpful in other situations, such as introducing cooperative projects to children used to working individually.

• **Orientation Period.** A formal orientation period, extending for several months, may be necessary before children are comfortable with independent work. During this time, teachers may use a series of group meetings to show children materials from each of the learning centers and explain key ideas, procedures, and rules. Immediately following the group meeting, children can explore the materials that were just discussed. Teacher-directed large-group activities are well suited to the orientation period, since children will need more guidance during this time than they will later on.

The orientation period serves three purposes. First, it acquaints children with the procedures for choosing and carrying out activities in the learning centers. Second, it gives them an early opportunity to explore all of the domains, particularly those of special interest. Finally, it enables teachers to gain an initial sense of children's strengths and interests.

• **Implementing the Activities.** Following the orientation period, teachers can conduct their learning centers in a variety of ways, depending on the structure of the classroom. In the Spectrum classrooms, teachers opened two to four learning centers at least twice a week for 2 hours at a time. In addition, learning centers might be available during free-choice time, recess, before and after the regular school day, or for children who finished work early.

Teachers can gear the learning centers to helping children explore different aspects of a unit they are currently studying, or to offer material not covered at all during the school day. They can introduce a new activity to the whole class, or to a small group of children while the rest of the children work on activities that were introduced during the orientation period. Finally, teachers can invite specialists or parents into the classroom to help supervise some learning centers, such as art or music.

During the orientation period, teachers may assign children to particular centers. As the children gain more exposure and experience, teachers gradually can provide more opportunities for students to choose an area or activity for themselves. The goal is to make sure that children have the opportunity to explore all the domains. When the children become accustomed to working independently, teachers will be better able to circulate among centers to observe and work with individual children or small groups.

• **Classroom Design.** If it is possible to set aside areas of the classroom as learning centers devoted to domain-specific activities, each center might include a work surface, a display surface, and a storage area for materials. The centers can also be color coded to help children identify them and match the materials with the domain.

In terms of room arrangement, placing the science and art centers near a sink can make cleanup easier. The language and the social centers might be set up together because they share materials, as do movement and music, which both use musical recordings and instruments. If space is available, the music and movement learning centers may be placed away from the others to reduce noise level.

• **Establishing Rules.** Although the child's decision making and self-management are ultimate goals in the classroom, they can be attained more easily if teachers provide an initial structure, clear directions, and a set of rules for using the learning centers. During the orientation period, teachers can brainstorm with children to generate rules for each center. While establishing rules, teachers might mention to the children that the rules exist to help them play or work, and that if a rule doesn't work it can be changed.

Rules usually address such issues as safety, sharing materials, taking turns, limiting the number of participants, reducing noise level, and cleanup. Rules specific to each center can be written or depicted on tag board and displayed at the centers. For example, a picture of Oscar the Grouch in a trash can may illustrate a rule about cleaning up before leaving the center.

• **Mini-lessons.** Organizing, directing, and supporting 20 or more children who are performing activities in several different domains can be a monumental task for one teacher. Therefore, it is best to confront management issues as they arise during the first few months of school. Mini-lessons, as described by Lucy Calkins in *The Art of Teaching Writing* (1986), offer one way of talking about management issues with children.

Mini-lessons are usually short discussions or demonstrations, 5 to 10 minutes long, about specific topics related to learning center use. These discussions can help children review rules and procedures, and also understand their role in the learning process. Teachers can give children a sense of involvement and responsibility by posing such questions as: How do you know when you are finished with an activity? What do you do when you are finished? How do team members help each other during learning center time? Examples of mini-lessons are included in Table 3.

• **Activity Leaders and Cooperative Learning.** Teachers can train children to take turns as activity leaders. As previously discussed, an activity leader's job includes leading children to the activity; reminding children to sign in; answering other children's questions; managing materials and cleanup; and helping to train the next leader. This kind of leadership experience helps children see themselves as competent and capable in the classroom environment and may boost their self-esteem. Teachers can allow children to lead activities in their areas of strength, or have the leader roles rotate on a regular basis.

In addition to training activity leaders, teachers may also use a cooperative learning approach during learning center time. As explained by Robert Slavin in *Cooperative Learning: Theory, Research, and Practice* (1990), cooperative learning is a teaching strategy in which children participate in small group learning activities that promote positive interaction. Because the learning center format, as well as many of the activities in this guide, encourages students to work in small groups toward a common objective and to turn to each other (not just the activity leader) for knowledge, assistance, and encouragement, learning centers fit well in a cooperative classroom.

• **Sharing Time.** We found it most valuable to include time for reflection at the end of Spectrum activities. This reflection can be an individual process in which children draw a picture, write a sentence, or dictate a journal entry about what they learned during the activity. Or, teachers occasionally can devote 5 or 10 minutes to a "sharing time." This is not show-and-tell but rather an opportunity for the students to see each other's work, ask questions about it, discuss it, and generate new ideas for projects they can do during Spectrum activity time. It also helps them articulate their thoughts and test their hypotheses and ideas against those of the group.

The first time children try a sharing time, teachers might have a short discussion to set ground rules. It is important to discuss: (a) how children can ask each other questions that are clear and constructive; (b) why it is necessary to listen while other children speak; and (c) how students can express their opinions without hurting each other's feelings.

Documenting Children's Strengths

The most distinctive feature of the Spectrum approach, however it is implemented, is the conviction that each child possesses a unique pattern of cognitive strengths. Identifying and documenting children's areas of strength, therefore, are critical to an effective use of the approach. As discussed in the section "Identifying Children's Strengths," the key abilities, listed in the front of each guide, can help teachers make specific observations about a child's interests, abilities, and approach to different types of tasks.

• **Teacher Observations.** Although recording these observations can be time consuming, we encourage teachers to develop a notation system compatible with their teaching practice. Table 4 provides one format for recording observations as children work. Another strategy is to attach Post-It sticky tags to a clipboard and write down one comment per tag. The tags can be labeled by domain and then placed directly in the appropriate child's file. Tape-recording discussions and presentations, photographing student work, or even video-taping performances if resources permit are several other methods of documentation. These all can be useful in writing a student profile, conducting a parent conference, or trying to devise an educational "treatment" suited to a child's intellectual profile.

Over the course of a semester, teachers should try to observe each child working in each of the domains. More information about using activities to assess and document children's abilities can be found in *Project Spectrum: Preschool Assessment Handbook*. Although the activities are geared to assessing preschool children, they might be adapted for an older age group if a teacher felt more formal assessment would be helpful for an individual child in a particular domain.

• **Children's Portfolios.** Portfolios—purposeful collections of children's work—offer another method of documenting children's efforts, strengths, progress, and achievements in one or more areas. Unlike standardized assessments that focus on a child's performance on a single occasion, portfolios can capture the evolution of a child's abilities over the course of the year. In the book *Portfolio Practices: Thinking Through the Assessment of Children's Work* (1997), Project Zero researchers Steve Seidel and Joseph Walters show that portfolios can take their shape from the student's own investigations—as manifested by artwork, poems, journal entries, data-recording sheets, clay structures, or other products—and thus provide a revealing portrait of the child as learner. Portfolios also can be used to involve children in the process of selecting and judging the quality of their work.

In *The Work Sampling System* (1993), Samuel Meisels recommends collecting two kinds of work in a child's portfolio: core items and other items. Core items are examples of work that was performed by all the children on several different occasions and that represent several different domains. These items are collected at least three times over the course of the school year and can provide a basis for making group comparisons of quality of performance as well as tracing individual progress. Other items include two or three additional work samples in one or more domains. These samples can be different for each child and provide an opportunity to keep track of the idiosyncratic preferences and abilities that individual children demonstrate.

Improving Children's Academic Performance

Identifying and documenting areas of strength is particularly important in helping children who are struggling with academics. When these children have opportunities to explore and pursue a wide range of learning areas, their skills and areas of competence, overlooked in more traditional programs, often become apparent. The process of drawing attention to and nurturing at-risk children's areas of strength offers a promising alternative to the all too typical characterization of this population as deficient. Building on children's strengths diversifies the content of intervention and provides alternative means for teachers to help children develop basic skills.

In fact, one long-term goal of the Spectrum approach is to reduce the need for special services, such as classroom "pull-out," by providing classroom-based support and enhancing the teacher's ability to reach at-risk children during first grade. This approach, however, is not recommended for all circumstances. For example, if schools or teachers are committed to a strongly academic focus, Spectrum is unlikely to be appealing or effective. Also, the Spectrum approach may be inappropriate for at-risk students who have severe emotional, physical, or learning problems. Recognition of the limits of the approach is important to its successful implementation.

For many teachers, however, we hope that the Spectrum approach can contribute some new and exciting ideas about reaching children, who each bring to school a different combination of strengths and weaknesses, interests and behaviors. We also hope it will help many children like Donnie and Charlie and Linda experience the joy of learning and see themselves as active and successful learners.

TABLE 2: ANTICIPATED LEARNING CENTER PROBLEMS AND REMEDIES

Problem:

Children are unable to work well without supervision.

Remedies:

- Have students work with you or student leader before they try the activities alone.

- Screen student leaders carefully.

- Group students so that personalities are compatible.

- Have entire class work on Spectrum activities at once so that you are free to float from activity to activity as children need help.

- Limit the number of activities that students can choose from at any given time.

- Make rules and closure clear.

Problem:

The planning involved in introducing a new activity is too time consuming.

Remedies:

- Have entire class work in one domain at a time.

- Introduce only one new activity at a time.

- Keep open several "old favorites" that everyone knows well.

- Introduce activities for which you already have the materials on hand.

Problem:

The logistics of implementing learning centers seem overwhelming.

Remedies:

- Introduce the centers gradually, making sure you are comfortable with one before you introduce another.

- Try the simpler activities first.

- Don't try to introduce too many new activities at the same time.

- Limit the number of activities available at one time.

- Make sure you are familiar with the activity yourself before introducing it.

- Team up with another teacher.

How do you know when you've finished an activity?

Objective: to help children reflect on their work and understand what it means to be finished with an activity. Finishing seems to be a central issue for some children. Try to elicit specific clues that identify "finished" products.

In addition to discussing the questions below, you might coach the children during activity time by repeating the rules and goals of the activities in which they are engaged. You might also model the activities more than once before the children begin to work on their own. Finally, you might have students write or draw in journals when they think the task is completed, or indicate what they want to do next at the center.

Suggested Questions:

1. If you are playing a game, when is it over?
2. If you are making something, when is your piece finished?
3. What are the clues that tell that you you're finished?
4. What feelings do you have when you have finished something?
5. What do you do if you're not sure you're finished?

What do you do when you're finished?

Objective: to help children verbalize what they should do when they are finished with an activity. This mini-lesson may be given immediately after the previous one or on the following day.

Suggested Questions:

1. What do you need to do as soon as you finish an activity? (Clean up! Encourage children to articulate the cleanup rules.)
2. What do you do next? (Children should articulate all the different activities they can pursue. The following are some possibilities.)

   - Write in your journal about the activity. (What was most fun? What did you learn?)
   - Draw a picture about what you were doing.
   - Talk about what you did into a tape recorder. Tell what you thought was most fun and what you learned.
   - Read a book related to the topic of the activity.
   - Help another child.
   - Choose a take-home activity.
   - Plan what you want to do next time.

How can we help each other?

Objective: to model how children can help each other and to foster children's independence. You might pose a problem like this: "You and a friend are doing an activity together. You think you know exactly what to do, but the person you're working with is having trouble figuring it out. How can you help your friend?"

Try to elicit many responses and reinforce those that are the most constructive. Observe which children think of suggestions readily and skillfully—they may be good choices for activity leaders.

Suggested Questions:

1. How can you help your friend? What are the best ways to help your friend?

2. What kinds of things can you say to your friend that will help her solve her problem?

3. What kinds of things shouldn't you say? What kinds of things may hurt her feelings?

4. Sometimes you might feel that the easiest way to help your friend is to do the activity for her. Why isn't this always the best way to help your friend? (The point of this question is to help children see that they can be most helpful by teaching the friend how to do the activity herself.)

Refocusing Activities

Objective: to help children organize and structure their activities in accord with curricular goals. If children are using the materials in such a way that they are distracted from these goals, or you are unable to observe key abilities, you may need to help them refocus.

For your discussion, choose two or three popular activities that you would like to redirect. Discuss one activity at a time, focusing on a few key issues. While supporting their creativity, help children understand the ways in which they should use the materials to develop or demonstrate key abilities.

Suggested Questions:

1. Can someone explain to me how you are playing this game?

2. How are other people playing this game?

3. Here is what I want you to try when you play this game next. . . . (Give clear directions. Perhaps have two children model the activity. They could become the class leaders for the activity or learning center, so that children could direct further questions to them.)

TABLE 4: CLASSROOM OBSERVATION SHEET

Teacher:_____   Date:_____

Child	Date/Activities	Domain/Key Abilities	Evidence/Examples

☐ _____

Calkins, L. M. (1986). *The art of teaching writing.* Portsmouth, NH: Heinemann.

Cohen, D. (1990). A revolution in one classroom: The case of Mrs. Oublier. *Educational Evaluation and Policy Analysis, 12,* 311–329.

Feldman, D. H. (1980). *Beyond universals in cognitive development.* Norwood, NJ: Ablex.

Feuerstein, R. (1980). *Instrumental enrichment: An intervention program for cognitive modifiability.* Baltimore, MD: University Park Press.

Gardner, H. (1983). *Frames of mind: The theory of multiple intelligences.* New York: Basic Books.

Gardner, H. (1998). Are there additional intelligences? In J. Kane (Ed.), *Education, information, and transformation.* Englewood, NJ: Prentice Hall.

Meisels, S. J. (1993). *The work sampling system.* Ann Arbor, MI: Rebus Planning Associates.

Slavin, R. E. (1990). *Cooperative learning: Theory, research, and practice.* Englewood Cliffs, NJ: Prentice Hall.

Seidel, S., Walters, J., Kirby, E., Olff, N., Powell, K., Scripp, L., & Veenema, S. (1997). *Portfolio practices: Thinking through the assessment of children's work.* Washington, DC: National Education Association Publishing Library.

MECHANICS AND CONSTRUCTION ACTIVITIES

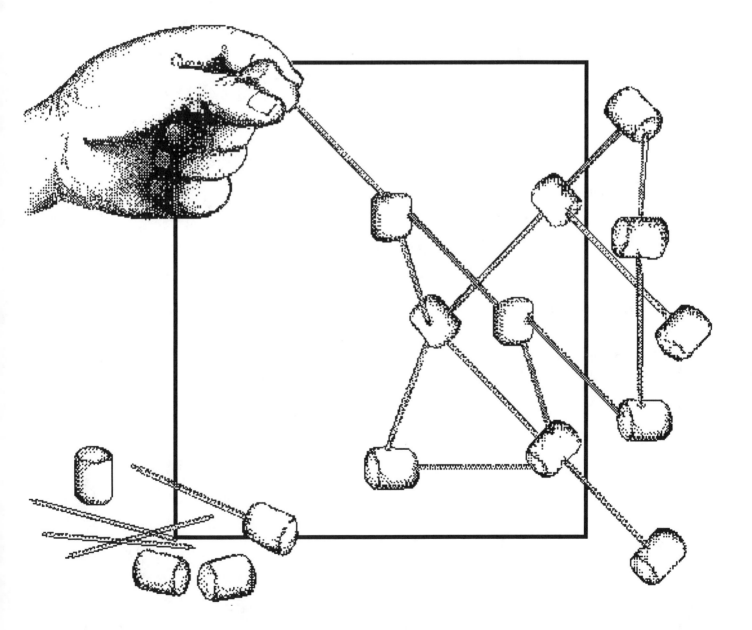

CONTENTS

Introduction

An Overview of the Mechanics and Construction Activities 25

Description of Key Abilities 26

Mechanics and Construction Activities

Understanding of Causal and Functional Relationships
Working with Tools 27
A Picture Dictionary of Tools 29
Take Apart 30
Assembly 31

Visual-Spatial Abilities
Mobiles 32
Clay Construction 33
Wood Construction 34
Super Structures 35
Paper Bridges 37
Our Town 39

Problem-Solving Approach with Mechanical Objects
Levers 40
Inclined Planes 41
Ramp and Roll 42
Wheels and Axles 43

Take-Home Activities

1 Take It Apart 45

2 Look, No Hands! 46

3 Can You Build a House? 47

Resources and References 48

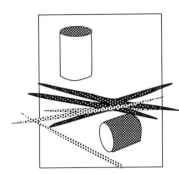

The mechanics and construction activities in this chapter give children the opportunity to use tools, repair gadgets, assemble machines, and solve other simple mechanical problems. These activities are particularly appealing to children for several reasons. First, they are "authentic"; children see their parents working with tools and machines at home and may sometimes be asked to help. Thus, the link between in-school learning and "real-world" challenges is especially easy for children to see.

Second, these activities draw upon intellectual strengths that may not be tapped by a more traditional curriculum. Children with scant interest in paper-and-pencil tasks may be engaged by—and excel at—the challenges posed in the following pages, such as figuring out how to build a house out of toothpicks or how to move objects without touching them. Thus, the activities can be used both to boost children's self-esteem and to bridge to other areas of learning. For example, some children might be interested in reading and writing about tools, machines, and structures.

The activities that follow are designed to give children practice in manipulating tools, to foster problem-solving abilities, and to deepen their understanding of principles governing the physical world. The guide is organized according to three key abilities: understanding causal and functional relationships, focusing on parts of machines and the way in which they are assembled; visual-spatial relationships, with an emphasis on construction; and a problem-solving approach with mechanical objects, introducing children to several simple machines. A fourth key ability, fine motor skill, is fostered by virtually all the activities.

Some of the activities, such as taking apart a food grinder and putting it back together, teach formal assembly and promote mechanical skills involving accuracy and precision. Technically, there is a "right" way to complete these tasks. Other activities, such as woodworking and building with clay, give children an opportunity for free exploration, creative construction, and experimenting with different solutions to the same problem.

Although these activities emphasize mechanical abilities, they also embody many other academic and nonacademic areas of learning, such as number concepts, new vocabulary, and cooperative learning skills. For example, children can learn to present information in charts and graphs as they conduct experiments and record results. They can develop their ability to express ideas, negotiate, and help each other as they design and build a tabletop town.

When you introduce the mechanics and construction activities, whether you use the activities at a learning center, as a curricular unit, or individually as a "weekly challenge," present them to the children as an adventure. You might introduce the activities by asking children questions such as the following: Can you tell me what the word *mechanical* means? Do you know someone who does mechanical work? What kind of work does this person do? What kinds of mechanical tasks are done at home?

Explain to the children that they will not only learn about machines—they will also have the chance to take some apart and put them back together again. And they will be able to use hammers, screwdrivers, and other tools to do their work! The children also might such as to know that they will be solving, on a small scale, the kinds of problems that grown-ups do, like building stable structures and moving heavy objects.

This type of orientation session would be a good time to emphasize safety in regard to using tools. Work with the class to develop safety rules, such as setting up a separate area for mechanics and construction activities, or using tools only when a teacher is available to help. After the orientation, have children explore some of the materials, such as blocks, wood scraps, nuts and bolts, and tools to the extent that you are able to supervise.

Understanding of Causal and Functional Relationships

- infers relationships based on observation

- understands relationship of parts to whole, the function of these parts, and how parts are put together

Visual-Spatial Abilities

- is able to construct or reconstruct physical objects and simple machines in two or three dimensions

- understands spatial relationships between parts of a mechanical object

Problem-Solving Approach with Mechanical Objects

- uses and learns from trial-and-error approach

- uses systematic approach in solving mechanical problems

- compares and generalizes information

Fine Motor Skills

- is adept at manipulating small parts or objects

- exhibits good hand-eye coordination
  (e.g., hammers on head of nail rather than on fingers)

☐ WORKING WITH TOOLS

Objective: Learn to use different tools

Core Components: Manipulating objects
Hand-eye coordination
Understanding functional relationships

Materials:

Group One—Making Wire Designs
4 wire cutters
Assorted wires
Contact paper

Group Two—Driving Screws
4 regular screwdrivers of different sizes
4 Phillips-head screwdrivers of different sizes
Assorted screws of various sizes and different heads
4 pieces of board with pre-drilled holes of different sizes

Group Three—Woodworking
4 hammers
Assorted small pieces of wood
Small nails
Wood glue

Group Four—Straightening Paper Clips
4 pliers
Paper clips of different sizes

Procedures:

1. Before class, put the four groups of materials on four separate trays. Begin the activity by talking about safety and the possibility of injury if tools are not used properly. Review any safety rules that the class developed during the mechanics and construction orientation.

2. Place the four trays in front of the children and explain that today's mechanical activity involves working with tools. Children will be able to use four different kinds of tools: pliers, hammers, wire cutters, and screwdrivers. Divide the class into four groups and explain that these groups will take turns using the different tools.

    The first group of children will start by using wire cutters to cut all sorts of wires. Explain that these wires are made of different materials and also vary in size. Give all the children a piece of contact paper. Let them cut the wires and place the pieces on the contact paper to make a design.

    The children in the second group are going to use screwdrivers to drive screws into a piece of board. Give them different-sized screws with different types of heads. Ask them to find the screwdriver that works best to complete the job.

    The third group of children will work like carpenters, using hammers and nails. Explain that they can make anything they like, and also use glue to help their construction work. If they wish, they can hammer nails into the wood so that the nails spell out their names or make a design.

☐ _____

Finally, the fourth group will use pliers to straighten paper clips. They can take the straightened clips and twist them together or make different shapes, such as a circle or a star.

3. Circulate through the room to supervise the four groups. Encourage the groups to stay with their assigned activity for at least 15 minutes before exchanging materials.

Variations:

1. Invite children to explore the mechanics of the classroom. Inspect what makes the cabinet door stay closed and how the drawers roll. Let the children try locking and unlocking the door. Investigations can also be conducted in other areas of the school, such as the playground or the office.

2. Make a sample of geometric shapes from straightened paper clips. Ask children to make any geometric design except the one that you demonstrated.

3. Invite parents who work with tools to come to the classroom and demonstrate the ways in which they use different tools.

4. Take a field trip to a hardware store to examine all kinds of simple hardware, such as springs, hinges, nuts, and bolts, and explore how these items are used. Have the children examine different tools, look at how the parts fit together, and try to figure out how the tools are used.

5. Read books about tools and machines to the children. Discuss any tools with which they are familiar, particularly those tools you have not yet introduced.

Notes to the Teacher:

1. If it is not possible to supervise the four different activities at the same time, introduce the tools more slowly, one or two at a time, to ensure children's safety.

2. Tools, as permanent materials in the classroom, should be kept in a toolbox. For safety reasons, you may wish to lock the toolbox and have children ask you when they need a tool.

3. Woodwork is potentially very noisy; some kind of acoustical shelter might help diminish the noise. You may wish to set up an area in a corner using corrugated cardboard panels or foam to deaden the noise.

□ A PICTURE DICTIONARY OF TOOLS

Objective:	Learn names and functions of different tools by creating a picture dictionary
Core Components:	Fine motor skills Understanding functional relationships Ability to express ideas
Materials:	A variety of tools (e.g., clamp, hammer, pliers, ruler, saw, screwdriver, wrench, hand drill) Books about tools Paper and pencils Markers or crayons

Procedures:

1. Introduce children to books about tools (a few suggestions follow). Tell children that they will create their own book, a picture dictionary of tools. They will draw pictures of different tools, write about them, and put them in alphabetical order.

2. Start with tools the children have used already (such as the wire cutters, screwdrivers, hammers, and pliers that they used in the Working with Tools activity). Then, introduce one new tool at a time. Encourage children to name the tool and explain how to use the tool. Create an activity so that children can use the tools (for example, use a screwdriver and screws to put together pieces of Styrofoam, or take something apart with a wrench).

3. Ask children to draw a picture of the tool. Encourage them write or dictate a short description of the tool, what it's used for, and their own experience using it.

4. Have children share their picture dictionaries of tools during group time.

Notes to the Teacher:

1. This and other projects can be used to bridge children's interest in mechanical work to the development of writing skills. For example, challenge children to write or draw an "instruction manual," giving step-by-step directions for using the tool to make something, fix something, or take something apart. Children can draw on their experience in the Take Apart, Assembly, and other activities that follow.

2. Here are several books about tools:

> Rockwell, A. & H. (1972). *The Tool Box*. New York: Macmillan.
> McPhail, D. (1984). *Fix-It*. New York: Dutton.
> Gibbons, G. (1982). *Tool Book*. New York: Holiday House.
> Homan, D. (1981). *In Christina's Tool Box*. Chapel Hill, NC: Lollipop Power.
> Morris, A. (1992). *Tools*. New York: Lothrop, Lee and Shepard.

3. Here are some sample definitions:

> drill—a tool for making holes
> wrench—a tool for holding or turning objects such as nuts or bolts
> screwdriver—a tool that turns screws
> saw—a cutting tool with sharp edges
> hammer—a tool used to insert or remove object
> pliers—a tool used for holding small things or bending and cutting wire

□ TAKE APART

Objectives:	Learn to use different tools
	Learn about machines by taking them apart
Core Components:	Understanding of causal and functional relationships
	Fine motor skills
	Attention to detail
Materials:	Broken appliances (e.g., clock, typewriter, phone)
	Tools (e.g., wrenches, pliers, screwdrivers, wire cutters)
	Containers for collecting parts

Procedures:

1. Divide the class into small groups. Give each group two broken appliances, several empty containers, and the tools that the children will need to do the work.

2. Ask the children to try to use different tools to take apart the broken appliances. Emphasize that their job is to take apart the machines, not to break or destroy them. Tell them that if they wish, they will be able to use the parts later to make collages, play math games, or make new machines.

3. As you circulate from one table to the next, talk with the children about the function of different tools as well as the structure of different machines. Ask the children questions, such as, How did screwdrivers help your work? Is it easier to take some of the pieces off with your hands or with the tools?

4. If space is available, you may wish to keep broken appliances available for children to explore throughout the year, whether for a few minutes at recess or for extended periods of time. Appliances can be replaced with different ones from time to time.

Variations:

1. After children have practiced taking apart the appliances, encourage them to use the parts to make new machines. This activity may be called the Inventing Shop. The purpose of the Inventing Shop is not to ask the children to invent a machine that works, but to give them an opportunity to make up their own design. Encourage children to name their design and make a list of its uses.

2. Encourage children to sort or classify parts after they have taken the appliances apart. Ask children how they want to sort—whether based on the parts' functions, shapes, sizes, or other characteristics.

□ ASSEMBLY

Objective: Learn about machines by taking them apart and putting them back together again

Core Components: Understanding of causal and functional relationships
Fine motor skills
Attention to detail

Materials: Oil pumps
Food grinders
Gear assembly set

Procedures:

1. Show children a food grinder, an oil pump, and a commercial gear assembly set. Start a discussion by asking questions such as the following: What can the children tell you about these machines? Does anyone know their names and functions? Where might they find one of these machines?

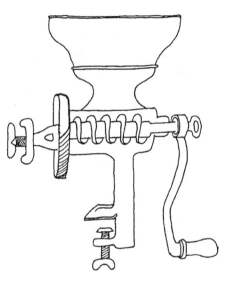

2. Explain to the children that they will be taking the machines apart and trying to put them back together. Tell them that they will be working in small groups and that it's OK if they cannot get their machines back together. They will all help one other.

3. Divide the class into groups of two or three. Distribute one machine to each group. Encourage the children to work together to take apart and reassemble the machines. After about 15 minutes, have children exchange machines.

Variations:

1. Ask children to use the oil pump and food grinder to do work. Squeeze water from the pump to water plants and grind food (e.g., apples, nuts, and potatoes) to make snacks. You might ask children questions such as these: How do these kitchen machines work? What might happen if you used other foods—softer foods, harder foods? What else could these machines do? How can you make the food finer or coarser? (Show the different cutting mechanisms.) When feasible, test out children's hypotheses.

2. Encourage the children to draw pictures of the machines and their parts. Ask the children how their pictures could help them put the machines back together. Do they think it would be helpful to draw as they take apart the machines?

3. Give children other household gadgets, such as flashlights or pencil sharpeners, to take apart and assemble. Encourage the children to examine various pieces of the gadgets and to talk about their functions.

☐ MOBILES

Objectives:	Make simple mobiles
	Observe variables that affect mobile balance
Core Components:	Understanding spatial relationships
	Fine motor skills
	Trial-and-error strategy
Materials:	Lightweight cardboard
	Markers or paint and paint brushes
	Scissors
	Yarn
	Dowels (2 per child, approximately 12" long)
	Twine or wire

Procedures:

1. In this activity, children learn, through trial and error, to assemble a balanced mobile. In preparation, ask the children (perhaps as an art project) to make ornaments they can put together into mobiles. Encourage them to make at least four ornaments each, of different shapes and sizes. Use cardboard or another lightweight but durable material, because children may need to experiment quite a bit in order to balance the ornaments.

2. When you are ready to assemble the mobiles, give each child his or her ornaments, two dowels, and the yarn. Help children cut the yarn into pieces 6" long or less, and attach a piece to each ornament. Show them a completed mobile with two tiers and explain that they can arrange their own ornaments however they please, trying to make the dowels hang as straight as possible. Let them arrange the ornaments flat on a table.

3. Demonstrate how to start the mobile by tying a piece of yarn in the middle section of one dowel. The dowel will be suspended from this piece of yarn. Next, children should tie half their ornaments to the dowel (a double knot works best). Encourage them to slide their ornaments back and forth along the dowel until they balance. Point out that they can shift the yarn in the middle of the dowel, too. Ask them questions about their work. What happens when they shift the yarn close to the heavier ornament? to a lighter ornament? What happens when they shift the heavier ornament close to the middle of the dowel? close to the end of the dowel?

4. Children should tie the remaining ornaments to the second dowel, then tie the two dowels together.

5. Hang the mobiles where children can reach them easily; you might suspend the mobiles from a piece of a heavy twine or wire stretched between the classroom walls. When children hang up their mobiles, they may find that if they make a change in one tier, it will throw the other tier off balance. With some experimentation—and your guidance if necessary—they will discover that it is easiest to balance a mobile if they complete the lower tier first, and then the upper tier. Discuss these and other discoveries with the children.

This activity is adapted from Elementary Science Study. (1976). *Mobiles.*
St. Louis: McGraw-Hill.

☐ CLAY CONSTRUCTION

Objective:	Learn about balance by constructing representational and nonrepresentational structures out of clay
Core Components:	Constructing three-dimensional objects Design and planning Testing hypotheses
Materials:	Modeling clay (about 1/2 lb. per child) Yardstick or ruler String Popsicle sticks Paper clips Copper wire Cardboard

Procedures:

1. Encourage children to play with clay and the other materials listed above, creating whatever objects they wish.

2. After the free-play session, give all the children the same amount of clay (about 1/2 lb. each). Challenge them to build the tallest structure they can. Measure each creation and point out the tallest ones. Ask children to compare the different sizes and shapes of the bases. Encourage children to develop their own hypotheses about how to build a tall structure that doesn't fall down.

3. Challenge the children to test their hypotheses by trying once again to build the tallest structure they can. How tall are their structures this time?

4. If you wish, give the children pieces of string to measure the height of their structures and the perimeter of the base. Which is longer? Help the children compare their results. They can draw bar graphs comparing height and base, or tape their pieces of string onto a poster.

5. Challenge the children to create a structure with a height greater than the perimeter of the base. Tell children that they can experiment with using the other materials on the table (popsicle sticks, cardboard, etc.) to make their buildings stronger and taller.

6. Ask children to describe their structures to the whole group. Encourage them to describe any construction problems they encountered and how they solved them.

Notes to the Teacher:

As children work on their own structures, they might enjoy visiting a construction site. If possible, arrange for them to talk with someone involved in the construction. Encourage them to draw pictures or write about the visit.

This activity is adapted from Elementary Science Study. (1968).
Structures. St. Louis: McGraw-Hill.

☐ WOOD CONSTRUCTION

Objective:	Learn about balance by building representational and nonrepresentational structures out of wood
Core Components:	Ability to balance one object upon another Sense of design Planning strategies
Materials:	Wood scraps, different shapes and sizes Paint Wood glue Masking tape Paint brushes

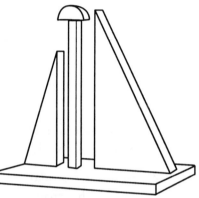

Procedures:

1. Tell children that they will be making structures out of wood, but that this time they will hold the pieces together with wood glue and masking tape instead of hammers and nails. Show them how to use the glue and the tape. Talk about what they learned about building a solid base in the Clay Construction activity.

2. Encourage children to create their own imaginative designs, combining scraps of different shapes and sizes. As they work, prompt them to think about balance with questions like the following: How can you balance a wide piece on top of a thinner one? a rectangular piece on top of a round one? three pieces on top of two pieces? Where could you add a piece of wood to make your design stronger? Where could you remove a piece without making it fall down?

3. After they have finished assembling and gluing their structures, let the glue dry for at least a day. Then give the children paint and brushes for decorating their work.

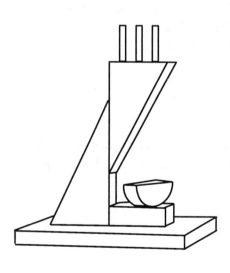

4. Set up a display of the wood structures. Encourage children to write a few comments to accompany their work, explaining how they put it together or made it balance.

Variations:

1. Show children pictures (from books or travel magazines) of real but unusual structures, such as the Empire State Building, the Sears Tower, the Eiffel Tower, the Golden Gate Bridge, the Coliseum, the Great Pyramids, and the Taj Mahal. Then, encourage children to use pieces of wood to create specific structures, such as a tower, a pyramid, an arch. You might suggest that they draw a sketch of their proposed building before they start. When they are finished, they can explain which parts of their plans worked, which parts didn't, what changes they made, and why.

2. Make available commercial games, such as Jenga or Timber, in which players try to remove individual building blocks without causing the structure to fall down.

□ SUPER STRUCTURES

Objectives:	Learn about the properties of different materials by building representational and nonrepresentational structures
Core Components:	Understanding spatial relationships Fine motor skills Working with others
Materials:	Package of toothpicks Package of small marshmallows Clay, playdough, Styrofoam peanuts, and tape (optional)

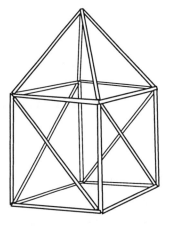

Procedures:

1. Tell the children that they will be making imaginative structures out of toothpicks, using marshmallows for the joints (modeling clay, playdough, or Styrofoam peanuts can be used instead of marshmallows). Encourage children to try some basic shapes.

2. Urge children to help each other (marshmallows encourage cooperative work, because they are soft until exposed to the air and thus may not hold the toothpicks in place). One child can hold pieces up while another attaches enough toothpicks to hold the structure together. When children are finished with their projects, encourage them to talk about any problems they encountered and how they solved them.

3. The next day, review the project and encourage children to build structures different from the ones they have made already. Suggest that they model their work after real buildings, such as bridges, houses, and skyscrapers, or after objects in nature, such as skeletons or trees.

4. Discuss the hypotheses that children developed during their work with clay and wood. Do the same strategies apply to building with toothpicks? What shapes make the most stable bases? the tallest walls? If a structure collapses, can they try again using extra toothpicks as reinforcements? What happens if they add a diagonal toothpick to a rectangle? if they add two toothpicks in an X-shape? What happens if they take toothpicks away? How many toothpicks can they remove before the building falls?

5. After the children have finished, ask them to describe their structures, their discoveries, and any problems they resolved while building. Display the structures. In fact, you may wish to use them as a starting point for creating a model town in your classroom (see Our Town activity on p. 39).

Variations:

1. Building a house out of newspaper logs makes a good group activity. Show children how to take a sheet of newspaper, roll it tightly into a tube, and secure the edge with masking tape. They can make logs of different sizes by cutting logs in pieces, or rolling newspaper the long way instead of the short way. Children can take turns at different tasks—making logs, holding logs together, taping on

new logs. Encourage children to find different ways to attach the logs and support the structure. If necessary, show them how to reinforce a corner with a log placed on the diagonal.

2. Make other building materials available to the children. For example:
    - Substitute drinking straws for the toothpicks. Ask children to figure out whether glue, tape, or string holds the straws together best.
    - Use toothpicks, but encourage children to experiment with different materials for fastening them (e.g., modeling clay, playdough, Styrofoam, tape). Which fasteners are the easiest to use? the hardest?
    - Try wire construction. Suggest that children try to use pipe cleaners to make a structures as tall as a milk carton, or thin wire to make an object the shape of a cereal box.
    - Make commercial construction materials (e.g., Legos, Tinker Toys, Erector sets, gear assembly sets) available in the classroom. Ask children to follow instructions or copy models as they put together the materials. Encourage children to work together to see how many different structures they can build.

3. Ask children to bring in yogurt and margarine containers, paper-towel tubes, and other "trash" for a junk sculpture project. Include materials that can be rolled, folded, or cut into different shapes, such as construction paper, paper plates, paper bags, and cardboard. You can do this activity on Earth Day, and incorporate the theme of protecting the environment.

☐ PAPER BRIDGES

Objective:	Construct paper bridges to learn how factors such as shape, size, and material affect their strength
Core Components:	Constructing three-dimensional objects Hypothesis testing Recording experimental results
Materials:	Paper (bond, construction, oak tag) Scissors Matchboxes or paper cups Pennies or washers (about 100) Blocks or books String

Procedures:

1. Before the activity, prepare the matchboxes to hold weights by making a handle out of string.

2. Explain to the children that real bridges must be strong enough to support the weight of heavy trucks and cars. Tell the children that they will experiment with different materials and shapes to see what types of paper bridges are the strongest. As a model, make a bridge out of a piece of oak tag and two equal stacks of books or blocks. Then, give children scissors and different kinds of paper and ask them to create their own bridges. Encourage them to experiment with different designs (e.g., narrow, wide, long, short, creased, folded) and different supports (resting on top of the stack of blocks or books, anchored underneath a block or book).

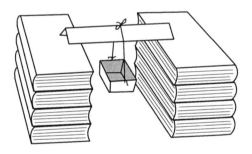

3. Ask children to compare the strength of the different bridges. Hang the matchbox from one of the bridges and ask children to fill it, one penny (or washer) at a time. How many weights can they add before the bridge collapses? Encourage them to test a number of bridges and to develop a system for recording their results. Discuss the different variables they are considering—for example, the material used to make the bridge, its length (both the distance between supports and the overlap with the supports), its width, and its shape. Can they develop a hypothesis about what shapes make a strong paper bridge?

4. Challenge the children to use their discoveries to build (individually or in small groups) the strongest bridge they can out of a small piece of construction paper. Make sure all the pieces are the same size (say, 2" by 8"). Which design is the strongest? How many pennies can it support? If the matchbox won't hold enough pennies, you might try using the bottom half of a paper or Styrofoam cup.

5. If the children are still interested, they can repeat the experiment with pieces of oak tag (once again, all the pieces should be the same size). You may need to use heavier washers or sinkers as their bridges get stronger.

Variations:

You may wish to introduce or extend this activity by examining bridges in a variety of ways:

• Go for walks and visit bridges. Encourage children to draw pictures of them and notice what they are made of and how they are designed.

• Make available reference books with drawings of different types of bridges (i.e., suspension, arch, cantilever, truss). Discuss the different designs and the materials.

• Ask children to bring in pictures of bridges — photos, postcards, cutouts from magazines. Encourage them to sort the pictures in different ways.

• Challenge children to construct bridges using other materials in the classroom (blocks, straws, clay). What shapes work best with different materials?

This activity is adapted from Elementary Science Study. (1968). *Structures.* St. Louis: McGraw-Hill.

□ OUR TOWN

Objective:	Use experiences with construction to build a model town
Core Components:	Constructing three-dimensional objects
	Designing and planning
	Development of social skills
Materials:	Choice of construction materials (e.g., recycled cardboard cartons and tubes, modeling clay, or wood scraps)
	Appropriate tools
	Paint and paint brushes

Procedures:

1. Tell children that over the next few weeks they will be building a small model town (or neighborhood, community, city, or whatever is most appropriate to your class) to display in the classroom. Explain that they will be working together not just to build the town, but also to plan it.

2. Take a walk through the center of your town, city, or neighborhood. Encourage children to record—in a map, words, or pictures—some of the different types of buildings they see (post office, police and fire stations, schools, restaurants, stores). If possible, arrange field trips to talk with owners and managers to find out what buildings look like inside and what goes on there.

3. Help the children decide what materials to use for their model. They may wish to use structures they already have made. Or, they may wish to start afresh, using recycled materials such as plastic containers, paper towel tubes, and cardboard.

4. For a structured approach, you might encourage the children to start with a detailed map of the town, thinking carefully about the best places to locate a fire station or a grocery superstore with lots of traffic. They could volunteer to make different buildings and work with graph paper in an effort to build their structures to scale.

   Or, they could start with a few buildings and allow the town to grow. Children could examine the model (or try to move toy figures through it) and add what they think is needed, such as roads, traffic signals, bridges, or a hospital. Challenge them to think about what buildings and other structures are essential to a town.

5. Encourage children to pursue their own interests. Some may wish to fill the town with cars, buses, and trucks; others, with human figures. Some children may enjoy using the parts from broken appliances to design machines that could clean streets, repair telephone lines, or perform other tasks. They could even connect small light bulbs to batteries to make street lights and traffic lights.

Variation:

You could extend this project into a study of your community and the services it provides. You could share books, invite parents and other community members into the classroom to talk about their careers, and have students write stories or keep a journal. You could even hold a campaign for town council or publish a newspaper.

☐ *LEVERS*

Objective: To figure out how to lift an object by constructing a lever

Core Components: Problem-solving skills
                          Observational skills

Materials: Cardboard block or cereal box
                          Sandbox
                          12" ruler
                          Magnets
                          Small blocks
                          String
                          Tape
                          Popsicle sticks

Procedures:

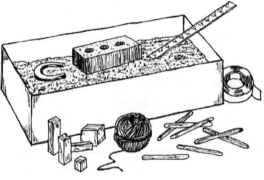

1. Tell children that they are going to solve a special problem. Put a brick-sized cardboard block (or comparable block) in the sandbox, and ask the children to lift it out without touching it with their hands. (If your school does not have a sandbox, you can make one or a number of small ones out of shoe boxes.) Give children a variety of supplies—magnets, small blocks, string, tape, a ruler, and popsicle sticks—and ask them how many different ways they can solve the problem.

2. After children have experimented with several ways to get the block out of the box, have them discuss their methods with each other. Ask them which way they think is the easiest, the fastest, the hardest, and the messiest.

3. Ask children to record their strategies in picture or written form. Keep the list of strategies near the sandbox so that other children can test them. Explain that by using one object to move another one, they were creating a simple machine.

Variations:

Challenge the children to conduct more experiments with levers. Give them a three-foot-long wooden board and a wooden cylinder to use as a fulcrum. Place the fulcrum in the center of the board. How many reams of paper can they lift to the height of a chair? Children should record results. Ask them to move the fulcrum closer to the paper and take measurements. How many reams can they lift? Move the fulcrum farther from the paper. How many reams can they lift? Urge them to try different positions for the fulcrum, take measurements, and record their results.

Talk with the children about the way in which the lever can make work easier. The longer the lever, the easier it is to do work (the less force must be applied). The shorter the lever, the harder it is to do work (the more force must be applied).

□ INCLINED PLANES

Objective:	To explore the ways in which ramps can make work easier
Core Components:	Testing hypotheses Comparing and contrasting
Materials:	3' long wooden board 18 to 24" long wooden board Blocks or books Brick Spring scale (a hand-held scale available in the fishing department of sporting goods stores) String

Procedures:

1. This activity builds on the concepts introduced in the previous activity, Levers. Talk with children about the ways that ramps, a type of inclined plane, are used to make work easier. You might even take a walk and look for ramps—ramps for loading and unloading trucks, for providing wheelchair access to buildings, for sliding down at the playground. Ask children to think about their own experiences with inclined planes (e.g., biking or sledding down a hill, hiking up a hill). Is it harder to pull an object up a steep ramp or a gradual ramp? Tell children that they will conduct an experiment to find out.

2. Children can work as a class or in small groups. They can use the boards and blocks (or books) to build two ramps of different lengths (one about three feet long, the other shorter) but the same height, 6" high at one end. Next, challenge children to figure out how to attach the spring scale to the brick (e.g., tie it up with string like a present, and hook the spring scale onto the string). Explain that they will use the spring scale to measure how much force is needed to move the brick. Encourage them to practice using the scale. How much force is needed to lift the brick straight up 6", to the top of the ramp? Record their findings.

3. Challenge children to predict whether it will take more force to pull the brick up the steep ramp or the gradual ramp. After they conduct the experiment and record the results, discuss the findings. As in the lever experiment, the longer the distance, the less force must be applied. (Note to the teacher: Although it feels easier, it takes the same amount of work to pull the brick up the gradual ramp as the steep one, because the brick must be pulled farther. Work can be defined as the product of the force exerted and the distance through which the force moves.)

☐ RAMP AND ROLL

Objective:	To learn about ramps and how objects move on ramps
Core Components:	Testing hypotheses Recording and interpreting data
Materials:	2 or more 3 ' long wooden boards Blocks or books Two identical rubber balls Balls of different weights and sizes Tools for measuring (e.g., Unifix cubes, rulers, graph paper)

Procedures:

1. Organize children to work in small groups to conduct this experiment. Tell them they will be racing identical balls down ramps of the same length but different height. (The balls should be smaller than the width of the ramps.) Challenge them to build two ramps, one 3" high and the other 6" high (later, they can build additional ramps of greater heights). Ask them to predict whether the balls will travel faster down the high (steep) ramp or the low (gradual) ramp. Place a board at the bottom of the ramps; that way, they can see and hear which ball reaches the bottom first.

2. Encourage children to work together to take on different tasks (releasing the balls, doing the countdown), conduct the experiment and record their results. Then discuss the findings. How does the slope of the ramp affect the speed of the ball?

3. If they remove the board from the bottom of the ramps, which ball will travel farther? Ask children to figure out different ways to measure how far the balls travel, such as using Unifix cubes, string, floor tiles, or a ruler. Or, they can put graph paper at the bottom of the ramp and mark where the ball stops. Record and discuss the results.

4. What happens if the slope of the ramps are the same, but the balls are different? Make more balls available and have children make both ramps the same height. Challenge children to ask their own questions and devise experiments to find out the answer. For example, which will roll faster if they are both the same size— a heavy ball or a light ball? (Note to the teacher: The balls should reach the bottom at the same time.) Which will travel farther? Which will roll faster, a small ball or a large ball? Which will travel farther?

Variations:

1. Challenge children to roll different objects down the ramp (e.g., toy cars, pencils, batteries, screws). Which objects roll? Which objects slide if the ramp is steep enough? Which objects roll if they are placed on the ramp in some ways but not others? Which objects are the most stable after they reach the bottom of the ramp?

2. Give children playdough. Ask them to make different shapes and predict which will roll and which won't roll. Encourage them to test or race their shapes.

☐ WHEELS AND AXLES

Objective:	To predict and determine through experimentation the function of a simple machine, the axle
Core Components:	Testing hypotheses Recording data Fine motor skills
Materials:	Marbles Small boxes Wheel with a nail, pencil, or other axle through the middle, so that children can hold on to both ends of the axle Pizza cutter Tempera or other washable paint Styrofoam trays or dishes to hold paint Drawings of shapes, 3 copies per child (see following pages) Data recording chart (see following page)

Procedures:

1. Show children the drawings and challenge them to trace over the shapes using three different instruments: a marble, a wheel with an axle through the middle, and a pizza cutter. Ask them to predict which instrument will be the easiest to use and which will be the hardest, and to mark their answers on the data recording chart.

2. Give each child three copies of a full-page drawing of a shape, such as a circle or a square. Place once copy of the drawing in a small box. Show children how to roll a marble in paint, put the marble in the box, and then try to trace over the drawing with the marble by tilting the box. Tell children they cannot push the marble with their finger (then their finger would act like an axle by controlling the motion of the marble).

3. Put the two other copies of the drawing on the table. Show children how to roll the wheel in some paint, then trace over the drawing. Encourage them to repeat the experiment with the pizza cutter.

4. Ask children which instrument turned out to be the easiest to use and which turned out to be the hardest. They can write down their answers on the data recording chart.

5. Repeat the experiment with one or two more drawings of simple shapes, like a star or a scribble.

6. Discuss the experiment with the children. What do axles do? How do they help control a wheel? What do they do in a car? Why is the pizza cutter easier to use than the other wheel and axle?

Variations:

Some children might enjoy the challenge of building a small model car that uses wheels and axles to move across the floor or table. Give children wheels and axles from commercial construction sets, or the materials they need to make their own (wooden dowels or metal rods, and wheel disks or wooden spools). You also can supply a variety of materials for making the body of the car, along with the appropriate tools (wood scraps, small hand saw, clamps, sandpaper, nails, hammer, wood glue, and paint; or cardboard boxes and tubes, glue, scissors, and markers). Encourage children to draw several plans, think about how each would work, and pick the most efficient one before they begin construction.

You might also find books with instructions or pictures to serve as a guide for the children. For example, in the book *Design and Technology 5–12,* Pat Williams and David Jinks explain how children can make a car chassis from small pieces of wood, using cardboard triangles to secure the joints. They can then use cardboard to make their vehicle into a truck, bus, sports car, or whatever they please.

Wheels and Axles
Data Recording Chart

Which machine is the easiest to use to trace a drawing?

1 = easiest   2 = in the middle   3 = hardest

Predictions

	marble	wheel	pizza cutter
◯			
☆			
(scribble)			

Results

	marble	wheel	pizza cutter
◯			
☆			
(scribble)			

☐ TAKE IT APART

Objectives: Practice using and controlling simple tools
                      Explore how a machine is put together

Materials: Broken machine or appliance (e.g., typewriter, telephone, clock, flashlight)
                      Hammer
                      Phillips-head and regular screwdrivers
                      Wire cutters
                      2 medium-size boxes

Note to Parents:

1. This activity gives children the rare opportunity to take a machine apart and examine the pieces inside. Furthermore, they can go about it however they please; there is no right or wrong way to take apart the machines. During this project, you will have the chance to observe the way your child handles tools and his or her ideas about the way the parts of the machine fit together.

2. If you don't have all the tools listed above, don't worry. You can do this activity with whatever tools you have.

3. This activity requires close parental supervision. Parents need to help children learn how to use tools and use them safely.

Procedures:

1. Introduce your child to the tools. If your child is unfamiliar with them, discuss what each one is used for. Discuss any rules you would like to set regarding how and when your child may use the tools.

2. Give your child a broken machine or appliance to take apart. Stress that work on this project can take place only when you are present.

3. As your child begins to take apart the machine, ask questions about the work. For example:
   - Which parts will the screwdriver help take apart?
   - When do you use a Phillips-head screwdriver?
   - What do the pliers help you do?
   - Can you find screws or parts in one place that fit in another place?
   - What patterns do you see inside the machine?
   - Are there patterns in the way the parts are put together? (For example, are there washers on every screw?)

4. When your child is finished for the day, suggest that he or she put the machine in one box and the parts in another box. If you have the space, save the parts. Your child can use them to make some great inventions.

Sharing:

Your child may want to bring some of the parts to class. Your child can describe each part to the class and tell which tool was used to take it out of the machine. Classmates will want to know every detail.

□ LOOK, NO HANDS!

Objective:	Solve a problem by developing strategies or constructions
	Think of different solutions to the same problem
Materials:	2 paper plates
	6 to 10 Ping-Pong balls
	Film canisters
	Styrofoam popcorn or any other light, small objects
	Envelope
	1/2" piece of masking tape or 1" piece of cellophane tape
	"Twist" for plastic bags
	12" piece of string
	8 1/2" by 11" sheet of paper
	Straw
	Ballpoint pen or pencil
	Paper or Styrofoam cup
	Plastic bag
	Popsicle stick, toothpick, or wooden skewer
	Birthday candle

Note to Parents:

Problem solving is an essential skill for both school and everyday life. This activity asks your child to solve a mechanical problem when given certain materials and instructions. As your child works on this problem, notice the strategies he or she uses. Does he or she use trial-and-error, simply guessing at strategies, or take a more systematic approach? How does your child use the information he or she has learned from experimenting? Many children enjoy coming up with their own solutions to problems and this activity invites them to come up with as many solutions as they can.

Procedures:

1. Tell your child that you have a special problem to solve. How can you move the Ping-Pong balls from one plate to another without touching the balls or the plates with your hands? Pretend that the balls are poisonous! Ask your child to figure out a way to move a ball, then try it out. Your child can use any or all of the materials you have collected, but needs to move each ball in a different way.

2. Let your child explore, plan, and construct for as long as he or she is interested.

3. When your child is finished coming up with solutions, ask questions about them. For example:
   - Which solution was the easiest? Why?
     Which solution was the most complicated? Why?
   - Which solution was the most surprising? Why?

Sharing:

This activity is a terrific challenge for other family members. Your child can be the one to introduce and supervise it.

☐ CAN YOU BUILD A HOUSE?

Objective: Build a house of cards

Materials: One deck of playing cards
                     A flat, sturdy, smooth surface (tabletop, bare floor)

Note to Parents:

Building a house of playing cards is a popular and well-known activity. It requires few materials but demands a lot of thinking and problem solving. In order to build a house of cards, your child will need to think about balance, weight, and design. Notice how your child addresses these issues as he or she builds. Some children find this activity so engrossing that they will build for long stretches of time. See the illustration for one way to build card houses.

Procedures:

1. You can introduce this activity with a challenge. Give your child two playing cards and see if he or she can make them stand up by leaning against each other, like an upside-down V.

2. After your child has figured out how to make the upside down V, ask him or her to make two upside-down Vs, one next to the other. Then ask your child how to build a house out of Vs. If your child is stuck, suggest laying a card across the points of the Vs. Then ask your child to continue.

3. It is fun to think of other ways to construct a house of cards. What different ideas does your child have? Urge your child to try some of them. Some questions you might want to ask include:

   - What helps the cards stand up?
   - What seems to make them fall down?
   - How many levels of cards can you build before they fall down?

4. For an extrahard challenge: Can you build something that will use all of your cards?

Sharing:

Building card houses is a fun family activity and can even be made into a game. Your child might want to do this with classmates in school.

RESOURCES AND REFERENCES

The activities on the preceding pages are just an introduction to the field. To help you conduct further explorations in the teaching of mechanics and construction, we offer a brief list of resources that have proved valuable to us or to our colleagues. It is intended to provide inspiration rather than a review of the literature. Sources used in the preparation of this volume are marked with an asterisk.

Brown, D. (1991). *How things were built*. New York: Random House.

Darling, D. (1991). *Spiderwebs to sky-scrapers: The science of structures*. New York: Dillon Press, Macmillan.

Dunn, S., & Larson, R. (1990). *Design technology: Children's engineering*. New York, London: Falmer Press.

* Educational Development Center, Inc. (1991). *Balls and ramps*. An Elementary Insights Hands-On Science Curriculum. Newton, MA: Author.

* Elementary Science Study. (1976). *Mobiles*. St. Louis: McGraw-Hill.

* Elementary Science Study. (1968). *Primary balancing*. St. Louis: McGraw-Hill.

* Elementary Science Study. (1968). *Structures*. St. Louis: McGraw-Hill.

Gibbons, G. (1982). *Tool book*. New York: Holiday House.

Homan, D. (1981). *In Christina's tool box*. Chapel Hill, NC: Lollipop Power.

Macaulay, D. (1975). *Pyramid*. Boston: Houghton Mifflin.

Macaulay, D. (1977). *Castle*. Boston: Houghton Mifflin.

Macaulay, D. (1988). *The way things work*. Boston: Houghton Mifflin.

McPhail, D. (1984). *Fix-It*. New York: Dutton.

* Nelson, L. W., & Lorbeer, G. C. (1984). *Science activities for elementary children* (8th ed.). Dubuque, IA: Brown.

Rickard, G. (1989). *Building homes*. Minneapolis, MN: Lerner Publications.

Rockwell, A. , & Rockwell, H. (1972). *The tool box*. New York: Macmillan.

Skeen, P., Garner, A. P., & Cartwright, S. (1984) *Woodworking for young children*. Washington, DC: National Association for the Education of Young Children.

* VanCleave, Janice. (1993). *Machines: Mind-boggling experiments you can turn into science fair projects*. New York: John Wiley & Sons.

* Williams, P., & Jinks, D. (1985). *Design and technology 5–12*. London: Falmer Press.

* Williams, R. A., Rockwell, R. E., & Sherwood, E. Q. (1987). *Mudpies to magnets: A preschool science curriculum*. Mt. Rainier, MD: Gryphon House.

Wilson, F. (1988). *What it feels like to be a building*. Washington, DC: Preservation Press.

SCIENCE
ACTIVITIES

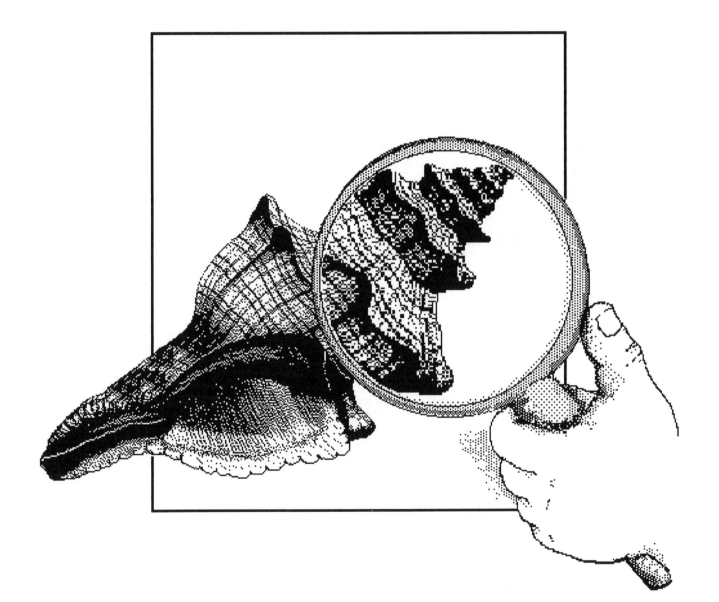

CONTENTS _____

Introduction

An Overview of the Science Activities 51

Description of Key Abilities 52

Science Activities

Short Experiments

What Tools Do Scientists Use? 53

How Can You Move the Toy Car? 55

How Are Light and Shadows Related? 57

What Do Mystery Drops Do? 58

Which of Your Senses Will Help You? 60

What Kinds of Food Contain Fat? 61

Long-Term Activities

Fall, Winter, Spring—What Changes Do They Bring? 62

What Can You Find Out by Playing with Water? 64

What Makes Bread Rise? 66

How Do Seeds Grow into Plants? 71

How Do You Record the Weather? 74

Take-Home Activities

1 Sprouting Seeds 77

2 Collections 79

Resources and References

. . . . 80

If a scientist is a person who wonders, who studies the world around her, and tries to figure out how it works, then young children are natural scientists. Children have abundant curiosity. This curiosity propels them into action—touching, tasting, weighing, mixing, pouring; from these experiences grows knowledge.

The activities in this guide are designed to show children different ways that they can use their curiosity to find out more about the world. As they monitor the growth of plants and animals, they develop observational skills. Through experiments that explore the nature of water, magnets, and chemical substances, they develop their abilities to generate questions, test hypotheses, and solve problems. Overall, the activities are intended to demystify the work of scientists, by showing children how much fun it can be to observe, experiment, classify, solve problems, and document one's work.

The Science guide is organized in two sections. The first contains short experiments, such as finding out which objects a magnet will attract, or what happens when you mix oil and water. These activities generally have focused objectives that the child is expected to accomplish within a given period of time. In contrast, the second section contains sets of projects, organized around a theme, that can continue throughout the year and often provide opportunities for free exploration and experimentation. Recording weather observations or taking nature walks to observe seasonal changes are examples of long-term activities that can begin in the fall and continue through the spring.

All activities suggested in this guide are centered around a question. The question is designed to arouse the child's curiosity and encourage her to explore the world around her in new ways. By asking questions, the teacher conveys to the child that learning is not the ability to give rote answers, but a process of thinking and experimenting. It is active rather than passive, creative rather than imitative.

To introduce your science unit or learning center, you might focus on the process of doing science. You might start a discussion with a question such as, Pretend that you want to find out how a new food tastes. What would you do? Or, You see a lot of teddy bears in a store, and you want to buy the one that is the softest. How will you decide which one to buy? These questions help children realize that they use their senses to get information about the world, and furthermore, that they act on objects in a number of ways to find out what they want to know. You might then suggest that children are scientists by nature and that they behave in many ways as scientists do.

To emphasize this point, ask questions such as, What are some things you want to know about? When you want to find out more about something, what do you do? Have children generate a list of terms that best describe what a scientist does when she wants to find out something new. Help children to understand some related terms such as *observing, exploring, experimenting, researching, analyzing,* and *examining.*

If possible, you might invite a scientist to the classroom to demonstrate laboratory equipment or an experiment. The visit gives children an opportunity to meet a professional scientist and see for themselves what scientists do in the real world.

Observational skills

- engages in close observation of materials to learn about their physical characteristics; uses one or more of the senses

- often notices changes in the environment (e.g., new leaves on plants, bugs on trees, subtle seasonal changes)

- shows interest in recording observations through drawings, charts, sequence cards, or other methods

Identification of similarities and differences

- likes to compare and contrast materials, events, or both

- classifies materials and often notices similarities, differences between specimens, or both (e.g., compares and contrasts crabs and spiders)

Hypothesis formation and experimentation

- makes predictions based on observations

- asks "what if"–type questions and offers explanations for why things are the way they are

- conducts simple experiments or generates ideas for experiments to test own or others' hypotheses (e.g., drops large and small rocks in water to see if one size sinks faster than the other; waters plant with paint instead of water)

Interest in/knowledge of natural/scientific phenomena

- exhibits extensive knowledge about various scientific topics; spontaneously offers information about these topics or reports on own or others' experience with natural world

- shows interest in natural phenomena, or related materials such as natural history books, over extended periods of time

- regularly asks questions about things observed

☐ What Tools Do Scientists Use?

Objective:	Learn to use different equipment for solving scientific problems
Core Components:	Observing
	Problem solving
Materials:	Group 1: "Biologists"
	Tray
	Microscopes
	Fabric scraps
	Feathers
	Magazine pictures
	Group 2: "Doctors"
	Tray
	Stethoscopes
	Group 3: "Inspectors"
	Tray
	Magnifying glasses
	Ink pads
	Paper
	Group 4: "Chemists"
	Tray
	Eyedroppers
	Ice cube trays
	Food coloring

Procedures:

1. Put the four sets of materials on four separate trays and place the trays in front of the children. Tell them that these are instruments that scientists use — and that they are going to use these instruments to work as real scientists do. Invite the children to identify the instruments and suggest different ways they can be used. Then, divide the class into four groups.

   a. Tell the first group of children that they will work as biologists. Place a microscope in front of them and ask if they can say what it is called and what it does. You might explain, "Microscopes can magnify—make things many, many times bigger than their actual size. They help our eyes see things that normally are much too small to see clearly, or to see at all." Ask the children to put the fabric scraps, feathers, and pictures under the microscope and compare how they look with and without the microscope. Show how to adjust the focus and angle of the mirror.

   b. Place the stethoscopes in front of the second group of children. Tell them that they will work as doctors, who are scientists of the human body. Ask them if they can tell you the name of the instrument on their tray, where they have seen it before, and what it is used for. You might explain, "A stethoscope is often used by doctors to check people's heartbeats. Just like the microscope that makes things look bigger, a stethoscope 'amplifies' sound—makes it sound louder. So things that are hard to hear, like a heartbeat, are louder and easier to hear." Ask the children to choose a partner and listen to each other's heartbeats.

Next, ask the children to find out how the heartbeat changes when their partner lies down, stands up, or jumps 10 times. Does it get louder and softer? Faster and slower? You may wish to help children develop a chart for recording these changes. Caution children not to talk or yell into the stethoscopes.

c. Tell the third group of children that they will be working as inspectors. Ask them what magnifying glasses are used for, and explain that this equipment, like the microscope, can make objects look bigger so that you can see small patterns and markings better.

Let them take their own fingerprints by carefully putting one finger at a time on the ink pad (one hand only) and then on a piece of paper. See if they can use the pictures below to figure out whether their fingerprints are whorls, arches, or loops. Show them that they can make the prints look clearer by placing the magnifying glass flat on the paper, then gradually lifting it up until the picture is in focus.

d. Tell the fourth group of children that they will work as chemists, scientists who study how different substances combine to create new ones. Ask the children what happens when you mix colors together. Give each of them two ice cube trays, one containing water, the other food coloring. Ask them how many different kinds of colored water they can mix. When they are finished, let them compare their colors and how they made them.

2. Let each group of children stay with their originally assigned activity for about 15 minutes. Then, switch the group to another activity.

Notes to the Teacher:

1. The purpose of this activity is to acquaint children with the scientific tools or equipment that they will be using all year. It may take more than one session.

2. If the children are interested, you might build upon the activities in the following ways:
   • Group 1: Let children select other items to examine under the microscope (e.g., hair, eraser crumbs, pulp from the pencil sharpener).
   • Group 2: Where can children find beats in their body (e.g., chest, wrist, neck, thumbs)?
   • Group 3: Use the magnifying glass to examine newspaper type, patterns on leaves, faces in photographs. Or, look at the items that Group 1 is examining (hair, pencil shavings, etc.) and compare the power of the magnifying glass with that of the microscope.
   • Group 4: Children may want to make "recipes" or color charts based on their findings.

My Fingerprint Pattern is:

Loop **Arch** **Whirl** **Other**

☐ HOW CAN YOU MOVE THE TOY CAR?

Objective:	Learn the function of magnets through experimentation
Core Components:	Hypothesis testing
	Comparing and contrasting
	Observing
Materials:	Metal toy cars
	Strong magnets
	Straws
	Ruler
	String
	Tape
	Wire
	Popsicle sticks

Procedures:

1. To introduce this activity, you might say that you have a problem for the children to solve. Show them a toy car and challenge them to move it across the table without touching it.

2. Arrange for children to work in small groups, with one car (or more) per group. Encourage children to try different materials to move their car across the table. You might also create and distribute a form on which children can note their "findings" by drawing or listing materials, how they were used, and whether they were successful.

3. After children have experimented with different kinds of materials, ask them, "What did you find out?" See if children have figured out that they can move the car with the magnet. If someone has another idea, encourage her to show you and ask the children whether they think this method works (other possible solutions might be pushing the car with a ruler or tipping the table). Watch and listen carefully to children's observations and explanations. Use their comments to suggest what types of activities might benefit them in the days to follow.

Variations:

1. Extend this activity with another magnet game. Divide the class into small groups and give each group a magnet and a box of small objects such as paper clips, nails, marbles, pennies, beads, and can openers. Ask children to act as scientists and find out what kinds of objects the magnet attracts (make sure they can tell you what *attract* means).

2. Explain that scientists always record the results of their experiments so they can look for patterns and remember what they find out. Tell children that they can record the results of their magnet experiment by sticking two labels on a table, one saying *yes* and the other *no*. They can line up objects under the appropriate label and then compare and contrast the two columns. Or, help them develop a chart, like the one below, so that they can save the results of their experiment.

3. Have a follow-up group discussion and ask children if they see any similarities among the objects that stick to the magnet. See if they can formulate — and articulate — the idea that most metal things stick, but some do not. After some discussion, share with children that the metals that magnets attract have a "hidden ingredient," and that it is iron or steel (which contains iron).

Magnet Experiment Recording Chart

Does a magnet attract this object? Circle either "yes" or "no."

Nail	Yes	No
Paper Clip	Yes	No
Marble	Yes	No
Bead	Yes	No
Can Opener	Yes	No
Penny	Yes	No
*	Yes	No
*	Yes	No

* Choose your own objects for these two boxes.

□ How Are Light and Shadows Related?

Objective:	Explore the relationship of light to shadows
Core Components:	Understanding spatial relationships
	Comparing and contrasting
	Observing
Materials:	*Bear Shadow* by Frank Asch
	flashlight
	chalk

Procedures:

1. Read children *Bear Shadow* by Frank Asch, a book about a bear that tries to get rid of its shadow. Ask children questions about shadows, such as, What do you know about shadows? Where have you seen shadows? When do you see shadows?

2. Ask children if they see any shadows in the classroom. Ask them what they could do to make shadows. Then, encourage them to try out their ideas. Provide materials they might need, such as a flashlight.

3. Take the children outside on a sunny day. Ask children to try to "lose" their shadows. Can they do it? What happens if they stand inside a larger shadow, or on the shaded side of the playground? How else can children change their shadows? Can they make their shadows grow bigger? smaller? thinner? wider? Ask children to make shadows with different objects, such as an umbrella or a book. How can they change the shape of the shadows?

4. Ask children to work in pairs to trace each other's shadows on the sidewalk or an asphalt play area. Return to the same spot every 2 or 3 hours. Have the shadows changed at all? Are they bigger? smaller? wider? pointing in a different direction?

5. Play shadow tag. The child who is "it" tries to tag other children by stepping on their shadows. Try tagging in different ways: by touching someone's shadow with your shadow, or with the shadow of your hand.

□ WHAT DO MYSTERY DROPS DO?

Objective: Conduct an experiment to compare and contrast the behavior of water droplets on different types of paper

Core Components: Comparing and contrasting
Experimenting

Materials: Different types of paper (e.g., typing paper, wax paper, newspaper, paper towels)
Different types of wrappers (aluminum foil, plastic wrap)
Water
Eyedropper
Magnifying glass

Procedures:

1. In small groups or with the whole class, have children put drops of water on different surfaces. Start with the aluminum foil. Does the water stay in one spot or spread out? sit on the surface or soak through?

2. Invite children to experiment, alone or in small groups, with using an eyedropper to make drops and drop piles on a piece of aluminum foil. How can they make giant drops? tiny drops? piles of drops? What different shapes can they make by pulling on the edge of the drops with the eyedropper? Can they push a drop from one spot to another? How close can they put drops and still keep the drops separate?

3. Introduce new surfaces as seems appropriate. Ask the children how water drops change on different kinds of surfaces. Do the drops look the same on the foil and on the paper towel? Do they form the same shapes and piles? Discuss the experiment with the children and ask what discoveries they have made. Write down children's responses.

4. Talk with the children about the properties of the papers and wrappers they are using. How are the surfaces different from each other? Which material absorbs, or soaks up, the most water? the least?

5. Ask children to make two groups: surfaces that absorb water and those that don't. How does the material's ability to absorb water relate to its function—the way that it's used? For example, why do you use paper towels to mop up a spill, and aluminum foil to save leftovers?

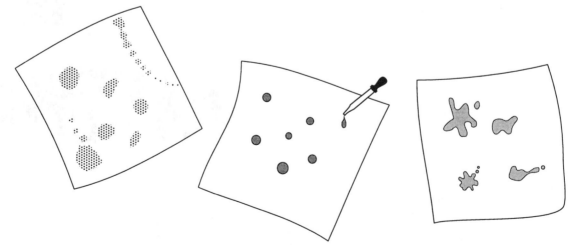

Variations:

1. Encourage children to experiment with different liquids, such as vinegar, oil, and molasses. Let them think of other liquids they might like to test: milk, apple juice, tea, or coffee.

2. Ask children to use magnifying glasses to examine both the edge and the middle of drops of different liquids, finding out whether drops of different liquids look alike. If not, how are they different?

3. Encourage children to make drop pictures with different liquids. Which liquids dry quickly? slowly? As time passes, which drops change in appearance?

4. Record children's questions and discoveries. Ask the children to make drawings and collect the pages into a big book.

This activity was adapted from Elementary Science Study. (1971). *Drops, streams, and containers.* St. Louis: McGraw-Hill.

□ WHICH OF YOUR SENSES WILL HELP YOU?

Objective:	Learn how your senses can help you solve problems
Core Components:	Comparing and contrasting
	Hypothesis testing
	Drawing conclusions
Materials:	Clear liquids (water, sugar water, and salt water)
	Amber-colored liquids (honey water, cider vinegar, and apple juice)
	Dark liquids (coffee, cola, and soy sauce)
	9 clear plastic bottles with caps
	Newspaper or cloth
	Paper cups

Procedures:

1. To prepare, pour the different liquids into bottles and cover the work tables with newspapers or cloth.

2. Tell the children that you have an interesting problem for them to solve. There are three sets of bottles on the table with liquid inside. Can they figure out which bottles contain your favorite drinks—apple juice, water, and cola? How might they solve the problem? The children usually will try to identify the bottles based on visual observation. Encourage them to try other methods with questions such as, How do you know? The liquids in these bottles look very similar. How can you be sure one is apple juice and the other is not?

3. Lead children's discussion to the different human senses. Explain that whereas they can use their eyes to identify the drinks in some cases, they must use other senses for liquids with a similar color. Ask them which of their senses can help. Encourage the children to smell the different liquids. Tell them that they can pour a small amount of each liquid into a paper cup and taste it.

4. Ask children to tell the group their findings. Help children draw conclusions about the functions of human senses.

Notes to the Teacher:

As a safety measure, you might emphasize that children shouldn't drink out of bottles without labels, unless they are being supervised by a parent, teacher, or other responsible adult.

☐ WHAT KINDS OF FOOD CONTAIN FAT?

Objectives:	Conduct a simple experiment and record results
	Learn about a healthy diet
Core Components:	Observing
	Recording and interpreting observations
	Drawing conclusions
Materials:	6 different foods, such as
	Dry breakfast cereal
	Cookie
	Cracker
	Mayonnaise
	Piece of apple, grape, or other fruit
	Frankfurter
	Paper
	Recording chart

Procedures:

1. Have a discussion with children about healthy food. You might want to use this opportunity to introduce the U. S. Food and Drug Administration's food pyramid. Ask children to give examples of junk food and healthy food. Write down children's responses. Discuss what the foods in each group have in common, focusing on what makes junk food unhealthy (fat, sugar, salt, lack of vitamins and minerals).

2. Introduce the activity by telling the children that they will conduct an experiment to discover which foods contain fat. They will examine six different kinds of food. Give the children six pieces of paper each. Ask them to rub one food firmly on one sheet of paper; hold the paper up to a light and observe the spot where they just rubbed; and write down on a recording chart what they observe. Does the food seem to have a lot of fat? Some fat? No fat?

3. Ask children to repeat the procedure with each food, then compare the results across foods. Ask questions such as, Based on our experiment, how might we know whether one food has more fat than another food?

This activity is adapted from L. W. Nelson & G. C. Lorbeer. (1984). *Science activities for elementary children* (8th ed.). Dubuque, IA: W. C. Brown.

☐ FALL, WINTER, SPRING—
WHAT CHANGES DO THEY BRING?

Objectives:	Learn to observe and study seasonal changes
	Learn to protect the surrounding environment
Core Components:	Observing
	Comparing and contrasting
	Recording and interpreting observations
	Interest in nature
Materials:	Plastic or paper bags (one for each child)
	Observation folders (one for each child)

Notes to the Teacher:

1. This activity is carried out primarily through nature walks. Give each of your walks a different theme or topic, such as a spring walk for observing seasonal changes, a summer walk for finding as many green things as possible, a fall walk for collecting leaves, an Earth Day walk for picking up trash, or a "nature scavenger hunt" for testing observational skills (a sample scavenger hunt is reprinted on the following page). The theme of the nature walk is designed to focus children's attention, not to constrain their own agendas or interests. Nature walks work best if the children are free to observe and explore the surrounding environment to the extent that they are safe.

2. If you are going to follow the same route each time, you can invite each child to "stake a claim" to a plot of ground or an object along the path. Mark the children's areas or objects in a permanent enough way that they will be able to locate them in different seasons. You can even map the route and mark the children's spots. Encourage children to notice the qualities or characteristics that make their spots unique: shade versus sun; grass versus asphalt; an object (tree or rock) versus an empty space. Before children pick their spots, explain that they will use that plot of ground or object all year to study outdoor science, observe the changes that different seasons bring, and look for living things. The children will each make a folder to collect their observations. They should be allowed from time to time to claim an additional area or object, but they must identify a reason for wanting to extend their space.

3. During or after each walk, all the children should keep written or drawn accounts or both of their observations, particularly of their special area. How has it changed? Remained the same? Structured checklists or worksheets may help the children remember what they saw. For example, provide a list or pictures of common objects, plants, insects, and so on. Distribute the list, and ask each child to mark the things that can be found in her area or on her object.

4. Follow-up discussions often extend children's spontaneous observations and enrich their knowledge of the surrounding environment. You can also supplement the walks with a variety of projects. For example, students can make leaf collages, create pictures with natural objects (see p. 231 and 245 of the Visual Arts guide), or make trash creatures.

☐

5. Nature walks offer great opportunities for children to collect natural objects that interest them. They also give you a chance to observe how each child brings her own agenda to activities, and differs from others in the way she approaches the natural world.

This scavenger hunt is from L. N. Gertz (1993). *Let nature be the teacher.* Belmont, MA: Habitat Institute for the Environment. Illustrations by N. Childs.

☐ WHAT CAN YOU FIND OUT BY PLAYING WITH WATER?

Objectives:	Learn about experimental procedures through water play
Core Components:	Hypothesis testing
	Comparing and contrasting
	Measuring
Materials:	Water tubs
	Aprons or smocks
	Assorted objects for free play with water

Plastic containers	Tubes
Bottles	Waterwheels
Sieves	Cups
Strawberry baskets	Eyedroppers
Pumps	

Notes to the Teacher:

1. The water tubs, which will be needed for all four activities, should be located near a water source with a mop and towels nearby. Remind children to keep the water in the tub and to clean up spills immediately. Limit the number of children allowed to play at any given time, based on the size of the tub.

2. Occasionally make the water tubs available at recess time or after the children finish other activities. Sometimes, the tubs should be available for free play in which children simply fill and pour water without any objectives. Other times, science experiments should be introduced that require children to form hypotheses, make careful observations, manipulate materials, and examine results.

3. The water experiments are all open ended. Materials needed for specific experiments are listed below, and in many cases can be recycled or donated. Questions are provided to assist the child in forming hypotheses and in drawing conclusions from the experiments.

Activity 1: Filling and Pouring

Materials:	Teaspoon	Cotton balls
	Cups	Drinking straw
	Eyedropper	
	Different-sized funnels and tube extensions	
	Hypodermic plunger without needle	

Questions:

1. How long does it take for a cup of water to flow through a funnel? (To count seconds, children can say "one thousand one," "one thousand two.")

2. Can you find materials or invent a device to make the water flow more slowly? (Have on display a range of possibilities: different-sized funnels, tube extensions, cotton balls and other partial "plugs.")

3. Can you figure out which tool fills a cup with water the fastest? (Provide an eyedropper, a teaspoon, a drinking straw, and a hypodermic plunger without a needle.)

Activity 2: Floaters and Sinkers

Materials: A variety of materials that sink and that float, such as

Film canisters	Sponges
Plastic eggs	Washers
Corks	Coins
Rocks	Wooden blocks
Aluminum foil	

Questions:

1. Which objects do you think are floaters?

2. Which objects do you think are sinkers?

3. Why do some objects float in water whereas other objects sink?

4. What could you do to find out whether light things always float and heavy things always sink? (Ask this if the child has suggested that floating and sinking are based upon an object's weight.)

5. Can you find a floater that will support a sinker?

6. Can you make a floater sink? Can you make a sinker float?

Activity 3: Dissolve It In Water

Materials: Plastic containers
Eye droppers
Spoons
A variety of liquids and solids, such as

Cooking oil	Cornstarch
Food coloring	Flour
Paints	Salt
Shampoo	Sugar
Sand	

Questions:

1. What do you think the water will look like if you pour _____ into it?

2. Can you tell which bottle has sugar in it and which bottle has salt? How?

3. Does the water look the same when you add food coloring and when you add paint?

Notes to the Teacher:

You might label each item A, B, C, D, and so on. Tell children that they can record their experiments by using letters. For example, A + B + D = the result. Also, make sure that the children do their mixing in the containers rather than in the water tub.

Activity 4: Volume and Conservation

Materials: Assorted plastic containers, measuring cups, and bottles
Questions:

1. Do you think this bottle has more water than the other?

2. Why do you think this bottle has more water?

3. How can we check to see if these two bottles have the same amount of water?

☐ WHAT MAKES BREAD RISE?

Objective: Learn about chemical change by conducting experiments and baking bread

Core Components: Observing
Measuring
Hypothesis testing
Recording and interpreting observations

Notes to the Teacher:

1. Every day, an incredible chemistry demonstration is going on in kitchens around the world. Ordinary ingredients such as flour, sugar, and salt are mixed together and turned into warm, nutritious, good-smelling bread. In this activity, children conduct a series of experiments to determine the ingredients that make bread rise. In the process, they grow to understand one of the many ways that chemistry affects their daily lives.

2. To the extent possible, encourage children to conduct the experiments and to do the cooking themselves. Talk with them about how they can work together as a group to conduct an experiment or make a recipe. Will they take turns? volunteer for different tasks? Once they get started, provide support by asking appropriate questions, such as, What is the difference between a teaspoon and a tablespoon? How can you make sure you have measured *exactly* one tablespoon? *exactly* one cup?

3. This activity can be extended in many different ways. For example, children are developing language and math skills as they read recipes and make measurements; in addition, they might hold a bake sale and price and label their bread, make change, and total their earnings. To promote social understanding, you can ask parents to send in a bread recipe unique to their family or their culture. You can collect the recipes into a class cookbook, and bake some of the breads in class. You also can use bread baking as the focus of a discussion or unit about nutrition.

Activity 1: What Would Happen If . . . ?

Materials: Baking utensils
Ingredients for 3–5 loaves of bread (suggested recipe follows)
Chalkboard and chalk or chart paper and markers

Procedures:

1. What would happen if you wanted to bake a loaf of bread but couldn't find the baking soda? What would happen if you ran out of flour? sugar? With the children, brainstorm a list of ingredients that are needed to make a loaf of bread and write it on the chalkboard or chart paper. Tell students that they will conduct a series of bread-baking experiments to find out which ingredients really are essential. They also will find out some answers to the question, What makes bread rise?

2. Select a bread recipe that is relatively simple to prepare. You might use one of your own favorites, the recipe that follows, or a special family recipe.

3. Bake the bread with the children, following the recipe exactly so children know what the bread is supposed to look and taste like. Challenge the children to predict which ingredient or ingredients in the recipe are needed to make the bread rise.

4. Bake the bread again, but this time leave out one of the ingredients that the children have named. Encourage the children to taste as well as look at the bread. Discuss the differences between the two loaves of bread the children have baked. Was the ingredient they left out essential to making a good loaf of bread? What does it do? Does it make bread rise? If so, the children probably have identified a leavening agent (baking soda, baking powder, or yeast).

5. Ask the children what other ingredients they would like to leave out. Bake the bread a few more times, leaving out one, and only one, ingredient at a time. Each time, talk with the children about what the ingredient contributes to the dough or batter. Does it help the bread rise? Is it needed for another reason? Why?

AUNT AMY'S BANANA BREAD
© 1998 Sara Evans, Belmont, Massachusetts

Ingredients:
   l/2 cup butter or margarine
   1 cup sugar
   1 egg
   4 tablespoons plain yogurt
   1 teaspoon baking soda
   2 ripe bananas, mashed
   1 1/2 cups flour
   1/4 teaspoon salt

Preheat oven to 350°.
In a large bowl, cream together the butter (or margarine) and sugar. Add the egg, mashed banana, and mix well.
Sift the flour with the salt. In a separate bowl, mix together the yogurt and baking soda. Add the flour and the yogurt mixture to the banana mixture in alternate portions.
Grease and flour a 9" x 5" loaf pan. Pour in the batter and bake for 55 minutes or until done (if you stick a toothpick into the loaf, it should come out clean). Let the loaf cool before cutting.

Activity 2: What's the difference between baking powder and baking soda?

Materials:	Baking soda	Flour
	Baking powder	6 paper cups
	Vinegar	Measuring spoons
	Recording chart	Water

1. By doing the bread-baking experiment, the children probably discovered that baking soda or baking powder (or perhaps both) can make bread rise. Do these ingredients work all by themselves, or do they need help? Tell children that in the following experiments, they will combine baking soda and baking powder with different ingredients and see what happens.

2. Ask children to set up three pairs of paper cups and number the cups from 1 through 6. Next, they should put one teaspoon of baking soda in Cups 1, 3, and 5. Ask them to clean and dry the measuring spoon and put one teaspoon of baking powder in Cups 2, 4, and 6.

3. Children should perform the following experiments and use the chart to record their results (e.g., "foam" or "no foam"). If it would be helpful to the children, write the ingredients for each cup on a chalkboard or chart paper.

    a. Add 1/4 cup water to Cup 1 and 1/4 cup water to Cup 2. What happens?

    b. Mix 1/4 cup flour and 1/2 cup water. Add half the mixture to Cup 3 and half to Cup 4. What happens?

    c. Add 1/4 cup vinegar to Cup 5 and 1/4 cup vinegar to Cup 6. What happens?

	baking soda	baking powder
1 water		
2 water		
3 flour mixture		
4 flour mixture		
5 vinegar		
6 vinegar		

4. Ask children to review their results. What do they think makes the baking powder foam? What do they think makes the baking soda foam? What do the bubbles do in a loaf of bread? (When acids and bases combine, they often produce carbon dioxide gas. Baking powder is made of sodium bicarbonate, a base, plus powdered acid; it is activated by water and other liquids. Baking soda contains sodium bicarbonate, but no acid. Therefore, an acid must be added to baking soda before carbon dioxide can be released. A bread recipe that uses baking soda as the leaven must also include vinegar, fruit juice, buttermilk, or another acid. Examine a piece of the bread with the children to see the tiny pockets left by bubbles of carbon dioxide.)

5. Ask children what they could add to Cups 1 and 3 to make the baking soda mixture foam. Try it.

Activity 3: Yeast! It's Alive!

Materials: 3 or 4 packages yeast   4 balloons
                     Sugar   4 one-liter bottles
                     Flour   2 bowls
                     Salt   Measuring cups
                     Apple juice   Funnel
                     Recording chart

Procedures:

1. Open a package of the yeast and encourage children to look at it, touch it, and smell it. Explain that it is a leavening agent like baking powder and baking soda. But unlike these other two ingredients, it is made up of tiny living organisms that, given the right conditions, will grow and multiply. Yeast (a single-celled plant) has been used by people throughout the ages to make bread rise. But in this experiment, children will be using yeast to blow up balloons!

2. Tell the children that they will be testing four different foods, all possible ingredients in baking, to find out which is the best "food" for yeast. First, have children empty three packages of yeast into a bowl and mix it thoroughly with one cup of warm water (the temperature is important, as you will see in the next experiment).

3. Next, have the children label four identical one-liter bottles, each with the name of one of the foods they will test: sugar, flour, salt, and apple juice. Challenge them to prepare the bottles as follows:

   a. In the bowl, mix 1/2 cup sugar and 1/2 cup warm water. Add 1/4 cup of the yeast mixture. Use the funnel to pour the mixture into the first bottle. Take a balloon and fasten it securely over the mouth of the bottle. Lay the bottle on its side.

   b. Wash out the bowl and funnel. Mix 1/2 cup flour and 1/2 cup warm water. Add 1/4 cup of the yeast mixture. Pour the mixture into the second bottle. Fasten the balloon over the mouth of the bottle and lay the bottle on its side.

   c. Use the same procedure to set up the third bottle with 1/2 cup salt, 1/2 cup water, and 1/4 cup of the yeast mixture.

   d. Use the same procedure to set up the fourth bottle with 1/2 cup apple juice and 1/4 cup of the yeast mixture. The apple juice should be at room temperature.

4. Challenge the children to predict which food is best for the yeast. To find out the answer, encourage them to check the bottles every half hour and record their observations on the following chart, using pictures, words, or both. What do the balloons look like? Which is the biggest? the smallest? What do the mixtures inside the bottles look like? Are there bubbles? clumps of bubbles?

5. How are the bubbles produced? Ask children for their ideas. Explain that yeast breaks down starches, like flour, into sugars, and converts sugar into alcohol. During these processes, carbon dioxide gas is produced. Ask children what they think happens when yeast is mixed with flour, sugar, salt, or fruit juice in bread dough.

Yeast Experiment Recording Chart

	after 1/2 hour	after 1 hour	after 1 1/2 hours	after 2 hours
flour				
sugar				
salt				
apple juice				

Activity 4: Hot and Cold

Materials:
- 3 packages yeast
- Flour
- 3 one-liter bottles
- 2 bowls
- Paper and pencils
- 3 balloons
- Funnel
- Measuring cups
- Stovetop or microwave

Procedures:

1. In each of the experiments above, a liquid — usually water — is added to the yeast. Does the temperature of the liquid make any difference? To find out, tell children that they will do another round of experiments with yeast. This time, however, the same type and amount of "food" will be used in each of the bottles. What will change is the temperature of the water.

2. Label the bottles *hot, warm,* and *cold.* Provide the guidance that children need to set up the experiments as follows (however, do the steps involving boiling water yourself):

   a. Mix 1/2 cup flour and 1/2 cup water. Use the funnel to pour the mixture into the first bottle. Boil water on the stove or in the microwave. Dissolve one package yeast in l/2 cup of the hot water, stir well, and use the funnel to pour the mixture into the bottle. Fasten a balloon securely over the mouth of the bottle and lay the bottle on its side.

   b. Pour a mixture of 1/2 cup flour and 1/2 cup water into the second bottle. Dissolve one package of yeast in 1/2 cup warm water (about 80° or so) and add that to the bottle. Fasten a balloon securely over the mouth of the bottle and lay the bottle on its side.

   c. Set up the third bottle the same way, but dissolve the yeast in 1/2 cup cold water.

3. Ask the children to predict which conditions will help the yeast grow. Once again, encourage them to check the bottles every half hour and record their results. Help children articulate what they learned from the experiment — that the water should be warm enough to help the yeast grow, but not hot enough to kill it. (Yeast begins to activate at about 50°, works best at about 80°, and begins to die at temperatures of 120° and higher.)

☐ How Do Seeds Grow Into Plants?

Objectives: Design and perform experiments to learn about the nature of seeds and plants

Core Components: Observing
Classifying
Comparing and contrasting
Formulating and testing hypotheses
Recording and interpreting observations

Notes to the Teacher:

1. Children enjoy planting seeds and watching plants grow. With the aid of a few simple materials — seeds and some containers to grow them in — children can start a series of projects that they themselves can plan, direct, and complete.

2. These activities also offer children the experience of conducting experiments with a control. To reinforce this concept, you can help children design experiments to answer questions that arise as they observe and think about seeds and plants. Guide them as they form hypotheses and think of ways to test them. Whenever possible, observe the children as they work to determine what interests them and what they want to learn more about.

3. Have children discuss their projects. Help children draw charts or develop other methods to document their activities, observations, and results.

4. If you have access to a plot of ground, planting a garden can be a rewarding way to study the growth of plants, as well as a variety of other topics: insects, nutrition, the food chain, seasonal change. Consult local nurseries to learn about plants appropriate to your climate that can be harvested before the end of the school year.

—Activity 1: Sorting Seeds

Materials: All kinds of seeds (e.g., fruit seeds and pits, peas and beans, pinecones, burrs, maple "helicopters")
Plastic bags

Procedures:

1. If possible, go for a walk to look at seeds and, if appropriate, collect them. Show that seeds can come in many different forms, including nuts, pinecones, fruits, and berries. What different types of seeds can the children find? What kind of plants did the seeds come from? What kind of plants will the seeds grow into? If the seeds are on the ground, how far are they from the "parent" plant?

2. When you return to the classroom, give children the seeds they have collected or some seeds that you have put together in advance. Ask children to look at and touch the seeds, and sort them however they wish (e.g., by size, texture, color, or type). When children are finished, encourage them to explain how they sorted the seeds.

3. Tell children you'd like to suggest another way to sort seeds — according to the way that they travel! Many plants have clever methods for disbursing seeds, so that the new plants can grow some distance away from the parent. That way, the plants won't be competing for light, water, and nutrients from the soil. Some seeds (like those from maple trees and

dandelions) are carried by the wind. Other seeds (like burrs) are covered with little hooks or spikes that allow them to "hitchhike" by sticking to animal fur. Still other seeds (like sunflower seeds and raspberries) are eaten by birds and animals and pass through their digestive systems. Encourage children to study their seeds and how they might travel.

Activity 2: What do plants need?

Materials: Plastic cups or other containers   Potting soil
   Radish seeds   Paper and pencil
   Chalkboard and chalk or chart paper and marker

Procedures:

1. Brainstorm with children about the different things that seeds might need to grow into plants (e.g., air, water, light, soil, fertilizer). Make a list.

2. Challenge the children to design experiments that will test whether radish seeds (or whatever seeds you've selected) really need the different items on their list. For example, how might they test whether the seeds need air? (They might drop the seeds into a cup of water.) Remind them to set up a control for each of their experiments, and to record their observations on a regular basis.

3. Keep watching the sprouts for a few weeks to see if their needs change. For example, seeds can germinate in the dark, but plants need light to keep growing.

4. What other questions do the children have about plants? Can they make a prediction and test it? Here are a few questions that are fun to explore (be sure to label the containers if they look the same):

   - Will radish seeds grow if you nick them? If you cut them in half?
   - Does it make a difference if you plant the seeds in soil, sand, or gravel?
   - Does it make a difference if you water the seeds with clean water or polluted water, such as soapy dishwater?
   - Do the sprouts grow better when it's warm or when it's cold?
   - Will the sprouts grow faster if you talk to them? sing to them? fertilize them?
   - Does it make a difference if you use a different type of seed? (For example, might other seeds survive with less warmth or sandier soil?)

Activity 3: Rooting Around

Materials: Potato, carrot and onion   Bowls of water
   Pot or other container   Dirt or potting soil
   Knife

Procedures:

1. Explain to the children that you don't always need a seed to grow a new plant. Tell them that they will grow a new plant from a potato. The potatoes we eat are called tubers, part of the root system of the plant that acts as an underground storehouse of energy. Some plants, such as the potato, can be grown from tubers or bulbs.

2. Find a small potato that has at least two eyes, the small dents on the surface of the potato. Put it in a bowl and keep it partially covered with water. Encourage children to observe the potato and record what it looks like twice a week. Do shoots grow? Where? Do roots grow? Where? How long does it take?

3. Once children have observed the new growth, they can plant the potato in a pot of soil. Children can put the pot in a sunny spot and water it regularly as part of a classroom "garden."

4. Try to grow new plants from the carrot and the onion, which also grow underground. Cut the vegetables into large pieces. Ask children to predict which of the pieces will have new growth (e.g., the top of the carrot) and where. Put the pieces in bowls, partially cover them with water, and observe how they grow.

☐ HOW DO YOU RECORD THE WEATHER?

Objectives: Observe and record changes in the weather
                        Learn about seasonal changes

Core Components: Observing changes in the environment
                        Recording and interpreting observations
                        Measuring
                        Hypothesis testing

Materials: Posterboard
                        Markers or crayons
                        Pushpins
                        Outdoor thermometer

Notes to the Teacher:

1. The purpose of this year-long weather recording activity is to help children become careful observers of changes in the weather and the seasons. Before introducing the activity to the children, prepare weather picture cards (e.g., sun, clouds, rain, wind, snow) and a calendar grid with spaces large enough to hold the cards. The children can draw the weather pictures during their art activity time.

2. Every child should have a turn to be the weather reporter for a week. Whole-group time is usually the best time for the weather report, so that the entire class feels involved and responsible. The weatherperson can pin the appropriate weather picture card to the calendar and explain how she made her decision (e.g., observing, listening to the radio).

3. Encourage the children to report other information as well, such as temperature, wind direction, and wind speed. Show children how to find this information in the newspaper, or hang a thermometer outside the window and ask children to take their own readings. You can even make your own wind vane (see instructions on following page).

4. If you wish, use different types of graphs to compare and contrast measurements taken at different times. Challenge the children to find ways to answer questions such as the following:

   • This year, which month was warmer, September or April? Which month was colder, December or January?
   • This month, which week was the rainiest? the sunniest?
   • This week, in which direction did the wind blow most often?

5. To extend this activity, conduct projects throughout the year that explore various weather conditions and the way that weather changes with the seasons. What follows is a sample calendar, geared toward a climate with cold winters and warm summers.

September: Which Way Is the Wind Blowing?

Work with the children to make a simple weather vane. Make the base of the weather vane from a one-pint plastic container. Cut a hole in the center of the lid and have children mark the compass points (N, E, S, and W) around the edge. Push an extralong nail through the bottom of the container and the hole in the lid. For the pointer, cut a long arrow out of posterboard; make sure the tail has more surface area than the head. Staple the center of the arrow to the top of a drinking straw and place the straw over the nail and through the hole in the lid. Make sure that the hole is large enough that the straw can spin freely. (More detailed instructions for making a weather vane and other instruments can be found in Melvin Berger's *Make Your Own Weather Station*.)

Children should take the vane outside, use a compass to find north, and point the N on the vane in that direction. The head of the arrow should point *into* the wind, so that if the arrow points west, that means that the wind is blowing from the west.

October: Leaf Art

Take a nature walk and ask children to collect their favorite leaves. Suggest that they look for leaves with different shapes and colors. Take the opportunity to observe which trees are losing their leaves and which are not, and discuss the reasons why. When you return to class, give each child two identical pieces of wax paper. Ask the children to arrange the leaves on one sheet of wax paper, sprinkle on some crayon shavings, and cover the picture with the other sheet of wax paper. Next, iron the two sheets together.

November: Feeding the Birds

In late fall, animals start getting ready for the cold days ahead. Squirrels scamper around looking for nuts to stash away, and many birds fly south. Those birds that stay behind may have a hard time finding fruit and nuts to eat. So why not make them a Thanksgiving feast? Give each child a large pinecone, or if possible, take children on a walk to collect their own. Mix one part peanut butter to one part shortening. Let children stuff the mixture into the pine cones, then roll the pinecones in bird seed. Use yarn to hang the "bird feeders" from a tree, or send them home with the children.

December: Keeping Warm

Talk with the children about different ways that animals keep warm in winter (e.g., dogs grow a thicker coat, frogs bury themselves in the mud under ponds, bears hibernate). Try this experiment to show how animals "winterize" their homes.

On a cold day, mix gelatin with boiling water (follow directions on the package) and pour the liquid into film canisters or other small containers. Take the canisters outside and ask children to pretend that the canisters are small animals that need a warm home. Tell children to find the warmest spot they can, and to place their "animal" there. Encourage them to test different locations—an open, sunny spot; underneath the snow; beneath a pile of leaves. Go away for 15 minutes (can exercise help the children stay warm?) and then check the canisters. Which spots were warm enough to keep the gelatin from turning solid? Children may be surprised to find that snow makes good insulation! If they were animals, where would they put their home in the winter? What materials might keep it warm?

January: Keeping Cold

Sometimes we want items to stay cold, such as ice cream in the freezer. Make a tray of ice cubes and wrap the cubes in different materials—bubble wrap, aluminum foil, plastic wrap, layers of newspaper. Build on the December experiment and pack an ice cube in a snowball or wrap it with leaves. Put the ice cubes on a tray and challenge the children to predict which one will take the longest to melt. Check the ice cubes periodically and graph the results. Which material makes the best insulation? If you wanted your sandwich to stay cool until lunchtime, what kind of wrapper would you use?

February: Snowflakes

Bring a container of snow into the classroom and examine the flakes with magnifying glasses or, if possible, a microscope. What makes the snowflakes different from each other? What do they have in common?

You also can make snowflakes as an art project. Give each child a circle of white paper about 6" in diameter. Show children how to fold the paper in half, and then in thirds (snowflakes are six sided). Show them how to cut a pattern into all the sides, then open the paper. Display the snowflakes on classroom walls or windows.

March: Measuring Rainfall

On a rainy day, take outside a variety of containers—wastebaskets, washbasins, yogurt cups, jelly jars. After a few hours, bring the containers back inside and use a ruler to measure how much water was collected. Are the measurements the same or different? Why? Next, use measuring cups to measure the amount of water in each container. Are the amounts the same or different? Why?

April: Signs of Spring

Tell the children to pretend that they are nature detectives as they take a walk in search of signs of spring. Give them each a pencil or crayon, a sheet of paper, and a piece of cardboard to use as a clipboard and ask them to write or draw their findings. Urge them to make observations about the weather. Is it windy? Are there puddles on the ground? Challenge them to use different senses. What smells are in the air? What sounds do they hear? What colors do they see? Are spring colors different from winter colors? Encourage the children to make observations about plant and animal life, and how growth and activity increase in the spring. Can the children find any flowers? Can they find any signs of animal activity—tracks, nests, holes in the ground, partially eaten nuts or seeds? When they return to the classroom, encourage children to reflect on their observations and create a picture, a poem, or a story.

May: Cloud Study

Go outside every day for a week or more and ask children to draw pictures of the clouds they see in the sky. What color are the clouds? What are they shaped like? How high are they in the sky? What is the weather like? Ask children to consult a cloud chart or book and use their observations to identify and label the clouds they have drawn.

At the end of the week, ask children to reflect on their observations. Which clouds are associated with fair weather? rain? After observing the clouds, can they make a good guess about the weather the next day?

□ SPROUTING SEEDS

Objectives:	Sprout seeds under different conditions
	Consider which conditions produce the best results
Materials:	Several small plastic bags
	Paper towels
	A packet of seeds or a handful of beans (lima beans, kidney beans, peas)

Note to Parents:

What makes one plant grow taller than another? Why do plants die when there is no rain? Children have lots of ideas about what happens in nature. Setting up experiments that test these ideas can be a powerful way to help children think about cause and effect and the conditions that help plants grow.

Procedures:

1. Discuss with your child what plants need in order to grow. Water, light, and warmth are important factors. Encourage your child to ask questions about plants, to try to come up with possible answers to these questions, and to share knowledge that he or she has gained at school or home.

2. Some questions you can ask your child include:
   - What happens to a seed if one of the things it needs to grow into a plant (water, light, or warmth) is missing?
   - What happens if a seed has light and warmth but no water?
   - What happens if it has water, but no light?
   - What happens if a seed has water and light but is in a very cold place?

   Ask your child to help you figure out an experiment to answer these questions.

3. Help your child set up the experiment:
   - Sprinkle a few seeds or beans onto a paper towel.
   - Dampen the paper towel with water, put it in a plastic bag, and place the bag in a warm, sunny place.
   - Have your child make a label, with either words or pictures, showing that these seeds have water, light, and heat.

4. Go on to the next steps:
   - Take another paper towel and sprinkle it with a few seeds or beans (use the same type of seed or bean for all the experiments).
   - Do not dampen the towel. Put it in a plastic bag in a warm, sunny place.
   - Have your child make a label showing that these seeds have light and heat, but no water.

5. Test what happens under as many different conditions as your child would like. These conditions might include:
   - putting the seeds in a damp towel, then placing the bag outdoors in a sunny spot—in the wintertime. (Make sure the animals can't reach it). Make a label

that shows that this bag has water and sun but no heat.
- putting the seeds in a damp towel, then placing the bag in the closet. The label should show that this bag has water and heat, but no light.

6. Watch the plastic bags every day for a week. You can use the attached chart to keep track of what happens. Or, you can help your child make his or her own chart and invent some symbols.

7. Ask your child questions about the experiment, such as:
   - Which seeds sprouted first?
   - What was the best place for the seed? What things do seeds seem to need most in order to grow?

8. You might wish to plant the seeds in a small container of dirt. As the seeds continue to grow, you might ask your child:
   - Which ones stay healthy?
   - What happened to the others? Why?

9. Help your child make a true statement about the results of the experiment.

Sharing:

If you wish, your child can carefully bring the sprouting seeds, the chart, or both to school. He or she can explain the experiments to the class and describe what he or she found out.

Sprouting Seeds Chart
(Draw a picture)

	Sun.	Mon.	Tues.	Wed.	Thurs.	Fri.	Sat.
Water Light Heat							
Light Heat No water							
Water Light No heat							
Water Heat No light							

☐ COLLECTIONS

Objective: Put together, identify, describe, and classify a nature collection

Materials: A collection of items from nature, such as

       Bugs   Butterflies
       Shells   Rocks
       Flowers   Leaves

      Large box or large sheet of paper
      Glue or tape
      Pen or marker
      Paper

Note to Parents:

Many children have a collection of one kind or another. They may collect stamps, or baseball cards, or shells, or coins, or butterflies. These collections serve as sources of learning as well as pleasure when children compare the pieces to see what is the same or different about them. They can classify their treasures by color, size, where the items were found, or any other category they think of (for example, "beach things").

Procedures:

1. Go outside and collect interesting items with your child. Back indoors, ask your child to describe each item; help out if necessary. What does your child notice about the item? Is it soft? hard? colorful? round? flat?

2. Have your child make a label for each object on small pieces of paper, using either words or pictures. Your child may want to include information about where it was found, when it was found, its color, shape, size, name if she knows it, and so forth.

3. Tell your child that he or she can display each item with its label. Your child can use a box, attach the items to a big sheet of paper, or think up another method.

4. Discuss with your child the idea that there are many different ways of organizing or classifying a collection so that people can learn from it and enjoy it. Ask your child to organize the items in different ways. He or she may come up with ways that you haven't thought of! Some helpful questions you can ask your child include:
   - How will you display the items?
   - Will you put all the ones of the same color together?
   - Will you put all the ones of the same size together?
   - Will you put all the ones of the same name together?

5. Encourage your child to look at the collection and make any changes that he or she wants. Stress that there are many different ways to classify items in a collection.

Sharing:

Your child can make a display area in his or her bedroom and invite friends and family to see the exhibit. Your child's class would like to see it, too. You can help find a safe way to take the collection to school and display it.

RESOURCES AND REFERENCES

The activities on the preceding pages are just an introduction to the field. To help you conduct further explorations in the teaching of science, we offer a brief list of resources that have proved valuable to us or to our colleagues. It is intended to provide inspiration rather than a review of the literature. Sources used in the preparation of this volume are marked with an asterisk.

Agler, L. (1991). *Involving dissolving* (rev. ed.). A GEMS Teacher's Guide. Berkeley: Lawrence Hall of Science, University of California.

Agler, L. (1991). *Liquid explorations* (rev. ed.) A GEMS Teacher's Guide. Berkeley: Lawrence Hall of Science, University of California.

* Berger, M. (1991). *Make your own weather station.* New York: Scholastic.

Braus, J. (Ed.). (1987). *NatureScope: Incredible insects.* Available from National Wildlife Federation, 1400 Sixteenth St., Washington, DC 20036.

Cohen, J. (1990). *GrowLab: Activities for growing minds.* Available from National Gardening Association, 180 Flynn Ave., Burlington, VT 05401.

Doris, E. (1991). *Doing what scientists do.* Portsmouth, NH: Heinemann.

* Elementary science study. (1971). *Drops, streams, and containers.* St. Louis: McGraw-Hill.

* Elementary science study. (1968). *Light and shadows.* St. Louis: McGraw-Hill.

* Gertz, L. (1993). *Let nature be the teacher: Seasonal natural history activities for parents and other educators to share with young children.* Belmont, MA: Habitat Institute for the Environment.

Gold, C. (1991). *Science express: 50 scientific stunts from the Ontario Science Centre.* Reading, MA: Addison-Wesley.

* Herbert, D. (1959). *Mr. Wizard's experiments for young scientists.* New York: Doubleday.

* Holt, B. G. (1982). *Science with young children.* Washington, DC: National Association for the Education of Young Children.

* Katz, L. G., & Chard, S. C. (1990). *Engaging children's minds: The project approach.* Norwood, NJ: Ablex.

* Nelson, L. W., & Lorbeer, G. C. (1984). *Science activities for elementary children* (8th ed.). Dubuque, IA: W. C. Brown.

Petrash, C. (1994). *Earthways.* Mt. Rainier, MD: Gryphon House.

* Pitcher, E. V., Feinburg, S. G., & Alexander, D. A. (1989). *Helping young children learn* (5th ed.). Columbus, OH: Merrill.

Richards, R., Collis, M. & Kincaid, D. (1990). *An early start to science.* Hemel-Hempstead, UK: Macdonald Educational.

* Sprung, B., Froschl, M., & Campbell, P. B. (1985). *What will happen if . . .* Brooklyn, NY: Faculty Press.

* VanCleave, J. (1989). *Chemistry for every kid.* New York: John Wiley & Sons.

* Williams, R. A., Rockwell, R. E., & Sherwood, E. A. (1987). *Mudpies to magnets: A preschool science curriculum.* Mt. Rainier, MD: Gryphon House.

Zubrowski, B. (1991) *Messing around with baking chemistry: A Children's Museum activity book.* Boston: Little, Brown.

MUSIC
ACTIVITIES

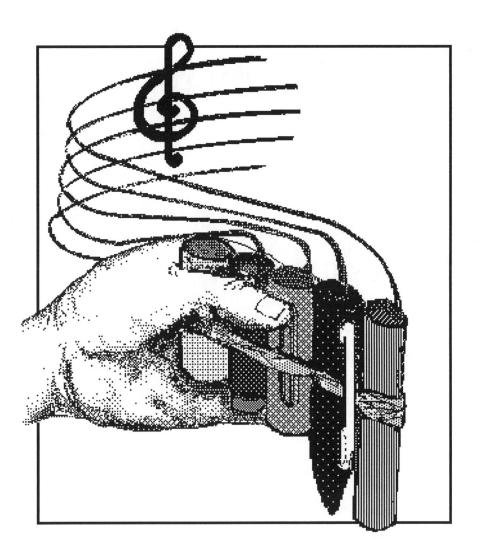

CONTENTS _____

Introduction

    An Overview of the Music Activities   83

    Description of Key Abilities   85

Activities

    Music Perception

        Loud and Soft Sound Cylinders   86

        Sound Cylinders Match-Up   87

        Music Lotto   88

        Name That Tune   89

        Xylophone Hide and Seek   90

        Picture the Music   91

        Water Bottle Xylophone   92

    Music Production

        Exploring Instrument Sounds   93

        Outdoor Sounds and Instruments   94

        Comb and Wax Paper Kazoo   95

        Rhythm Poem   96

        Pentatonic Performance Group   97

    Music Composition

        Notating a Song   98

        Rhythm Patterns   99

        Melody Steps   100

        Number Notation   101

        Composing a Tune with Music Blocks   102

        Film Scoring   103

Take-Home Activities

    1 I Hear a Train Coming!   104

    2 Family Favorites   105

Resources and References   106

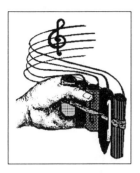

Music brings joy into our lives. Some of us play an instrument and read music. Almost all of us sing, dance, listen to performances and recordings, and compose, even if it's only a tune that we hum to ourselves. Music accompanies many of us throughout the day, either as background in the car, at home, and at the workplace, or as the highlight of artistic performances, parties, and other special events. Nevertheless, relatively few of us receive much formal instruction, perhaps because in Western culture music ability traditionally has been considered a "talent" possessed by a chosen few rather than an intellectual ability intrinsic to us all. The music activities in this guide are intended to expand the kind and depth of music-related offerings available to all children in the classroom.

Because not all children approach or enjoy music in the same way, this guide provides a broad range of activities, including music making, dramatic interpretation, and listening experiences. The activities are intended to immerse children in the world of music and to nurture three key music abilities: production, perception, and composition. Children explore the concepts of pitch, rhythm, and timbre (tone), as well as engage in simple notation and composition exercises. The music activities also invite children to use several simple percussion and melody instruments. Percussion instruments include triangles, drums, wood blocks, sand blocks (sandpaper on wood blocks), and tambourines. Simple melody instruments include bells, children's xylophones, a small electric keyboard, and tuned water glasses or bottles.

The activities can complement a school's ongoing music program and also be adapted to the children's tastes. To enrich children's experience with music, you can play recordings or allow children to use headphones to listen to tapes between structured activities. Feel free to select recordings that address children's music interests and their level of music understanding. These recordings also can illustrate specific instruments, groupings of instruments, types of voices, and musical styles and periods.

The majority of activities in this guide can be led by teachers who have not had musical training. Most activities do not call for group singing, although you can include it in many of the activities if you wish. You also might like to work together with the school music specialist, or invite parents into the classroom to sing or play instruments for the children.

Introduce the music activities (or the music area, if you are setting up a listening or instrument table) in a way that seems appropriate to your class and also makes you feel comfortable. You might begin by asking children, "What do you know about music?" Write down their responses. You can follow up with more specific questions, such as:

- Where do you hear music?
- Do you hear music at home? What kind of instruments do you hear?
- How would you sing to a baby?
- Can you hear music in a forest? What kind of music would you hear? Can you make whistling music like birds do?
- What kinds of music do you like most?

You might introduce the role of musician to children by pointing out that they listen to well-known musicians on tapes, CDs, the radio, TV, or live in concert. Ask them to name some singers or players they have heard on tapes, or watched on TV or in person. Emphasize that they themselves are musicians, too, when they sing or make music.

As children name their favorite musicians, ask them the reasons for their choices. Help children understand that music can arouse moods and emotions. Music can make us feel happy, sad, or silly. And we listen to certain music when we feel certain ways. Ask children questions such as, Do you ever sing when you are feeling happy? What kind of music do you like when you are feeling sad? If you wish, play or sing a happy and a sad song to children. Or ask children to volunteer to help.

Finally, you can introduce some of the instruments that will be used in music activities and let children play them. Ask children to name as many musical instruments as they can (e.g., guitar, piano, trumpet, violin). Show children the instruments, particularly such unconventional ones as the wood blocks, sand blocks, and tuned water bottles. Demonstrate how these instruments make music and reinforce the idea that there are many different ways to make music. Invite children to experiment with the instruments.

Music Perception

- is sensitive to dynamics (loud and soft)

- is sensitive to tempo and rhythmic patterns

- discriminates pitch

- identifies musical and musicians' styles

- identifies different instruments and sounds

Music Production

- is able to maintain accurate pitch

- is able to maintain accurate tempo and rhythmic patterns

- exhibits expressiveness when singing or playing instrument

- can recall and reproduce musical properties of songs and other compositions

Music Composition

- creates simple compositions with some sense of beginning, middle, and end

- creates simple notation system

☐ LOUD AND SOFT SOUND CYLINDERS

Objective: Use sound cylinders to learn about the role of different
                               sounds in music

Core Components: Music perception
                               Identification of different sounds

Materials: 6 different sound cylinders (either purchased or handmade)

Procedures:

1. Put the sound cylinders in front of children and tell them that each cylinder has different materials in it. Ask children to shake the cylinders and think of ways to categorize the cylinders (for example, by weight, types of sound, etc.)

2. Discuss the categories suggested by the children. Encourage children to question each other. Ask children questions such as, What senses did you use to classify (or group) the cylinders?

3. Suggest that children use their ears to arrange the cylinders from loudest to softest. Encourage children to try different methods to do this.

4. Discuss with children the methods they found most effective for ranking the cylinders. If necessary, help them generate the following system:

   • Shake the cylinders one at a time. Find the one that is the loudest and set it aside.
   • Of the ones that are left, find the one that is the loudest and set it beside the first one.
   • Of the ones that are left, find the loudest and set it beside the second.
   • Repeat until the sound cylinders are arranged in a row from loudest to softest.

5. Ask children to mix up the cylinders and try the game again.

6. Ask children to think of ways to use the loud and soft shakers in music. Which shakers would they use if they were trying to sing a baby to sleep? Which shakers would they use in a song about an elephant dance?

Variations:

Let children make their own sound cylinders. Give them empty film canisters and ask them what materials they might like to put inside in order to make shakers (e.g., paper clips, rice, or dried pasta). Glue the caps closed to prevent spilling. Once they are complete, make the sound cylinders available at appropriate times so that children can explore and experiment with the sounds.

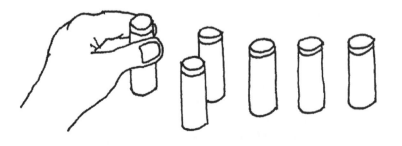

☐ SOUND CYLINDERS MATCH-UP

Objective: Practice listening skills by matching pairs of sound cylinders

Core Components: Music perception
                  Identification of different sounds

Materials: 6 pairs of sound cylinders, each pair filled with a different material
                  from the other pairs

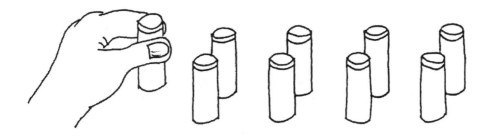

Procedures:

1. Show children the sound cylinders and tell them you have a secret about the sounds they make. Ask children if they can figure out the secret. Give them a hint: They need to shake all the cylinders and listen to the sounds carefully in order to find out the secret.

2. Give the cylinders to the children. Let them work in small groups to come up with ideas about what the secret might be. After they report on their findings, let the children discuss and question each other's ideas.

3. Reveal the secret: Each cylinder has a matching cylinder, filled with exactly the same material so it makes the same kind of sound.

4. Help children generate an effective way to find the cylinders that match.
    -   Pick up one of the cylinders and shake it.
    -   Hold it in one hand and shake it as you pick up another cylinder with the other hand and shake it also. Does it sound exactly like the first? If it doesn't, put the second cylinder down, pick up another one, and shake it.
    -   Keep trying until you find a cylinder that matches the first. Arrange the finished pairs of cylinders in a row or grid, with the matching ones side by side.

Variations:

1. Encourage children to make their own sets of matching sound cylinders. Children can challenge each other using these sets.

2. Use these cylinders as rhythm instruments to be played along with live or recorded music.

3. Encourage children to create dances using the sound cylinders as accompaniment.

□ Music Lotto

Objective:	Learn about instrument sounds
Core Components:	Sound discrimination
	Identification of different instruments
Materials:	Tape recorder
	Audiotape with different instrument sounds
	Photos or pictures of instruments featured on the audiotape

Procedures:

1. To prepare for this activity, play audiotapes of different instruments for the children so they become familiar with the sounds. If possible, bring in some instruments so children can see what they look like.

2. To play with one child: Play an audiotape featuring different instrument sounds. Ask the child to match the photos to the appropriate sounds for each instrument on the tape.

3. To play with a small group: Have children sit in a circle and give each child a photo of a musical instrument. When the child hears an instrument sound that she thinks matches her photo, she holds up the photo.

Variations:

Ask children to plan and record their own tape of musical instruments and other sounds, such as cars, machines, birds, bells, and different animals. They can make their own music matching game by drawing or photographing the sound sources, or cutting pictures out of magazines.

□ NAME THAT TUNE

Objective:	Learn about musical properties by guessing familiar tunes
Core Components:	Ability to recall musical properties of songs
	Ability to maintain accurate pitch
	Ability to maintain accurate rhythm
Materials:	A list of songs familiar to the children (include songs that they sing in class as well as popular melodies aired on radio and TV)

Procedures:

1. Let children take turns selecting a title from the list. The first player hums the tune without words and classmates try to "name that tune."

2. To make the game challenging, the player might hum the first three notes only, stop, and see whether others can recognize the tune. If the tune isn't recognized, the player can try humming the first four notes . . . then five notes . . . then six notes . . . adding a note each time until the tune is recognized.

3. Keep score and find out who can recognize and name the tunes after hearing the fewest notes.

Variations:

1. Instead of having the children hum the tune, let them use kazoos. Or, you can use recordings, playing the tape or record until someone identifies the song. Ask children to identify and discuss the features of the song that helped them recognize it (e.g., a voice, an instrument, a particular passage).

2. As children become more comfortable guessing and reproducing tunes, you can add variations to the game. You might ask questions like:
   - Can you change the rhythm of the song (the length of time you hold the notes, the time between the notes, or which notes are emphasized)?
   - Can you change the tempo, or speed, of the song?
   - Can you change how high or how low you hum the song?
   - What changes will make the song hard to recognize?
   - What changes can you make so that the song sounds almost the same?

☐ Xylophone Hide and Seek

Objective: Play a game to develop pitch-matching ability

Core Components: Pitch discrimination
                       Recall of musical properties

Materials: 2 xylophones (with individual, removable bars)
                       2 mallets
                       1 cardboard dividing screen (e.g., a manila folder)

Procedures:

1. As you introduce the activity point out how the two xylophones look and sound the same. Demonstrate by playing identical notes on each xylophone.

2. Invite two children to sit on opposite sides of the screen with a xylophone on each side. Children take turns playing a note and asking the partner to match the tone on her xylophone. (If necessary, start with only a few of the xylophone bars; for instance, remove all but three bars and add them back as children become adept at the exercise).

3. Make sure that children continue to strike the same note until the guesser has made a final guess. Children can name the color of the bar that they hit to check their guess, or look around the screen while their classmate continues to strike the key to check whether the note is correct.

4. After mastering the single tone discrimination skill, children could move on to matching more than one note at a time.

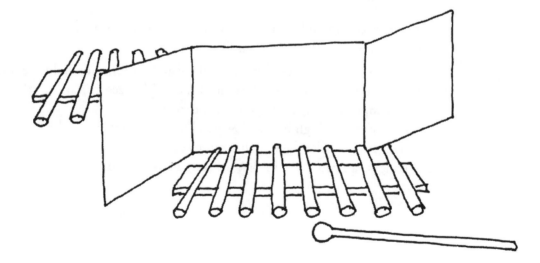

❑ PICTURE THE MUSIC

Objective:	Explore mood and dynamics of music by finding pictures that reflect musical selections
Core Component:	Sensitivity to dynamics and musical styles
Materials:	Tape recorder or record player
	Variety of tapes or records (including, if possible, Mussorgsky-Ravel's *Pictures at an Exhibition*)
	Old magazines
	Paper or posterboard
	Glue or tape

Procedures:

1. Ask children to close their eyes. Play various musical passages from a tape or record. Ask children how the music makes them feel. Ask them if the music reminds them of anything or anyone in particular. Discuss how music can stir specific thoughts or feelings.

    Mussorgsky-Ravel's *Pictures at an Exhibition* illustrates this concept well. The Russian composer Modest Mussorgsky composed the original piano suite, with each movement representing a different painting. The piece was later orchestrated by Maurice Ravel. If possible, play the music or a few passages for the children and talk about how the different movements actually sound like the pictures they represent.

2. Now play other music or sounds. Ask children to select characters, pictures, or action scenes from books or magazines that seem to illustrate the music they have heard. Model the activity, choosing a photo in a book or magazine as you listen to a piece. Children might find a tranquil nature scene to go along with some quiet music, and a busy urban scene to go along with faster, more involved music. Or they might choose a picture of birds to go along with some flute or piccolo music. Play musical passages that represent a range of styles and emotions. Ask children to explain the connections they have made. What aspects of the music led them to make their selections?

3. If they wish, children can mount the pictures they have cut out so that they have a poster or book that accompanies the music.

Note to the Teacher:

Disney's *Fantasia* is a good example of the way that pictures can be coordinated with music. You might rent this film or video and show children selected passages to illustrate how music can suggest different visual images.

☐ WATER BOTTLE XYLOPHONE

Objective:	Explore pitch by making a xylophone from bottles filled with different amounts of water
Core Components:	Pitch discrimination Music production Music composition
Materials:	8 identical glass bottles, approximately 1 liter each Water Pitcher Funnel Xylophone mallets (or dowels with a thick layer of tape or rubber bands at the end)

Procedures:

1. Fill the bottles with different amounts of water. Adjust the amount of water in each bottle to produce an approximate musical scale (more water raises the pitch). Let children use mallets to play the water bottle xylophone you created. Explore with children the reason the sound differs with the amount of water in the bottle. (As the bottle is filled with water, the column of air becomes shorter, producing faster vibrations and a higher pitch.)

2. Pour the water out and invite the children to fill the bottles with different amounts of water using the pitcher and funnel (or the faucet and sink). Children then play the water bottle xylophone they made themselves.

3. Children can take turns writing songs with these xylophones. Help them label each bottle with a symbol—either the traditional note or a symbol they suggest. Then, they can make up songs and record them by jotting down the symbols in the correct order, in effect creating their own sheet music. The children can help each other learn their songs by pairing up and sharing this sheet music (see the Music Composition section of this guide for related activities).

Variations:

1. Let children blow over the top of the bottles instead of hitting them with a mallet.

2. Put drinking straws in the bottles and let children blow bubbles in the water. Now you have an organ! (To ensure that children don't swallow the water by mistake, you can cut small holes at the top of the straws to prevent suction.)

□ EXPLORING INSTRUMENT SOUNDS

Objective: Experiment with and learn about sounds by playing simple instruments

Core Components: Expressiveness in playing an instrument
Identification of different instrument sounds

Materials: Drums, rhythm sticks, triangles, and other rhythm instruments
Xylophone
Keyboard (or piano, if available)
Rubber, wooden, and plastic mallets

Procedures:

1. Collect a variety of instruments that you plan to use with the children throughout the year. Tell them they will have time to explore the instruments, to experiment with different ways to use the instruments to make sounds, and eventually to make music. Invite one or two children at a time to pick up an instrument and see how many different sounds they can create.

2. Encourage children to experiment. Here are a few suggestions to guide their exploration, based on Bjornar Bergethon's recommendations in *Musical Growth in the Elementary School*:

   • drums—Tap in different places. Strike with fingertips, open hand, closed hand, different objects. Tap a large drum and a small drum.
   • xylophone —Strike the same bar with a rubber mallet, a plastic mallet, a wooden mallet. Touch the metal bar as it is struck.
   • rhythm sticks—Tap together near the tips, then near your hands. Strike on a desk, the floor, a book, the radiator. Try sticks of different lengths and diameters.
   • keyboard—Play the same note in lower and higher octaves. Play a series of notes individually and in a chord. If a piano is available, watch how sound is produced by the action of the hammer on the strings. Try using different pedals.

3. As children experiment, ask them to describe the sounds they create. Ask questions such as:
   • How does the sound change?
   • What happens to the sound when you . . . ?
   • How can you make the sound louder? softer?
   • How might you play the instrument for a lullaby? in the marching band at a football game? to celebrate a birthday? to say goodbye?

Variations:

1. Compare how different instruments sound when playing the same phrase. Ask for volunteers to take turns as conductor/composer. The conductor can make up a rhythm pattern and have the "orchestra" practice it in unison. Then, the conductor can signal individual instruments to play the phrase alone or in small groups. Discuss the variety of sounds that result from different combinations of instruments.

2. Improvise a piece as a group, with children playing one at a time or in small groups. Encourage them to think about which instruments they should use to create desired effects. For example, pick a theme such as "The Storm" or "The Circus." Which instrument should play the part of the elephant? the acrobat? the clown?

☐ OUTDOOR SOUNDS AND INSTRUMENTS

Objective:	Take a sound-finding walk to explore different sounds and how they are produced
Core Components:	Identification of different sounds Exploration of music in the environment
Materials:	Drumsticks Rhythm sticks Spoons Bell Bowl of water

Procedures:

1. Plan a short walk outside with a small group or the whole class. Explain to children that they will be using their ears to listen for sounds. To illustrate that sound can be caused by vibration, strike a bell. Let children touch the bell immediately and feel the vibrations. To extend the illustration, immediately lower the edge of the bell into a pan of water and point out the tiny rivulets formed by the vibrating bell. Tell children that on their sound-finding walk, they will be looking for things that vibrate and make sounds when tapped.

2. Give all the children a drumstick, rhythm stick, or spoon. Tell them that on the walk, they will be using these sticks or spoons to tap lightly on objects they see, and find out what sounds are produced. If necessary, talk about basic rules: tap gently, and don't hit anything living or anything that could break. Let the children tap on fences, trash cans, signs and signposts, trees, and mailboxes. Ask them to share their findings with classmates. Others should stop tapping during the demonstrations. Give children some questions to think about: Which items sound pleasant? Which sound not so pleasant? Which items make a high sound? Which ones make a low sound? Notice that some sounds last a long time and gradually die away, while other sounds are very short.

3. Consider which items or "instruments" discovered on the walk could be safely taken back to school. Group the instruments into those that make high sounds or low sounds, and those that make loud sounds or soft sounds. Use the instruments in a rhythm band and accompany recorded music. Or, if the newly found instruments are varied enough, have the children form a small band and make their own music.

4. Lead a discussion about outdoor sounds and instruments. Ask children to close their eyes to recapture the sounds they have heard on their walk. Help children think of words to describe sounds: clanging, tapping, clicking, booming, scraping, ringing, and so forth.

Variation:

Take a tape recorder on the walk and record sounds you hear outside (e.g., the sounds of nature—wind, birds, animals; and the sounds of mechanical things —machines, bells, whistles, sirens, cars). All these can become part of the "music" of everyday life. Come back to the classroom and see how many of the sounds the children can identify.

☐ COMB AND WAX PAPER KAZOO

Objective:	Make your own instrument (a kazoo) and use it to play a simple tune
Core Components:	Music production Expressiveness Music composition
Materials:	Small plastic comb for each child Wax paper Tissue paper and other types of paper

Procedures:

1. Give each child a comb and a piece of wax paper about the same size as the comb. Ask children to fold the paper over the comb.

2. Tell them to hold the flat side of the comb against their lips and hum. The wax paper should vibrate, producing a buzzing sound.

3. Suggest that children form a Kazoo Choir and perform a few familiar songs such as "Mary Had a Little Lamb," "Yankee Doodle," or "Be Kind To Your Web-Footed Friends."

4. Encourage children to try using tissue paper and other types of paper on the comb. Ask them to compare the sounds that the different papers produce.

Variations:

Let children try to make different kinds of instruments. Provide a variety of materials and plenty of time to experiment. Here are a few suggestions:

- Take the top off a small, sturdy box and stretch different-sized rubber bands around it to make a rubber band harp. Children can make a more elaborate instrument by putting the lid back on and cutting a hole in it to make a "sound board," or placing a pencil underneath the rubber bands to act as a "bridge."

- Make panpipes from marker caps. Collect four or five marker caps of different sizes. Let children blow across the top of the caps, then arrange them in order from highest sound to lowest sound. Tape the caps securely to a popsicle stick. Generally, the larger the cap, the clearer the pitch.

- Make sound cylinders (described on p. 86), or larger shakers from oatmeal or baking powder containers. Avoid metal cans that might have sharp or jagged edges. What types of "fillings" (e.g., rice, pennies, paper clips) can children think of?

- If an adult is available to supervise, children can make a different kind of shaker by placing two bottle caps back-to-back and nailing the pair to the end of a stick. Let children make several pairs and experiment with different ways to arrange them on the stick. For example, children could place all the bottlecaps at one end of the stick, or place a few pairs at each end and hold the stick in the middle.

- Cut a one-liter plastic soda bottle in half. Let children make a drum out of the bottom piece by putting wax paper over the top and holding it in place with rubber bands.

□ RHYTHM POEM

Objective:	Learn about rhythm and tempo by clapping to poems
Core Components:	Ability to maintain accurate rhythm
Materials:	Blackboard and chalk or chart paper and markers
	Audiotape or record

Procedures:

1. Play recorded rap music or any music with a very strong beat. Have children clap along to the beat. Later, try clapping with more complex rhythms.

2. Teach children the following poem, emphasizing the rhythm by clapping on the accented syllables. Keep the rhythm steady as the syllables in each line increase. Show children the words on the chart paper or blackboard. If you think the children would like to sing, you can make up a tune to go with it. Introduce the word *rhythm* if you wish (see the Movement guide for more rhythm activities).

   (1) Sleep, sleep, sleep, sleep.

   (2) Lit-tle fair-ies tip-toe in and

   (3) fly through the air and they spar-kle like gold as they

   (4) tick-le all our nos-es and they sprink-le us with ros-es while we

   (5) sleep, sleep, sleep, sleep.

   This poem demonstrates the following time values: quarter notes in the first line, eighth notes in the second, triplets in the third, sixteenth notes in the fourth, and quarter notes in the fifth.

3. Encourage children to write their own rhythm poems during language activity or writing time. As one example, children could group their classmates' names by accented syllables. Improvise if there aren't enough names of class members with the appropriate accented syllables.

   Jane, Kim, Luke, Juan,

   Robert, William, Trini, Heather,

   Helena, Jennifer, Estefan, Cynthia,

   Pollyanna, Christiana, Thumbelina, Rosemaria,

   Lee, Mike, Sun, Steve.

☐ PENTATONIC PERFORMANCE GROUP

Objectives: Compose and perform music on a xylophone to learn about the pentatonic (five-tone) scale

Core Components: Music production
Expressiveness
Music composition

Materials: Xylophones (with removable bars)
Two or more rhythm instruments (e.g., finger cymbals, maracas or shakers, African drums)

Procedures:

1. Introduce the word *pentatonic*. Explain that the pentatonic scale consists of only five tones or sounds. On a small xylophone (eight bars) the pentatonic scale is played on the first, second, third, fifth, and sixth bars. Ask children to remove the other bars to make pentatonic xylophones. On a piano the black notes form a pentatonic scale.

2. Encourage children to make up a song on the pentatonic scale and play it for the class. Ask children to make up a song with a loud part, a soft part, a fast part, and a slow part. Also ask them to vary the *notes*, the *rhythm*, and the *tempo* they played. Review those terms if necessary. Help children notice the way some notes are high and others are low, but they all can be played loudly and softly. Try to find different combinations of loud and soft with high and low.

3. After children become familiar with the pentatonic scale, ask a small group of children to work together to compose a piece using the pentatonic scale. Practice and rehearse the music.

4. Ask the group to perform the music for the class. Add other rhythm instruments. Choose a conductor or leader to introduce the members of the performing group, describe their instruments, and announce the name of the piece. Encourage children to think of ways that the conductor could show the performers when they should begin, when only one child should play, and whether they should play softly or loudly, fast or slow.

Notes to the Teacher:

The pentatonic scale is used here because its five notes almost always sound pleasant when played together.

☐ NOTATING A SONG

Objective:	Learn how to use symbols to represent musical sounds in written form
Core Components:	Pitch discrimination
	Recall of musical properties of songs
	Creation of simple notation system
Materials:	Paper
	Musical staff paper
	Colored pens, pencils, or markers
	Tape recorder
	Audiotape of very familiar songs

Procedures:

1. Play a song on the audiotape (e.g., "Row, Row, Row Your Boat" or "Twinkle, Twinkle, Little Star"). Make sure you select a song that the children know well—perhaps one that you have sung together as a class.

2. Ask children to figure out a way to write the song's tune or music (not words) on a piece of paper so that someone who doesn't know the song can sing it back. Tell children that they may use either the plain white paper or the music paper with staff lines on it. If they wish, they can use different colored pencils or markers to represent the rhythm and melody of the song.

3. After children finish their notations ask if they would like to sing the song while reading what they wrote on the paper. Do they think their notation would help someone who couldn't remember the tune?

4. Show children sheet music and explain that this is the "official" system that people use to remember and play back songs. It is not necessarily a better system than the ones they devised, but it is used by musicians and composers all around the world so they can read each other's music. Show children that the notation conveys both melody (through the position of the notes on the staff) and rhythm (through time signatures and the appearance of the notes—filled in, empty, dotted, etc.) Ask children to compare the official music notation system with the ones they created.

Notes to the Teacher:

1. To make the activity easier, you may play the song on a xylophone or other keyboard as well as on the tape. This will help children see the progression of notes and the relationships between them.

2. You can save samples of the children's notations in a notebook or in their own portfolios, to compare with work they do later in the year.

This activity is adapted from L. Davidson & L. Scripp. (1988). Young children's musical representations: Windows on music cognition. In J. Sloboda (Ed.), *Generative processes in music.* Oxford: Clarendon Press.

□ RHYTHM PATTERNS

Objective:	Learn that rhythms can be recorded with musical notation
Core Components:	Rhythm discrimination Creation of simple rhythm notation system
Materials:	Rhythm instruments (including ones that children have made) Pencils, crayons, markers Paper

Procedures:

1. Invite individual children to improvise interesting rhythm patterns. At first, their patterns may be somewhat erratic and nonmetric (irregular). Encourage the children to be imaginative, and try to avoid forcing their patterns into traditional metric groupings.

2. Encourage children to repeat the patterns they have developed so that they can remember them. Ask children to write down their patterns, too, using whatever system helps them remember the rhythm.

4. After children have notated their rhythm patterns, help them play the pieces, one after another, as a "percussion composition." Try the patterns in different sequences; play the same pattern on different instruments; and discuss the resulting differences.

Variations:

1. Ask one child to improvise rhythm patterns while other children develop movements to match the sounds they hear.

2. Sing a familiar song and then repeat it, changing the rhythm patterns or varying the tempo. Ask questions, such as, Does the song sound different? Why? Can you think of ways to vary the tempo that might improve this song? What words can you use to describe the changes in tempo?

☐ MELODY STEPS

Objective:	Use a staircase to help children visualize the relationship between musical sounds and written notes
Core Components:	Creation of simple notation system Pitch discrimination
Materials:	Building blocks Checkers Paper and pencils Xylophone

Procedures:

1. Use blocks to build a miniature staircase with eight steps. Talk about how the notes of the xylophone are like stair steps. Play a scale on the xylophone, striking the bars one at a time from left to right as you point to the steps, from lowest to highest.

2. Ask children to take turns placing one checker on the steps each time you play a note on the xylophone. As you go up the scale from the lowest note to the highest note, they should place the checkers on the corresponding steps, from lowest to highest. Then, go down the scale, and ask children to start with the top step and go down as they add their checkers.

3. Call the highest step number 8. Ask children to sing the numbers as they count the steps on the staircase.

4. Play three to five notes on the xylophone. Let children guess which notes you have played and place the checkers on that staircase. Ask them to identify the notes—and steps—by number to reinforce the relationship.

5. Encourage children to invent a new method to illustrate the scale, such as drawing a staircase, birds flying low and high, or a large family arranged from the tallest to the shortest member.

6. Encourage children to write a short melody using their notation system. Have them sing and explain their songs.

□ NUMBER NOTATION

Objective:	Use numbers to notate and play familiar and original melodies
Core Components:	Pitch discrimination Use of number notation system in music
Materials:	Xylophone Pencil and paper

Procedures:

1. Use the Melody Steps activity to introduce the concept that numbers can be used to represent musical notes. (Children may find it easier to see the relationship of notes to numbers than to letters or position on the staff.)

2. Use number notation to write out some simple, familiar melodies or portions of melodies (see examples below). Sing or play the melodies on a xylophone as you write. You might help children see the correspondence between notes and numbers by writing or taping the numbers on the xylophone bars.

3. Let the children play the xylophone based on the number notations.

4. Encourage children to use the number notation system to write their own melodies and play them for the class.

Mary Had A Little Lamb

3 2 1 2 3 3 3   2 2 2   3 5 5
Ma-ry had a lit-tle lamb, lit-tle lamb, lit-tle lamb.

3 2 1 2 3 3 3   3   2   2   3 2 1
Ma-ry had a lit-tle lamb whose fleece was white as snow.

Row, Row, Row Your Boat

1   1   1   2   3   3 2 3   4 5
Row, row, row, your boat. Gent-ly down the stream.

8   8   5   5   3   3 1   1   5 4 3 2 1
Mer-rily, mer-rily, mer-rily, mer-rily. Life is but a dream.

☐ COMPOSING A TUNE WITH MUSIC BLOCKS

Objective:	Arrange music blocks and play the notes on a xylophone to learn about musical notation
Core Components:	Music composition
Materials:	Xylophone
	Pencil
	Staff paper
	Music blocks (see Notes to the Teacher)

Procedures:

1. Explain to children that the notes in music are sometimes called by their letter names: A, B, C, D, E, F, and G. Point to these letters on the xylophone (you may need to add them).

2. After you have practiced the scale, try naming some notes and see if children can find them on the xylophone. Next, let one child call out notes while another child finds them on the xylophone.

3. Introduce the music blocks. Explain to children that by arranging the letters in different ways they can write simple tunes. Demonstrate the concept by arranging the blocks randomly, playing the notes on the xylophone, rearranging the blocks, and playing the new tune.

4. Ask children to compose a tune by arranging the music blocks any way they want. Tell them to try several arrangements until they find one that they like. Encourage them to use pencil and paper to write down the tunes that they compose, using letters to represent the notes. Those who wish may draw the notes on the music staff paper and write the letters underneath. Children can use this notation to perform their own and each other's tunes.

Notes to the Teacher:

To make the music blocks, take a set of wood blocks, all the same size, and paint or glue on the letters *A* through *G*, one letter per block. Or, write the letters on staff paper, along with the musical notation. Glue the staff paper onto the blocks so that when the blocks are lined up the staff is continuous, like sheet music.

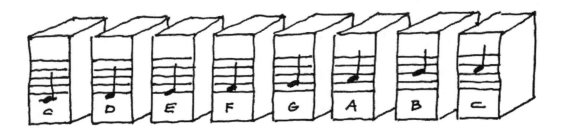

☐ FILM SCORING

Objective:	Produce and record vocal and instrumental music for a film segment to learn about the role of music in movies
Core Components:	Creation of simple compositions Relating musical styles to visual images
Materials:	Short movie, video, or cartoon Tape recorder and blank tape

Procedures:

1. Select a cartoon, short video, or a 2- to 5-minute section of a movie on videotape, preferably including lots of action. Watch the movie or video segment *without* sound. As you watch, pause occasionally and lead the group in a discussion of what the voices of the characters *might* sound like. What kind of music would work best as background music? Explain that in TV and movies, the main characters may each have special music that is played when they are approaching or appearing in a scene. Music can also create a mood or warn the viewer that something scary or important is about to happen. Talk about what kind of music might introduce the characters in this movie and accompany the action.

2. After the discussion, help children make an audiotape with music and sound effects for the drama they have just watched. Help children consider the following:

   - How can they use their voices as well as the classroom instruments (including ones they made themselves) to compose a film score for the drama?
   - How can different children play different characters in the drama?
   - How can they use props from the classroom to produce the sound effects they want?
   - How can they coordinate the voices and music they created with the film's characters and action?

3. Synchronize the film score with the film and let the class enjoy the show.

Notes to the Teacher:

Producing a film score is a long-term project. Children need to watch the film and rehearse the voice, music, and sound effects many times to complete the task successfully. For a less structured activity, you can turn off the sound of the video and let them have the fun of playing along, without recording their efforts.

□ I Hear a Train Coming!

Objectives: Learn about pitch by using sound to figure out whether a vehicle is approaching or moving away
Learn how to imitate different sounds

Materials: None

Note to Parents:

You're driving down the street and hear a siren wail. Without thinking, you know whether the ambulance is approaching or moving away. How can you tell? Because of the *Doppler effect*: the pitch of the sound seems higher when the ambulance draws near, and lower (or deeper) when the ambulance moves away.

Using sound to figure out whether an ambulance, train, car, or other vehicle is moving toward you or away from you is a good way for your child to learn about pitch and to practice careful listening.

Procedures:

1. You can try this activity in front of your home, on a walk, at a bus stop or train station, or in any outdoor place where vehicles pass. Explain to your child that trains and other vehicles make a high-pitched sound as they approach, and that the sound changes to a low rumble as the vehicles pass and move away. Have your child listen to and imitate the sounds of passing cars, trucks, or buses. Encourage your child to ask questions about these changes in sound.

2. Now try a game. When you see a car (or bus, train, or other vehicle) approaching, ask your child to close his or her eyes and listen carefully to the sound of the vehicle. Ask your child, "Does it sound like the car [bus, train, etc.] is coming toward us or moving farther away?" Ask the question again as the vehicle passes in front of you, and then once more as the vehicle moves away.

3. You and your child can make up other games. For example, your child can pretend that he or she was just hired to produce sound effects for a radio show. Ask your child to use his or her voice to sound like a train that pulls into the station, passes in front of you, and moves way; a police cruiser on a high speed chase; a fire engine racing to a fire; the high school band on its way to the football game.

Sharing:

Have your child ask other family members if they can figure out whether vehicles are approaching or moving away. Your child also can teach the game to classmates during outdoor time at school.

□ FAMILY FAVORITES

Objectives:	Collect and compare the lullabies, birthday songs, and holiday songs sung by your family and by other families Learn to sing these traditional songs
Materials:	None

Note to Parents:

Music can be an important part of family tradition. Many families have special songs that they sing at bedtime, birthdays, religious holidays, and other celebrations. Each family may have its own way of singing these songs. For example, there are many variations of the song "Happy Birthday," and it can be exciting for a child to discover these different versions. In this activity, your child will be practicing music memory and figuring out the differences between songs. Your child will also be exploring the origins of songs and their role in preserving family and cultural traditions.

Procedures:

1. Choose a song that your family sings often. Do you have a special lullaby, or a song your child enjoys hearing at holidays or other family celebrations? Teach your child the song.

2. Next, have your child ask a friend (or a neighbor, grandparent, or other relative) to share the song that his or her family sings for the same occasion. Let your child learn this song, too.

3. Ask your child questions that will help him or her compare different aspects of the songs. For example:
   - How are the songs alike? Do they have the same tune?
   - Do they talk about the same subject, but use different words?
   - Do they use basically the same words, but in different languages?
   - In what other ways are the songs different?
   - Where do the songs come from? Do they tell you anything special about your family and your friend's family?
   - How did the members of your family and your friend's family learn these songs over the years?

Sharing:

You can do this activity on your own or coordinate with the teacher, who may choose one birthday or holiday for letting children compare family songs.

RESOURCES AND REFERENCES

The activities on the preceding pages are just an introduction to the field. To help you conduct further explorations in the teaching of music, we offer a brief list of resources that have proven valuable to us or to our colleagues. It is intended to offer inspiration rather than a review of the literature. Sources used in the preparation of this volume are marked with an asterisk.

Bayless, K. M., & Ramsey, M. E. (1987). *Music: A way of life for the young child* (3rd ed.). Columbus, OH: Merrill.

Beall, P., & Nipp, S. (1984). *Wee sing and play.* Los Angeles: Price/Stern/Sloan.

* Bergethon, B. (1980). *Musical growth in the elementary school.* New York: Holt, Reinhart & Winston.

Birkenshaw, L. (1982.) *Music for fun, music for learning* (3rd ed.). Toronto: Holt, Reinhart & Winston.

Cohn, A. (1993). *From sea to shining sea.* New York: Scholastic.

* Davidson, L. & Scripp, L. (1988). Young children's musical representations: Windows on music cognition. In J. Sloboda (Ed.), *Generative processes in music.* Oxford: Clarendon Press.

DeBeer, S. (Ed.). (1995). *Open ears: Musical adventures for a new generation.* Roslyn, NY: Ellipsis Kids.

Dunleavy, D. (1992). *The language beat.* Portsmouth, NH: Heinemann.

* Flemming, B. (1977). *Resources for creative teaching in early childhood education.* New York: Harcourt Brace Jovanovich.

Jalongo, M. (1996, July). Using recorded music with young children: A guide for nonmusicians. *Young Children, 51,* 11–14.

Jenkins, E. (1984). *Learning can be fun* [video]. Washington, DC: National Association for the Education of Young Children.

Hart, A., & Mantell, P. (1993). *Kids make music! Clapping and tapping from Bach to rock!* Charlotte, VT: Williamson.

* Krone, B. (1959). *Help yourselves to music.* San Francisco: Howard Chandler.

McDonald, D. T. (1979). *Music in our lives: The early years.* Washington, DC: National Association for the Education of Young Children.

Nichols, B. (1989). *Beethoven lives upstairs.* [audiocassette]. Toronto, Ontario: Classical Kids.

Page, N. (1995). *Sing and shine on! The classroom teacher's guide to multicultural song leading.* Portsmouth, NH: Heinemann.

Prokofiev, S. (1977). *Peter and the wolf* [audiocasette]. New York: Columbia Records.

Upitis, R. (1990). *This too is music.* Portsmouth, NH: Heinemann.

Upitis, R. (1992). *Can I play you my song?* Portsmouth, NH: Heinemann.

MOVEMENT ACTIVITIES

CONTENTS

Introduction

An Overview of the Movement Activities 109

Description of Key Abilities 111

Movement Activities

Basic Techniques

"On the Farm" Warm-Up 112

Warm-Up Stretches 114

Cool-Down Exercise 115

Body Control

Mirror Game 116

Statue Game 117

Four Square 118

Obstacle Course 119

Sensitivity to Rhythm

Heartbeats 121

I've Got Rhythm 122

Hum Drums 123

Expressiveness

Oh, What a Feeling! 124

Can I Move Like . . . ? 125

Dance A Story 126

Generation of Movement Ideas

Anatomy Boogie 127

Making Shapes 128

Hop, Skip, Jump 129

Body Machines 130

Responsiveness to Music

Free Dance 131

Take-Home Activities

1 Stretching 132

2 Slow Motion 133

3 Dance Fever 134

Resources and References 135

Physical activity is an important part of the development of all young children. Children use their bodies to express emotions and ideas, explore athletic skills, and test the limits of their physical capacities. The movement activities described in this guide provide children with opportunities to experiment with creative and athletic styles of movement. (We have emphasized creative movement, however, because most early elementary programs already include athletic games and exercises.) The activities are designed to foster children's abilities in body control, in sensitivity to rhythm, in generating movement ideas, and in using the body to express feelings, emotions, and thoughts.

Children's bodily-kinesthetic awareness generally occurs in sequential stages: (1) the child's recognition of the physical self, (2) the child's performance of a variety of movements and movement patterns, and (3) the child's movement as a source of creative expression. An understanding of these stages and the different rates at which children proceed through them can help guide the planning of movement sessions in a classroom.

The activities included in this guide are organized according to key ability, in an order that reflects the developmental stages. Each section starts with a basic introductory activity and is followed by more complex activities. For example, rhythm activities begin with finding and exploring one's own beat or rhythm—the heartbeat. This introductory exercise is followed by activities that involve recognizing and moving to various rhythms. Later, children are given the opportunity to create their own rhythm patterns. Note that there is only one Responsiveness to Music activity; this category is small because music is an important part of many of the other activities. You can assess children's responsiveness to music during any activity that includes music.

Also included is a section called Basic Techniques, presenting warm-up, cool-down, and relaxation exercises. The same warm-up/cool-down exercises can be used for each session to provide a consistent method of transition between movement and nonmovement activities. Movement activities are unique in the sense that most require teacher direction and can be disruptive to those children not included. The stretching and cool-down exercises, however, are both quiet and relaxing; once the teacher has explained them and held several practice sessions, children usually feel comfortable doing them on their own.

According to the theory of multiple intelligences, the ability to solve problems or fashion products with one's body is a distinct form of intelligence. Moving a basketball past the defense, telling a story through dance, and balancing in a difficult position are a few examples of the different ways in which children can "think" with their bodies. By providing children with opportunities to increase their movement vocabulary and bodily efficiency, you can help equip them to use their bodies as problem-solving tools. Moreover, movement activities can provide active and enjoyable experiences through which children can explore the world around them.

By the time they reach kindergarten and first grade, most children have played outdoor games and know many basic athletic movement activities. To introduce the activities in this guide, you might ask children to talk about what they know about movement in general and creative movement in particular. Write down their responses. Then, you can tell children that they will be participating in some creative movement activities in which they will use their heads, arms, legs, and entire bodies to express their thoughts and emotions. They can free their imaginations and pretend to be all kinds of things, using their bodies to express themselves.

Next, you might play the game Simon Says. Follow the traditional rules, but instead of giving instructions such as "Simon says 'touch your nose,' " challenge children to use their imaginations and pretend to "be" different things. Model several examples, such as pretending to act like a monkey and a flower, so that children have an idea of what they will do. Encourage children to make any gestures that they think are appropriate to Simon's instructions. Once they get used to playing the game this way, they can take turns being the leader. Here is a sample of creative movement ideas:

Simon says be . . .

> a tall tree on a windy day
> a seed growing into a flower
> popcorn popping
> spaghetti—before and after cooking
> a person walking through mud
> a dog walking through mud
> a person rowing a boat
> a robot
> the letter *o*
> a snowflake floating down from the sky.

You can tell children that they were acting very creatively because they used their imaginations—and their bodies—to pretend to be many different people and things. Explain that they will play more games like this during movement activity time.

A number of the movement activities involve remembering specific steps in sequence, a task that can be difficult for young children. Therefore, we sometimes provide a script to help you "talk" children through an exercise, describing each movement that the children are supposed to make. Feel free to substitute your own words.

Body Control

- shows an awareness of and ability to isolate and use different body parts

- plans, sequences, and executes moves efficiently—movements do not seem random or disjointed

- is able to replicate own movements and those of others

Sensitivity to Rhythm

- moves in synchrony with stable or changing rhythms, particularly in music (e.g., child attempts to move with the rhythm, as opposed to being unaware of or disregarding rhythmic changes)

- is able to set own rhythm and regulate it to achieve a desired effect

Expressiveness

- evokes moods and images through movement using gestures and body postures; stimulus can be a verbal image, a prop, or music

- is able to respond to mood or tonal quality of an instrument or music selection (e.g., uses light and fluid movements for lyrical music versus strong and staccato movements for a march)

Generation of Movement Ideas

- is able to invent interesting and novel movement ideas, verbally, physically, or both; or offer extensions of ideas (e.g., suggesting that children raise their arms to look like clouds floating in the sky)

- responds immediately to ideas and images with original movements

- choreographs a simple dance, perhaps teaching it to others

Responsiveness to Music

- responds differently to different kinds of music

- shows sensitivity to rhythm and expressiveness when responding to music

- explores available space (vertical and horizontal) comfortably using different levels, moving easily and fluidly around the space

- anticipates others in a shared space

- experiments with moving the body in space (e.g., turning and spinning)

□ "ON THE FARM" WARM-UP

Objective:	Warm-up and stretch out before creative movement activity
Core Components:	Flexibility
	Coordination
	Body control
Materials:	None

Procedures:

1. Ask children to stand up. Invite them to join you for an imaginary day on a farm as a fun way to gently stretch out and warm up for creative (or athletic) movement activities. You may want to start by having the children close their eyes and imagine being awakened by a rooster's crow.

2. Using this script or your own words, tell the children to jump out of bed and gently stretch out. Ask them to raise their right arm toward the ceiling, stretching out the right side of their rib cage and bending slightly to the left. They should repeat with the left arm and do both stretches a few more times.

3. Next, ask them to work the kinks out of their necks by nodding slowly up and down, then looking to the right, the left, and back again. Tell them to reach their shoulders up towards their ears, then down toward the ground. Ask them to move their shoulders in a circle—up towards the ears, way back as if their shoulders could touch each other, down, forward, and back to a resting position. After a few more shoulder circles, tell children its time to pull on their overalls (they should pretend to step into overalls) and go outside.

4. Tell children to take a few deep breaths. What do they smell? Fresh air? Hay? Pancakes and sausage? They'll have to do the chores before they can eat breakfast. Ask children to perform the following movements, or other ones that you make up, to stretch the major muscle groups.

   • *Pat the cat*:

   Barn cats are usually jumpy, so you want to move very slowly. Starting with your head, reach down toward the floor. Begin by dropping your chin to your chest and slowly letting your head carry you toward the floor. Follow with the shoulders and the back. Just hang and let your arms hang loosely. Pat the cat, then slowly roll up, straightening the back, shoulders, and head until you are standing straight. (*Repeat.*)

   • *Do the chicken*:

   On the visit, see how chickens' heads move back and forth as they walk. Can you move your neck and head like that, but not too fast?

- *Walk through mud* (knee lifts):

    Watch out—some parts of the farm are very muddy. You have to lift your knee clear up to hip level just to take a step! Feel the stretch in the top of your thigh each time you take a step. [*Have children alternate legs, holding the knee up for a count of three.*]

- *Rake the garden:*

    It's early spring and time to rake the garden to prepare it for planting. Stretch out those arms as you rake up the old plants and leaves.

- *Pull up weeds:*

    You got up a lot of the weeds while raking, but you'll have to bend down and pull out the rest. Stand with your legs slightly apart and slowly bend your knees. Now reach out, pull up a handful of weeds with each hand, stand up, and throw the weeds onto the compost pile.

- *Load hay:*

    Pretend to have a pitchfork in hand and pitch hay into the wagon. That hay sure is heavy! Feel the stretch in your arms.

- *Kick the tractor tires:*

    Is there enough air in those tires? Pretend to give a good kick to each tire, alternating your legs.

Notes to the Teacher:

Starting your movement session with a warm-up will help instill the habit of stretching out before exercise to prevent injury. Telling a story can help create a playful mood for the movement activities that follow; you may wish to make up different scenarios based on the children's interests, the seasons, or a unit you are teaching.

☐ WARM-UP STRETCHES

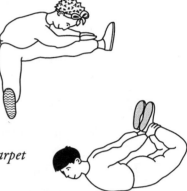

Objective:	Relax and stretch out to warm up
Core Components:	Flexibility
	Body control
Materials:	Carpet squares (optional)

Procedures:

• Stretch 1

Teacher's instructions to children:

1. Lie on the floor on your stomach, hands to your sides. [*Use carpet squares if they are available.*]

2. While taking a slow, deep breath, bend your legs at the knees, reach your hands back to grab your ankles, and gently pull. Breathe out. [*Repeat twice.*]

3. The next step is the same, only once you grab your ankles, try to gently rock back and forth as you breathe out.

4. Now lie on your back with your knees raised to your chest. Your arms should be straight out at your sides. Roll your hips from side to side, touching the floor with your knee with each roll. Breathe in as you roll and out as your knee touches the floor. [*Repeat three to five times.*]

• Stretch 2

Teacher's instructions to children:

1. Sit on the floor with your legs in front of you, bent slightly at the knee. While you breathe in, reach your arms forward toward your toes. Keep your head down. Keep reaching forward until you feel a little pull at the back of your legs. Hold that position while you count to three. Breathe out and slowly sit back up. [*Repeat three times.*]

2. Sit on the floor with your legs stretched out to both sides. Again, while you breathe in, reach forward with your arms toward the toes of your left leg. Keep your head down. Move forward until you feel a little pull at the back of your leg. Hold that position while you count to three, then breathe out and slowly sit back up. [*Repeat the stretch toward the right leg, then forward.*]

• Stretch 3 (Cat Stretch)

Teacher's instructions to children:

1. Now we're going to stretch like a cat. Close your eyes and imagine what a cat looks like and feels like when it stretches. Kneel down on all fours and arch your back up toward the ceiling. Let your head hang loosely toward the floor.

2. Hollow out your back and lift your head and shoulders, stretching your neck and looking at the ceiling. [*Hold a few seconds and repeat at least once.*]

Notes to the Teacher:

The Cat Stretch, based on the yoga stretch, is a good relaxation exercise. You can use it to help children calm down when they are tired or need to redirect their energy.

☐ COOL-DOWN EXERCISE

Objective:	Relax after creative movement activity
Core Components:	Flexibility
	Body control
Materials:	None

Procedures:

1. To start the cool-down exercises after a boisterous creative movement activity, gym class, or recess, ask the children to sit in a circle (or wherever there is room) and take slow, deep breaths. You might then suggest, "Close your eyes and drop your chin to your chest. After a moment, slowly lift your chin and open your eyes."

2. Use this script, or your own words, to lead the children in a gentle stretch. "Raise your hands over your head and reach toward the ceiling. Now lower your arms and gently start to lower your head toward the floor—first bend your head, then your neck, then your shoulders, then your back, one little bit at a time. Just hang and let your arms hang loosely. Slowly roll up reversing the order: back, shoulders, head, until you are standing straight. Now reach up to the ceiling again. Keep your hands over your head and stand on your tiptoes. Now, flatten your feet back on the floor and drop your arms."

3. Repeat this stretch/roll-down exercise several times. The last time, let the children roll down into a seated position on the floor.

4. Once children are seated, you might say, "Close your eyes and take a deep breath. Hold it for a second. Now let it out slowly." Repeat the deep breathing three more times, counting to three on the inhale and three on the exhale (e.g., inhale-two-three, exhale-two-three).

5. After the deep breathing, tell children to open their eyes slowly. Ask them to put their feet on the floor and push themselves up so that they are standing, but still crouched over their legs. Now ask them to take four long counts to roll up straight. Count aloud until everyone is standing.

6. Ask if everyone feels cooled down and ready to go on with other activities. Cool down a bit more if necessary.

Notes to the Teacher:

If possible, play soft music when you are leading the cool-down and other relaxation activities.

☐ Mirror Game

Objective:	Learn to isolate body parts by trying to mirror another person's movements as precisely as possible
Core Components:	Body control Generation of movement ideas
Materials:	None

Procedures:

1. Tell children that they will play the Mirror Game in pairs. Explain that one child will be the mirror, reflecting exactly each motion that her partner makes.

2. Ask one child to be your partner and help model the activity. Stand about an arm's length apart, facing each other. Ask the child to do exactly what you do, at the same time that you are doing it. Her motions should mirror yours. Move deliberately, isolating parts of your body. For example, turn your wrists, wiggle your fingers, move your hands from head to shoulders to waist to knees, and so forth.

3. After several different types of movements, switch roles with the child. Ask her to produce the movements while you act as the mirror.

4. After the demonstration, pair up the children and ask them to play the Mirror Game. If necessary, remind them that the point of the game is not to throw off your partner (by going too fast or changing movements suddenly), but to try and move at the same time as your partner, to be an exact mirror image.

Variations:

1. Children may want to work on the Mirror Game during recess or free-play time and prepare a piece to present to the rest of the class. With practice, they can perfect a relatively complex series of movements.

2. Children also can form a circle and pass around a movement, like a ripple.

Notes to the Teacher:

You can use the Mirror Game to explore various components of movement. For example, you can experiment with use of space (e.g., squat down, step back, stretch out) or with expressiveness and movement quality (e.g., make flowing movements, then choppy ones). Or, you can play a tape during the Mirror Game and ask children to move to the music, while you observe their responsiveness to music. Once they have learned the activity, children can play the Mirror Game in pairs between structured activities or during free-play time.

□ STATUE GAME

Objective:	Respond with movement to verbal and rhythmic cues
Core Components:	Body control
	Timing
	Sensitivity to rhythm
Materials:	Drum and mallet

Procedures:

1. Tell children how to play the Statue Game. Explain that you will beat the drum while they move around the room to the beat. As soon as the drumbeat stops, they should freeze like statues and hold whatever position they may be in.

2. Beat a steady four counts and stop. Remind children to freeze like statues. Beat a steady eight counts and stop. Freeze!

3. Change the tempo and the quality of the beat. For example, speed it up, slow it down, or add more beats.

4. Identify one rhythm pattern as the movement phrase and another as the hold phrase. That is, ask children to move on one phrase and to be a statue on the other. For example, move for eight steady counts, then freeze for four steady counts. Repeat two or three times. Change the rhythm pattern.

5. Assign specific poses for the statue phrases. For example, move for eight counts, squat and freeze for another eight counts; or move for eight counts, balance on one leg for four counts, and so on.

Notes to the Teacher:

1. You might prepare for this activity by playing Follow the Leader with the children. Ask children to line up behind you and to do exactly what you do as you move through the room. At first, tell children what you are doing. For example, say, "When I walk, you should walk. When I stop, you should stop. When I jump, you should jump!" Later, try a longer series of movements without talking. Ask children to pay very close attention to your movements and the way that you do them, being sure to stop when you stop. You can also encourage children to take turns being the leader.

2. Another way to prepare for Statue Game is by conducting the rhythm activities in this guide (Heartbeats and I've Got Rhythm) and in the Music guide (Rhythm Poem).

☐ FOUR SQUARE

Objective:	Practice body control and balance with a familiar game
Core Components:	Body control and balance
	Execution of planned movement
	Strategy
Materials:	Sidewalk chalk
	Ball

Procedures:

1. This game is played outside. Players draw a four-square grid on the ground with chalk and number the squares from one to four.

2. One child stands in each of the four boxes. Remaining children form a line near box 1.

3. The child in box 4 starts by bouncing the ball to another player's square. Children bounce the ball back and forth until one player misses.

4. When a child misses the ball, she must leave the square and go to the end of the line. Players rotate to fill her space and the first person in line steps into space 1.

Notes to the Teacher:

1. This is a good outdoor game because once children have been taught the rules, they can play independently.

2. Other familiar games, such as hopscotch, can also be used to help children develop body control, balance, and movement strategies. If you wish, vary the games by letting children make up and use their own rules. (Possibilities for hopscotch: Throw the marker while standing on one leg; close your eyes while throwing the marker; play with partners; change the diagram.)

3. Give children other materials (hula hoops, balls, jump ropes, beanbags) and encourage them to make up their own games. If necessary, start them off with a few suggestions. Maybe they could roll the hula hoops, or lay them on the ground for a ball bounce or obstacle course. Beanbags could be used for a pitch toss or a balancing contest. Let the children work in small groups, then demonstrate their games to the whole class.

□ OBSTACLE COURSE

Objective:	Practice a series of developmentally appropriate athletic skills
Core Components:	Body control, with particular emphasis on
	Balance
	Power (explosive force)
	Speed
	Agility (ability to make rapid, successive movements in different directions)
Materials:	Tape measure
	Wooden boards (one wide, for jump ramp; one narrow, for balance beam)
	Pylons or other markers
	Hurdles
	Mattress or mat

Procedures:

1. Select an area large enough to hold a six-station obstacle course. A playground is best, but if one is not available, then a gym or a room set aside for movement activities will suffice.

2. Set up an obstacle course. The stations described on the next page were designed to tap a wide range of athletic skills. However, feel free to design your own obstacle course tailored to the needs and interests of your class.

3. Try to use the equipment on hand in your classroom. For example, you can make the long jump by fastening a tape measure to the floor. Outdoors, you can chalk a line on the ground to serve as the balance beam, or fashion it from a piece of scrap lumber, tape, or ribbon; in a gym, you can use one of the lines painted on the floor. For pylons, you can use traffic cones, chairs, stacked-up tires or books, or any other safe, agreed-upon markers. The jump ramp can be made by securing a wide board to the ground at one end and to a raised support at the opposite end. You can make the hurdle out of blocks, ribbon, or bamboo sticks.

4. It may take some trial and error before you find the course layout that best suits your activities and your site. A horseshoe shape is an effective way to set up the Spectrum Obstacle Course, since it provides ample room to sprint at the end. For a course without the sprint, a circle or square shape generally is the simplest for teachers to build and for children to use. Each station leads directly to the next until the child arrives back at the beginning and rejoins the group. Figure-eight courses tend to confuse children while straight-line courses leave room for children to wander off.

5. Before you begin, make sure all the equipment is stable and secure. Then, walk through the course with the children, modeling the task they should perform at each station. You may wish to offer a "trial run" or a chance for the whole group to practice the exercises together.

6. Ask each child do the obstacle course on her own, to eliminate confusion and enable you to observe how she executes the individual tasks.

7. In subsequent sessions, you can change the exercises performed at the stations to provide variety or to suit your instructional program. You may wish to ask the children for their suggestions for props (such as hula hoops) or games (such as a bean bag toss).

Spectrum Obstacle Course

Station 1—The Long Jump

Children stand still at the start of the jump. Demonstrate and describe how to keep the feet together before and after jumping, and how to use arms and torso to propel the body forward. Knees should be slightly bent at the start of the jump. Demonstrate good arm swing: swing arms back to create the momentum needed for jumping while swinging the arms forward. Emphasize that horizontal, not vertical, movement is the goal of the long jump.

Station 2—Balance Beam

Children walk slowly across the beam. Behaviors that should be stressed and modeled are alternating feet, looking ahead when walking, and using the body to maintain balance. Spotting is necessary if you use a raised beam.

Station 3— Running Around Obstacles

At this point children are ready to run. Ask them to weave, as closely as possible, around five obstacles or pylons while running as quickly as they can. First, model a successful run: Look forward to the pylons, swing arms (not too inhibited or exaggerated), pay attention to lifting knees, and run lightly, pushing off balls of feet. Stress that the goal is to get as close to the pylons as possible while running as fast as you can. After the careful, deliberate movement of the balance beam, running around obstacles gives children a chance to let loose a bit.

Station 4—Jumping From Height

The ramp jump provides a good transition from running around obstacles to running and jumping over hurdles. Children tend to enjoy this station because they are generally skilled at this type of jump and find it to be an exhilarating movement. You can place a mattress on the ground to cushion their landing. Secure a wide board to the ground at one end and raise the other end approximately two feet off the ground. Ask the children to run up the ramp and jump, with feet together and knees bent, to the ground or mattress. Suggest that they use their arms to maintain balance.

Station 5—Hurdles

Set up three or four hurdles each about three feet apart, giving children enough room in between hurdles to regroup, take a couple of strides and prepare for the next hurdle. The hurdles can be made by placing plastic or bamboo rods onto supports, so that they easily give way. Show children how to run and jump over the hurdles without stopping in between. If a child is very hesitant or unwilling to jump, ask if she has another way in which she would like to complete the course (such as crawling). Or, you can raise the hurdles and ask children to walk underneath, bending backwards.

Station 6—Running

A relatively long sprint at the end of the course can give children a sense of accomplishment and completion. Try to find room to let children run approximately 20 yards, with a fence or finish line as the goal. To make sure that the children will not be running into dangerous areas, you may wish to set up blockades so they can't overrun the course.

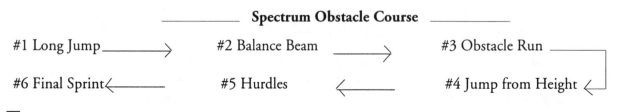

Spectrum Obstacle Course

#1 Long Jump ———→   #2 Balance Beam ———→   #3 Obstacle Run ——

#6 Final Sprint ←—— #5 Hurdles ←—— #4 Jump from Height ←

☐ HEARTBEATS

Objective:	Gain familiarity with rhythm by finding one's natural "beats"
Core Components:	Rhythm sensitivity, particularly rhythm identification Moving in rhythm
Materials:	Stethoscopes, if available Clock or stopwatch

Procedures:

1. Show children how to find the pulse in their necks or wrists. Explain, in as much detail as you would like, how the heart gives us our very own beat. It is just like having our own little drummer inside our body. As children find their pulse, have them tap their feet to the beat. (If stethoscopes are available, let children use them to listen to each other's heartbeat. They can clap or tap to each other's pulse or heartbeat.)

2. Explain that we can time our own heartbeat, or pulse, to see how fast or slow it is. Use a clock or stopwatch and have children take turns counting their pulses aloud for 15 seconds each. Each child should keep track of her own pulse rate. As a math activity, children can also prepare a graph showing pulse rates for all the members of the class. What is the fastest rate? the slowest? the most common?

3. Have children participate in increasingly strenuous aerobic activities. Let them walk, then hop, hop fast, do jumping jacks, and so on. If outside, have children run around. After each activity, ask children to time their heartbeats. What happens? Children can each make a graph showing how fast their heart beats during the different activities. Remember to do a cool-down after vigorous exercise.

4. Play different music for the children, asking them to keep time to the beat by clapping, tapping, or humming. Discuss each piece. Does the beat remind the children of walking, hopping, or running?

Note to the Teacher:

This activity can be extended over several sessions and can be used to introduce other graphing, rhythm, or music composition activities. For example, you could ask children to tap out their own beat using different percussion instruments, or to use instruments to show how the beat changes as they walk, jump and run. The compositions can be recorded and shared with classmates.

This activity is adapted from E. Nelson. (1979). *Movement games for children of all ages*. New York: Sterling.

☐ I've Got Rhythm

Objective:	Study rhythms by moving to a drum beat
Core Components:	Moving in synchrony with a changing rhythm
	Expressiveness
Materials:	Drum and mallet
	Bell or xylophone

Procedures:

1. Seat children in a circle on the floor. Tell them that they are about to experiment with rhythms and counting. Ask them to listen carefully while you beat a steady rhythm on the drum. After a little while, ask them to clap each time you beat the drum.

2. When they are confident of the rhythm, try a different one. Tell them to listen first, then clap with the drum. Beat a waltz rhythm (one-two-three, with the down or heavy beat on *one*) and let them clap with the drumbeat.

3. Ask the children to stand up and stamp in place, taking one step with each beat of the drum. Tell them that this exercise is very much like the time they moved to their own rhythm, except that this time they are stamping to the drumbeat.

4. Try other rhythms and vary the speed (couplets, four/four time, etc.). Let children move around the room as they keep the beat. Encourage them to develop their own pattern as they travel and to move different parts of their bodies. You might suggest: "Can you move your arms to the beat? your head? your feet?"

Variations:

1. After children have had some experience with the activity, assign specific movements to individual counts. For example, the first count of a sequence gets a jump, the second two get walking steps. A waltz time might be jump-walk-walk, jump-walk-walk. Have children make up different sequences.

2. Keep time with a bell as well as with the drum. For example, you might use the drums for a fast beat and the bell (or xylophone) for a slower beat. Play different rhythms and ask the children to identify them as fast or slow. Next, ask children to move around the room keeping time to the beat. When children seem comfortable, vary the beat. You can even let them take turns playing the drum and bell for the rest of the class.

☐ Hum Drums

Objective: Explore rhythm using voices and drums
Core Components: Rhythm sensitivity
                          Setting own rhythm
                          Expressiveness

Materials: Drums, other percussion instruments, or both

Procedures:

1. Like the heartbeat or pulse, the natural beats of speech are a wonderful way to help children explore rhythm. Begin by having children tap rhythm sticks, clap their hands, or beat on a drum to the rhythm of their own speech. Explain that each syllable gets a beat, and practice a few sentences together. Then, let children pretend that they are on the phone with a friend, meeting a new student, or engaged in another scenario you have created. Or, you might ask them to clap along with everything they say for the next 3 minutes.

2. Next, ask them to leave out the words and simply hum their message while they are beating or tapping. Point out how carefully they have to listen to the beat of the message in order to understand it.

3. Finally, encourage children to leave out their own voices altogether, and to use only the drum or other rhythm instruments to communicate.

4. Discuss why the drum messages can be hard to understand. How might children change the beat of the message to make the meaning more clear? If necessary, ask leading questions. What would good news sound like? What would bad or sad news sound like? What would a shy drumbeat sound like? Ask children to demonstrate their suggestions. You may also wish to write children's comments on chart paper, creating a set of "Tips for Drum Talk."

5. Play a guessing game. Ask children to work in pairs to send and guess messages, based on the "tips" they created. See if children can carry on an extended conversation. Afterward, ask them to discuss how well the tips worked.

6. Encourage children to act out the messages. One child beats the message on the drum, while another moves to the beat.

Notes to the Teacher:

For more practice in finding rhythm in the spoken word, see Rhythm Poem on p. 96 in the Music guide.

This activity is adapted from E. Nelson. (1979). *Movement games for children of all ages*. New York: Sterling.

☐ Oh, What a Feeling!

Objective:	Learn how to express different feelings through movement
Core Components:	Responding to verbal cues Evoking moods through movement
Materials:	"Feelings" music tape

Procedures:

1. Tell children that they are going to do a movement activity that explores feelings. They will listen to music and move around the room in lots of different ways, depending on how the music makes them feel. Ask children to spread out through the room. Play segments of music, preferably from a prerecorded tape. Ask students to describe the music in terms of feelings, helping them with the vocabulary. Does the music sound happy? sad? excited?

2. Begin playing music that exemplifies a particular feeling, such as happiness. Ask what feeling the music is. When children respond with "happy," prompt them to make different happy movements. "How do you hold your head when you feel happy? What happens to your back? Show me chipper shoulders, cheerful feet, pleased knees," you might suggest. Continue for 2 minutes and then let children rest.

3. Next, switch to music that sounds sad. Once again, offer suggestions. "How do you let your friends know you're sad without using words? What do sad shoulders look like? How do sad arms move? sad legs and toes? What about a sad head, and mouth, and eyebrows? What do all your different body parts look like and move like when they feel sad?" Continue for 1or two minutes and ask children to stop.

4. Continue this pattern, playing "scary," "mad," "excited," and other types of music. Use prompts, such as, "Let your body be (scared, angry, excited, surprised, etc.). Now move around the room." Another prompting strategy is to have children imagine situations: "You're having a birthday party!" "Your best friend is moving."

5. To extend this activity, urge children to think of (or bring in recordings of) songs that evoke a specific emotion or emotions. Encourage them to discuss the aspects of the song (beat, tempo, melody, words) that make them feel happy, angry, sad, and so on. They can work in small groups to choreograph movements to all or part of the song they have selected. Then, they can perform the movements for each other.

Notes to the Teacher:

You may wish to make (or buy) a "feelings" audiotape, composed of musical selections that conjure up different feelings (e.g., anger, happiness, sadness, calm, silliness). Some song examples include:

Sadness:	"Jeannie with the Light Brown Hair" (Stephen Foster)
Anger:	"Overture Coriolan" (Ludwig van Beethoven)
Fear:	"Night on Bald Mountain" (Modest Mussorgsky)
Joy:	"Isn't She Lovely?" (Stevie Wonder)
Confusion:	"Confusion" (Fela Kuti)

This activity is adapted from G. Hendricks and K. Hendricks. (1983). *The moving center: Exploring movement activities for the classroom.* Englewood Cliffs, NJ: Prentice Hall.

□ CAN I MOVE LIKE . . . ?

Objective:	Explore different ways in which movement can be used to create images
Core Components:	Expressiveness Generating movement ideas Observational skills
Materials:	None

Procedures:

1. Ask children to stand up. Explain that they will be playing a game in which they use their bodies to imitate different actions, people, and things. For example, how would they move their bodies if they were popcorn popping, or if they were walking through deep mud? Talk with the group about movement in terms of: the *quality* of movement (e.g., what is a light movement like? a heavy one? bouncy one? choppy one?); the *speed* of movement (e.g., what things move slowly? very slowly? quickly?); and the *orientation in space* (e.g., what things move on the ground? high in the air? in between?).

2. Ask children how they would move if they were a tiger stalking prey, a fish swimming in a fish tank, a leaf ruffled by the wind. Encourage them to act out these images.

3. With children's help, put together silly combinations. For example, ask children how they would fly if they were a bird wearing a jacket or a tiger with a broken foot. Encourage them to come up with their own combinations.

4. Pair up the children. Help them develop roles and prepare a short scene to demonstrate for others, such as:
   - rowing a boat and fishing
   - eating dinner
   - figure skating
   - getting caught in a sudden rainstorm
   - being birds and building a nest together

   Encourage them to come up with their own ideas for a scene.

Notes to the Teacher:

1. You can turn this exercise into charades. Make movements and ask children to guess who (or what) you are or what you are doing. Then, reverse roles and let the children perform.

2. You can lead a more structured game by preparing cards with pictures of different scenes (you can pick a theme, such as animals, sports activities, or books). One child picks a card and acts out the picture until a classmate guesses what is on the card. This classmate gets to "act" next.

☐ DANCE A STORY

Objective:	Explore the expressive potential of the body by using movement to act out a story
Core Components:	Expressiveness Generating movement ideas
Materials:	Books with many pictures, either with or without words (e.g., *Where the Wild Things Are* by Maurice Sendak)

Procedures:

1. Start by reading a short book. Talk about how the words and the pictures tell the story. Ask children to think about what a particular picture is telling them. If they couldn't talk, how might they tell the same story?

2. Model how you can use movement alone to act out part of a story. Pick a page with text that can be acted out clearly, such as "Mr. Smith closes the door." Act out closing the door.

3. Explain that whole stories can be acted out. Have children stand and act out a story that you have chosen. Go through the book page by page, reading the page, showing the picture, and having all the children act it out. Repeat from start to finish at least once.

4. As a project, you can let small groups of children choose a book they would like to act out. Assign different corners of the room (or different times) for groups to get together and work out their stories. Have one child in each group narrate the story while the others act it out. Circulate around the room helping the groups. Have each group perform its story for the rest of the class.

Notes to the Teacher:

If you take videotapes or photographs of the activity, you can create a classroom library of "stories in action."

□ ANATOMY BOOGIE

Objective: Explore and generate range of movement ideas by focused
                        movement of isolated body parts

Core Components: Body control and awareness
                        Generating movement ideas
                        Expressiveness

Materials: Scarves, if desired
                        Music audiotapes or radio

Procedures:

1. Tell the children that for this movement session they will be moving to music (but not
   dancing). Explain that our bodies are capable of many different movements, because we
   have different body parts that each can move independently. All together, one body can
   make many different combinations of movements. This activity will explore the different
   ways that each body part can move.

2. Have the children brainstorm a list of different body parts that they can move. Keep a list
   on chart paper. Make your own suggestions or prompt children to create a full list.

3. Ask the children to stand up. Starting at the top of the list, ask them to demonstrate
   different ways in which they can move each body part. As a group, come up with terms for
   those movements. For example, the list for "eyes" might include "close, blink, squeeze"; for
   shoulders, "shrug, shake, circle"; and so on.

4. Either on the same or a different day, repeat the exercise with music. Focus on one body
   part at a time, using the list as a guide. Play different types of music and see if children come
   up with new ideas. Encourage children to discuss how music helps them find new
   movement possibilities. When the music changes, do they change the way they move?

5. You can use music in different ways. For example, children can move different body parts to
   the same piece of music. What do the different body part movements have in common? Or,
   small groups of children can choreograph and demonstrate their own short dances based on
   movements from the Anatomy Boogie list.

Notes to the Teacher:

Music can inspire the children to create different movements, so try to have a range of
music on hand. You might encourage students to bring in their own favorites. Or, you can
use a radio, and stop randomly at stations playing different types of music. You might also
hand out scarves and let children experiment with the patterns they can create.

This activity is adapted from G. Hendricks and K. Hendricks. (1983). *The moving center:*
Exploring movement activities for the classroom. Englewood Cliffs, NJ: Prentice Hall.

☐ MAKING SHAPES

Objective:	Improve spatial awareness by using the body to create geometric shapes
Core Components:	Generating movement ideas Recognizing shapes Spatial awareness Problem solving
Materials:	Shape cards (cards with pictures of triangles, squares, circles, and other geometric shapes) or blocks

Procedures:

1. Divide the class into groups of five or six. Challenge the children to work together, in their groups, to use their bodies to make the shapes that you suggest. Start by showing them a picture of a square.

2. Direct children to different parts of the room and have them try to make the shape. Circulate among groups as they work. Then, ask them to make one or two other basic shapes.

3. Ask children to make more complex shapes, such as a hexagon. After each group has come up with a shape, they can show it to the whole class. Encourage all ideas that children come up with. If the children in a group do not make a shape successfully, help them rearrange themselves to form the right shape.

Variations:

Children can also use their bodies, individually or in groups, to form the letters of the alphabet. Encourage children to try different methods, such as lying down, sitting, and standing, and to point out ways in which their ideas are different from each other's.

Notes to the Teacher:

If children are having difficulty with this activity, let them use pipe cleaners to make the shapes or letters as a first step toward using their bodies.

☐ Hop, Skip, Jump

Objective:	Expand repertoire of movement ideas by figuring out different ways to cross the room or playground
Core Components:	Generating movement ideas Body control Expressiveness
Materials:	None

Procedures:

1. Ask children to line up at one end of the room or playground. Tell them that they each will get to cross to the other side. But they have to think of a new way to get across!

2. Challenge the children to describe or demonstrate different ways to cross (hop, skip, jump, gallop). You may need to prompt them. (What can you do with your arms or legs? Do you need to walk at all?)

3 Let children develop their own ideas, or give them the following suggestions:

   - squat-walk all the way
   - link arm and leg with a partner and slowly make your way
   - close your eyes and have someone guide you
   - tiptoe
   - stamp
   - zigzag
   - walk backwards
   - crawl on all fours
   - crawl on all fours and backwards
   - crabwalk
   - roll
   - cartwheel

4. Afterwards, discuss the activity with children, listing (on chart paper if you wish) the many different movement ideas they developed.

5. Add music to the activity, asking students to vary their movements in ways the music suggests.

This activity is adapted from G. Hendricks and K. Hendricks. (1983). *The moving center: Exploring movement activities for the classroom.* Englewood Cliffs, NJ: Prentice Hall.

□ BODY MACHINES

Objective:	Make a "machine" with bodies to explore the way that moving parts—and children—can work together
Core Components:	Generating movement ideas Understanding causal relationships
Materials:	Food grinder Other simple machines with moving parts (optional) Paper and crayons

Procedures:

1. Put a food grinder or other small machine on a table. Ask children to examine it and take turns operating it, if they haven't had the opportunity to do so as a mechanics activity (see Take Apart and Assembly in the Mechanics and Construction guide, pp. 30–31).

2. Lead a discussion about how this machine works in terms of cause-and-effect relationships (e.g., what happens to the food, the spiral core, the grinding disc when you turn the handle?). Demonstrate how one mechanism affects the next.

3. Tell children that they will be making machines with their own bodies. Each person will act as one part of the machine, just as each of the parts on the table fits with other parts to make a real machine. Use the food grinder as a model. Ask for volunteers and let each child pretend to be one part of the food grinder. Children can act out their parts one at a time, and then all together.

4. Divide the class into groups of five to eight children. Have groups brainstorm ideas about what machines they could produce, and what motion each child could make. Children can look around the classroom for a real machine to imitate (e.g., a pencil sharpener).

5. Or, children can invent an imaginary machine (like a radish-smasher). You might have groups start by sketching their machines. Help children consider what parts their machine would need (e.g., a part to smash the radish, an arm to lift the smasher up and down, a spring to move the arm); the cause-and-effect relationships between the different parts; and ways in which the children can move their bodies to act like the mechanical parts.

6. After a practice session, let each group member describe his or her part. Then, the group can demonstrate its machine for the rest of the class.

Variations:

1. Build a machine one child at a time. When you call a child's name, she should add herself to the machine as a new "part," until the whole class is involved. Videotape this activity if possible so children can watch it later.

2. Add verbal cues, such as "I am pouring peanut butter into this machine," or "I am oiling the gears." Have children show you how your actions will affect the way the machine moves.

3. Remove one "part" and ask the child to find another place to fit in. How do all the other parts adjust?

This activity is adapted from E. Nelson. (1979). *Movement games for children of all ages.* New York: Sterling.

☐ FREE DANCE

Objective:	Explore how different types of music suggest different kinds of movement and ways of dancing
Core Components:	Responsiveness to music Generating movement ideas Expressiveness Body control
Materials:	Tape recorder Tape featuring various types of music

Procedures:

1. Tell children that you are going to play a tape with many different kinds of music and that they are going to dance to it, responding to the way the different selections make them feel.

2. Start the tape and let children move freely through the space. Ask, "How does this music make you feel like moving?" If a child says, for instance, "This sounds like marching music to me," then march around the room with the children.

3. Add a new component. Ask children to keep dancing until the selection ends. Then they should stop as quickly as they can, and freeze in whatever position they're in.

4. Continue to dance to music, reminding children to freeze as a musical selection ends. End the dance session with music that the children choose.

5. Help the children calm down by playing slow, quiet music. Turn down the volume as well. Ask children to find a place on the floor and to sit down, slowly lowering their bodies to the ground. Have the children close their eyes and listen to the music.

6. Turn off the music and ask children to listen to their own breathing. Tell them to drop their chins to their chests and sit quietly, breathing deeply in and out. After a minute or two, tell the children to raise their heads and open their eyes; lift their arms over their heads and shake their hands; and slowly bring their arms back down to their sides. After a moment, the children may return to their seats.

Notes to the Teacher:

1. This is a good indoor activity for a rainy day. It can also be used when children seem unable to sit still.

2. Ask children to bring in tapes of music they enjoy.

3. Free Dance gives children the opportunity to display various key movement abilities. If possible, videotape the session. Note the following strengths:
   - rhythm—children who adjust to the rhythm changes from piece to piece and focus on rhythm throughout the song;
   - use of space—children who experiment with high and low movements and with moving in different directions through the room or work space;
   - expressiveness—children who show a great deal of expression and vary it from song to song;
   - generation of movement ideas—children who show or suggest to other children a wide variety of movements across the different songs.

☐ STRETCHING

Objectives:	Learn the function of different muscles
	Learn to relax and to tighten muscles
Materials:	None

Note to Parents:

Body awareness is an important element of both athletic and creative movement. This activity is designed to make your child more aware of individual muscles in the body. It also helps you observe how well your child can tell which muscles he or she is stretching, and whether your child can stretch or relax specific muscles without moving other muscles nearby.

Procedures:

1. Ask your child to lie down on the floor and stretch, just like he or she does after waking up in the morning. Now, ask your child to stretch, or lengthen, one group of muscles at a time and enjoy how it feels: neck, shoulder, arms, fingers, chest, tummy, legs, feet, toes.

2. Next, ask your child to tighten the muscles, one part of the body at a time. Once your child tightens a muscle, he or she should hold it until all the muscles in the body are tight. After a moment, let your child relax one muscle group at a time, until all the muscles are relaxed.

3. Ask your child to move one muscle (or set of muscles) without moving the muscles around it. For example, can he or she move the "ankle muscle" without moving the "toe muscle"? move the little finger without moving the ring finger?

Sharing:

Your child may want to demonstrate these exercises to friends at school, or share them with the teacher.

☐ SLOW MOTION

Objective: Plan a series of movements and carry them out

Materials: None

Note to Parents:

This activity emphasizes body control and movement memory. You can observe your child's ability to remember and imitate movements, and to plan a series of motions and carry them out.

Procedures:

1. Ask your child to close his or her eyes and imagine someone running a long distance. Your child should picture the person running in slow motion. What are the runner's legs doing? arms? face? fingers?

2. Ask your child to open his or her eyes and pretend to be running in slow motion.

3. Next, let your child pretend to be a pitcher, cyclist, piano player, truck driver, or someone else performing a physical activity. Remind your child to pay attention to all the parts of his or her body so that the action looks real.

Sharing:

At school, your child can act out a sport or other activity, and let the teacher or classmates guess what he or she is doing.

☐ DANCE FEVER

Objective:	Create a short dance based on the music your child hears on the radio and movements he or she sees on TV or videos
Materials:	Audiotape of dance music or a music video

Note To Parents:

Dancing gives children a chance to express their feelings and also sharpen a variety of movement skills. As your child dances, observe his or her sensitivity to rhythm, ability to use movement to communicate feelings or ideas, awareness of space, and responsiveness to music.

Procedures:

1. If you have a video with dance music, let your child pick out a song and watch and listen to it several times. Then, ask him or her to make up a dance that looks like the one on the video. As an alternative, you can use a tape or CD and let your child make up his or her own dance.

2. Help your child plan a dance that matches the music. Should the dance be fast or slow, happy or sad, forceful or gentle?

3. To help your child concentrate on his or her own dance, you might darken the TV screen and just listen to the music. Or, you can turn off the sound and let your child make up a new tune for the dance.

4. Encourage your child to give the dance a name that tells the audience what the music and movements mean.

5. If your child is shy about performing alone, you might dance along yourself. Or, ask older brothers and sisters to join in.

Sharing:

A performer needs an audience. Let your child put on a performance for you and the rest of the family, or even show friends or the teacher.

RESOURCES AND REFERENCES

The activities on the preceding pages are just an introduction to the teaching of movement. To help you explore further, we offer a brief list of resources that have proved valuable to us and to our colleagues. It is intended to provide inspiration rather than a review of the literature. Sources used in the preparation of this volume are marked with an asterisk.

Belknap, M. (1980). *Taming your dragons: A collection of creative and relaxation activities for home and school.* Buffalo, NY: DOK .

Benzwie, T. (1980). *A moving experience: Dance for lovers of children and the child within.* Tucson, AZ: Zephyr Press.

Boal, A. (1992). *Games for actors and non-actors.* New York: Routledge.

Carr, R. (1980). *See and be: Yoga and creative movement for children.* Englewood Cliffs, NJ: Prentice Hall.

Cole, J. (1989). *Anna banana, 101 jump rope rhymes.* New York: Scholastic.

Fluegelman, A. (1981). *New games book.* New York: Doubleday.

Fraser, D. L. (1991). *Playdancing: Discovering and developing creativity in young children.* Princeton, NJ: Princeton Books.

Gilbert, A. (1977). *Teaching the three Rs through movement experience.* New York: Macmillan.

Gregson, B. (1982). *The incredible indoor games book.* Belmont, CA: Fearon Teacher Aids.

* Hendricks, G. & Hendricks, K. (1983). *The moving center: Exploring movement activities for the classroom.* Englewood Cliffs, NJ: Prentice Hall.

Jenkins, E. (1989). *Adventures in rhythm* [audiocasette]. Washington, DC: Smithsonian/Folkways; Cambridge, MA: Rounder Records.

Jones, B. & Hawes, B. L. (1972). *Step it down: Games, plays, songs and stories from the Afro-American heritage.* Athens : University of Georgia Press.

Joyce, M. (1973). *First steps in teaching creative dance.* Palo Alto, CA: National Press.

Lowden, M. (1989). *Dancing to learn: Dance as a strategy in the primary school curriculum.* London: Falmer Press.

* Michaelis, B. & Michaelis, D. (1977). *Learning through non-competitive activities and play.* Palo Alto, CA: Learning Handbooks.

Nelson, E. (1989). *Dance sing and listen* [audiocasette]. Available from Dimension 5, Box 403 - Kingsbridge Station, Bronx, NY 10463.

Nelson, E. (1987). *Everybody sing and dance!* Available from Dimension 5, Box 403 Kingsbridge Station, Bronx, NY 10463.

* Nelson, E. (1979). *Movement games for children of all ages.* New York: Sterling.

Orlick, T. (1982). *The second cooperative sports and games book.* New York: Pantheon Books.

* Pangrazi, R., & Dauer, V. (1981). *Movement in early childhood and primary education.* Minneapolis, MN: Burgess.

Sullivan, M. (1982). *Feeling strong, feeling free: Movement exploration for young children.* Washington, DC: National Association for the Education of Young Children.

Yolen, J., (Ed.). (1992) *Street rhymes around the world.* Honesdale, PA: Wordsong/Boyds Mill Press.

MATH
ACTIVITIES

Contents

Introduction

An Overview of the Math Activities 139

Description of Key Abilities 140

Description of Materials 141

Activities

Numerical Reasoning

Estimating Games 142
Weights and Measures 143
Calendar Patterns 145
War 147
Fives 148
Dice Toss 149
Dinosaur Game 151

Spatial Reasoning

Pie Graph 153
Relating Area to Volume 155
Copycat Blocks 156
Copycat Geoboards 157
Treasure Hunt 158
Create a Quilt 160

Logical Problem Solving

NIM 161
Bakery Shop 162
Bus Game 163

Take-Home Activities

1 How Many Minutes Until Dinner? 164

2 How Tall Are You? 165

3 Cookie Math 166

Resources and References 168

This guide helps children develop logical-mathematical knowledge and thinking through "hands-on" and "minds-on" activities. The activities can enrich the early elementary curriculum by linking abstract concepts to concrete materials and familiar situations, thus reinforcing skills presented in curricula such as *Everyday Mathematics* or *Mathematics Their Way.* By combining cooperative play and individual challenge, the activities invite children to regard math as fun as well as useful, and as a way to answer many of their questions about the world.

In the pages that follow, you will find instructions for making two board games, the Dinosaur Game and the Bus Game, which were developed by the Spectrum staff to assess and reinforce specific math skills. Also included are several ways to adapt familiar games, such as the card games War and Fives, to encourage children to practice counting, adding, estimating, recognizing patterns, and other math skills. These activities can serve as models to help you use other well-known number and strategy games, such as Concentration and Ticktacktoe, as vehicles for math learning.

The games and other activities in this guide encourage children to think about numbers and quantities of objects, to make and compare sets, to develop strategies for problem solving, and to work and exchange ideas with each other. They are based on three principles: (a) helping children to explore many facets of numbers and the various relationships that exist between numbers; (b) asking children to act and to reflect upon the action in order to develop understanding; and (c) encouraging children to think actively and autonomously in a wide range of situations.

The guide is organized in three sections corresponding to three key abilities in the area of logical-mathematical intelligence: numerical reasoning, spatial reasoning, and logical problem solving. Within each category, activities progress from relatively simple, exploratory experiences with numbers, patterns, and relationships to more complex, goal- and project-oriented endeavors. Only a few activities are included in the logical problem-solving section because this ability is tapped in many activities in the other sections.

When you introduce the math activities, you may wish to start by describing some of the materials that children will encounter, including puzzles, games, blocks, and measuring devices. You might discuss the ways that activities they enjoy—cooking, buying candy, keeping score in sports—all depend upon math. Encourage children to share their own ideas about math by asking such questions as: What does math mean to you? How do you use it at home, outdoors, and at school? When do people need math? What purposes does it serve?

If you are setting aside a special area for math activities, let the children know that in this area they will be working with numbers, shapes, sizes, weights, heights, time, and money. They also will be able to play games and invent their own games. Explain that they will learn how to solve problems with some very special math tools, such as scales, Unifix cubes, clocks, rulers, and tape measures. If possible, show them these tools and talk about the different ways in which adults and children can use them.

Numerical Reasoning

- is adept at calculations (e.g., finds shortcuts)

- is able to estimate

- is adept at quantifying objects and information (e.g., by record keeping, creating effective notation, graphing)

- is able to identify numerical relationships (e.g., probability, ratio)

Spatial Reasoning

- finds spatial patterns

- is adept with puzzles

- uses imagery to visualize and conceptualize a problem

Logical Problem Solving

- focuses on relationships and overall structure of problem instead of isolated facts

- makes logical inferences

- generalizes rules

- develops and uses strategies (e.g., when playing games)

Spectrum Dinosaur Game

This game is easy to make using a foamcore board (we used one that was 27" by 31"), several small plastic dinosaurs, two number dice, and a directional die (see illustration). To make the game board, cut out of construction paper a large dinosaur and a background of rocks and trees, then glue them onto the foamcore board. Using markers, draw a path of 35 numbered spaces starting at the dinosaur's mouth, continuing along its back, and ending at the tip of its tail. Write *Start* or *S* under the space marked *15*. You can color the last space, number 35, a different color or mark it *Finish*. Use two store-bought dice or make them out of 1/2" cubes. You can make the directional die out of a cube by drawing a plus (+) sign on three sides and a minus (-) sign on the other three sides.

Spectrum Bus Game

This game is made up of a bus, a game board, bus stops, station, passengers, and writing materials for notations. To make the game board, use a large rectangular piece of foamcore (about 20" by 33"). The bus will travel from one corner to the next around the inside perimeter. Glue on colored contact paper to create a street-like path, and add trees or other scenery if you wish. You can cover the game board with clear contact paper to make it more durable.

Use your imagination to make four bus stops, each 3" to 4" high. The Spectrum version includes feather, key, toothbrush, and pinecone stops. Mount the materials in plasticine or set them in large plastic caps using a hardening resin. Place a station just past the last stop. You can make it out of a small cardboard box and use paint or colored contact paper to create a door, window, and sign saying *Bus Station.*

You can make the bus out of a small shoe box or other cardboard box (about 7" by 9" by 4") covered with foamcore. Paint or draw the windows rather than cut them out to keep "passengers" in the bus out of children's view. Near the front, cut out a door that can open and close to allow passengers to enter. At the back of the bus, cut a flap that opens like an exit door to allow easy removal of the passengers after each bus trip.

You can make the passengers—10 adults (4") and six children (2" to 3")—out of sturdy cardboard and mount them on small wooden or cardboard stands. Because players must keep track of how many adults versus children get on and off the bus, their sizes should be clearly distinguishable. You can draw your own characters, cut out magazine photos, or use store-bought figures (such as Playmobile).

□ ESTIMATING GAMES

Objective:	Play games to practice estimating skills
Core Components:	Counting and estimating
	Making and checking predictions
	Spatial reasoning
Materials:	Measuring cup
	Large bowl or pot
	Various containers (e.g., paper cups, small boxes)
	Nuts, beans, dried pasta, or rice
	Water

Procedures:

1. Ask children to guess how many cupfuls of water the bowl will hold, and to write down their guesses.

2. Use the measuring cup to fill the bowl while children count how many cupfuls you pour into it. Ask children to compare the actual count with their estimate. How close did they get?

3. Give children a variety of containers and "fillings" (e.g., nuts, beans, rice, or dried pasta). Ask them to design their own experiments. They should estimate how many cupfuls it will take to fill a container, and then check their estimate by filling the container.

Variations:

1. Give children some nuts and three or four paper cups, each a different size. Ask the children to answer the following questions, first by estimating, and later by filling the cups:

    •   How many nuts can the smallest cup hold?

    •   How many nuts can this bigger cup can hold?

    •   How many of these cups could hold more than 10 nuts? fewer than 5 nuts?

    •   Are there any cups that hold exactly 15 nuts?

□ WEIGHTS AND MEASURES

Objective:	Conduct a variety of hands-on tasks to learn about standard and nonstandard measurement tools
Core components:	Comparing and contrasting Learning from trial and error Logical reasoning

Materials:

Ruler	Small bag
Toothpicks	Styrofoam pieces
Paper clips	Wooden dowel
Pencils	Small paper cups
Colored paper	String
Playdough	Wire hanger
Wooden block	Bottles
Large bowl or bottle	

Procedures:

1. Measuring length: Give children a ruler, toothpicks, a chain of paper clips, and pencils. Ask them to measure the length of one side of the chalkboard, a book, a desk, a door, or the classroom wall. Encourage children to think of other ways of measuring the objects, such as using their feet or hands. Ask them to fill out the recording sheet and answer the questions on the next page, and then compare results with each other. Talk with the children about standard and nonstandard measuring tools. Nonstandard measuring tools may be convenient, but not very accurate—your hands and feet are always right there, but would you and your teacher get the same result?

2. Measuring area: Give each child a set of shapes cut out of different-colored paper. Ask them to put the shapes in order from smallest to largest, just by using their eyes. Next, ask them to try to figure out a way to measure the area of the shapes. After a while, you might suggest that they cut up the shapes and arrange them into new shapes that are easier to compare (e.g., make a triangle into a rectangle and see how many times the smallest rectangle fits into it). Ask children to put the shapes in order by size once again, and compare their new line-up to their "guesstimate."

3. Measuring weight: Give children three or four pieces of playdough and ask them to find out which is the heaviest and which is the lightest. As another exercise, give them a wooden block, a small bag, and some Styrofoam pieces and ask them to fill the bag with Styrofoam until it weighs the same as the block. Encourage children to try different ways to measure weight, such as using their hands to estimate, or building their own scales. For example, children can make weighing pans out of paper cups and suspend them from a hanger or dowel with string (they should attach the string to each cup in three or four places to hold the cups steady). Or, they can make a scale that looks like a seesaw by balancing a ruler across a pencil.

4. Measuring volume: Give children three or four bottles of different shapes and sizes, and fill them with water. Ask children to figure out which container has the most water. Encourage them to think about the difference between weight and volume. (If one of the bottles was filled with rice instead of water, would the volume be different? the weight?) Why would a large bowl or bottle be better than a scale for measuring volume?

Weights and Measures Recording Sheet

	chalkboard	book	desk	door	wall	other
Ruler (How long?)						
Toothpicks (How many?)						
Paper clips (How many?)						
Pencils (How many?)						
Feet (How many?)						
Other						

Which tool is the easiest to use to measure an object? _____

Why? _____

Which tool is the most difficult to use to measure and object? _____

Why? _____

☐ CALENDAR PATTERNS

Objectives:	Learn the relationship between days, weeks, and months
	Explore the number patterns on calendars
Core components:	Understanding the calendar
	Pattern recognition
	Addition and subtraction
Materials:	Markers or crayons
	Posterboard (approximately 16" by 20")
	Ruler or yardstick
	Clear contact paper
	Construction paper

Procedures:

1. Use the posterboard to prepare a calendar grid with seven blocks across and five blocks down. Tell children that they will help make a calendar for keeping track of important events. Discuss the grid. Why are there seven blocks across? Have the children tell you what days to write across the top, starting with Sunday.

2. Cover the grid with contact paper, so that the children can stick on numbers and pictures without damaging the calendar. Ask for a group of volunteers to cut the numbers 1 through 31 from construction paper.

3. On the first day of each month, children can take off the numbers and rearrange them for the next month. They can also cut pictures from construction paper to indicate special events, such as holidays, birthdays, and field trips. Or, you can use the calendar to record the weather (see p. 74) or weekly events (music class on Tuesday, gym on Friday).

4. Practice using the calendar with the children. Here are some questions you can use to explore the number patterns that make up the calendar; feel free to make up your own.

   - If you look down a column of days, what do these days have in common? (They are all the same day of the week.)
   - How many days are in a month? How many weeks are in a month?
   - If it is Wednesday, how many days until Friday?
   - If Wednesday is the 10th, what is Friday's date?

   The following questions are more challenging:

   - Make a list of the Tuesday dates, the Wednesday dates, and the Saturday dates. Do you see a pattern in these numbers? (You add seven to each one to get the next.)
   - Why does it work out that way? (There are 7 days in a week.)
   - What other patterns do you see in the calendar?

Variations:

1. Explore patterns by giving each child a small calendar grid (you may want the children to fill in the numbers). Ask the children to find the box with the number *2* and color it red. Ask them to add 2 and color that box red; add 2 again and color that box red; add 2 again and

color that box red, until they complete the calendar. Next, they should find the number *3* and color it blue. They should keep adding 3 and coloring those boxes blue until they complete the calendar (they can color some boxes both red and blue). What pattern do they see?

1	2 (red)	3 (blue)	4 (red)	5	6 (red) (blue)	7
8 (red)	9 (blue)	10 (red)	11	12 (red) (blue)	13	14 (red)
15 (blue)	16 (red)	17	18 (red) (blue)	19	20 (red)	21
22 (red)	23	24 (red) (blue)	25	26 (red)	27 (blue)	28 (red)

2. Give each child a 100-table with 10 boxes across and 10 down. What pattern do they make now if they color in all the even numbers? all the multiples of 3, using a different color? You can even make a large 100-table for the classroom, to show the patterns that result when children count by 2, 5, 10, and so on. You can also use the table as a calendar and celebrate after 100 days of school.

3. Encourage children to create their own grids and patterns. Some children may wish to make patterns on their grids without any numbers at all; others may enjoy adding the numbers and seeing how large a grid they can complete.

□ WAR

Objective:	Play a card game to practice comparing and adding numbers
Core Components:	Number identification
	Number comparison
	Addition
Materials:	Deck of cards

Procedures:

1. Show the children how to play War. In this version, you remove all the face cards from the deck. Ask children to divide the remaining cards (ace through 10) into two equal stacks and give one stack, face down, to each player.

2. The players turn over the top card on their stack and compare their cards. The one with the higher number takes both cards and puts them on the bottom of her stack. If the turned-up cards have the same number, players turn over another card (war!). The player with the higher number takes all four cards. The game continues until one player has won all the cards.

3. Next, try Double War. It's the same as War, but players turn over two cards at a time and compare the sums. The player with the higher sum takes all four cards. When players have the same sum, they both turn over a third card. The player with the higher sum takes all six cards. If children are having trouble with the addition, you can let them use chips to count out and add the numbers on the cards.

Variations:

Let three or four children play War together, so that they must compare more cards and thus more numbers.

Notes to the Teacher:

You can encourage children to play other card games, such as Concentration and Solitaire, to reinforce number recognition, pattern recognition, addition, and other math skills.

☐ FIVES

Objective:	Play a card game to practice addition skills
Core Components:	Addition
	Concept of sets
Materials:	2 decks of cards
	Tray

Procedures:

1. Take the two decks and ask children to find all the cards numbered from 1 through 4, for a total of 32 cards. Divide these cards evenly among two, three, or four players. Children should keep their cards in a pile, face down. Put any extra cards face up in the tray. Make sure that there is at least one card in the tray (i.e., if only two children are playing, the last two cards should go in the tray instead of to the players).

2. To start the game, each player should turn one card face up, then another card face up. If the two cards add up to 5, the player puts them aside. If the cards do not add up to 5, the player can discard one card into the tray and exchange it for any other card in the tray that, when combined with his or her remaining card, will add up to 5. If none of the cards add up to 5, the player waits until his or her next turn, then turns over two cards as usual (so that four cards may be face up). At this point, the player may be able to make more than one combination that add up to 5. The game continues until all the cards are used up.

3. Players compare and possibly record how many different combinations add up to 5.

Notes to the Teacher:

1. To make the game more challenging, use more cards and encourage children to add more than two cards to equal 5.

2. Games like Fives and Double War encourage active and autonomous learning. Children must figure out addition problems for themselves and reach agreement about the answers. Immediate feedback from peers or teachers is often more effective than simple correction. For example, if a child says that 4 + 2 = 5, instead of correcting her, you might ask, "How did you get 5?" In such a situation, as children try to explain their reasoning, they may correct themselves spontaneously.

□ DICE TOSS

Objective:	Play a game to learn about probability and graphing
Core Components:	Graphing
	Use of strategy
Materials:	Dice
	Recording sheets or graph paper
	Pencils

Procedures:

1. Give each child one die, a pencil, and a recording sheet (see sample on following page). Ask questions such as, How many sides does a die have? How many numbers does a die have? Does it seem that each number comes up as often as every other one? Or does one number come up the most? Let's do an experiment to see how often we toss each number.

2. Ask for a volunteer to roll the die. Each child can record the number tossed above the same number on her recording sheet.

3. Have children work independently. Ask them to keep tossing and writing the numbers on top of each other until one of the columns hits the top of the chart. Discuss the results with the children. Were the numbers they got very different, or almost the same? Have each child tell which number he or she tossed the most. Help children compare results and recognize that all the numbers are tossed approximately the same number of times.

4, To make the activity more challenging, ask children to roll two dice at a time, record the sum, and compare the results. You will need to supply, or help the children make, a recording sheet with 12 columns.

5, Next, play a game that requires strategic thinking. Ask children to make two columns on a sheet of paper. Then, they roll one die and decide whether to write down the number in the left or right column. They roll the die again and put the number in the empty column. If the number in the left column is smaller than the number in the right, the child gets a point. Ask children to think about strategies that could help them earn points (e.g., if they roll a 4, 5, or 6 on the first throw they might put it in the right column).

1	2	3	4	5	6

Dice Toss Recording Sheet

□ DINOSAUR GAME

Objective:	Play a game to learn number concepts, counting skills, and strategy
Core Components:	Counting skills
	Adherence to rules
	Ability to handle two variables
	Addition and subtraction
Materials:	Spectrum Dinosaur Game (see Description of Materials, p. 141)

Procedures:

1. Introduce the game at a group meeting. As you describe the rules and objective, model with the materials. Explain that players pretend to be small dinosaurs running along the back of a big diplodocus who wants to eat them. The goal of the game is to move the game pieces (small plastic dinosaurs) to the tip of the diplodocus's tail, as far as possible from the hungry dinosaur's mouth. Two or three children can play. To start, they put their game pieces on the space marked *S* on the board (space 15). Then, they take turns rolling the dice to move their game pieces from space to space.

2. Take time to model and discuss how the dice are used. Two dice have dots like a regular die, with one to six dots on each side. Players toss the dice and add the dots together to find out how many spaces to move forward. You might ask the children, "If I roll these numbers, how many spaces do I go forward? Remember you're trying to escape from the hungry mouth of the diplodocus so forward means moving away from the mouth and up to the tail."

   The third die has plus and minus signs that tell players whether to move their game pieces forward away from the mouth or backward toward the mouth. You might ask the children, "Which sign, plus or minus, do you think tells you to move forward? [+] If I roll all three dice like this, where should I move my dinosaur?" (Let the children practice throwing the dice and moving the pieces until you are sure that they understand that forward means moving towards the tail.)

3. A few more rules: If players have to move backwards and end up at the space right inside the diplodocus's mouth, they just stay there until they roll a plus sign telling them to move forward. The first person to reach the last space in the diplodocus's tail is the winner.

Variations:

1. Add another die, so that children add up three numbers to find out how many spaces to move.

2. Change the rules so that you use the die with the plus and minus signs to tell whether to add or subtract the numbers on the two number-dice, instead of to tell in which direction to move. Start the game pieces right at the diplodocus's mouth and always move forward, toward the tail.

   Before the children play this version, help them practice rolling the three dice. Ask them to make number sentences out loud. What happens if they throw 2, 5, and + ? or 1, 6, and - ? Explain that they can't take a bigger number from a smaller number, so they should make the number sentence 6 - 1 = ? Ask children what to do if they throw - , 4, and 4. What is 4 - 4? How many spaces should the player move forward?

3. Make sure that you have numbered each space on the game board. Ask children to use addition and subtraction to figure out where they should move on the game board, rather than counting out the move one space at a time. For example, if a player is on space 5 and rolls + , 3, and 5, he or she should do the calculations to figure out the move to space 13.

4. Encourage children to work in small groups to make up their own board games. Ask children to talk about number games that they play outside of school, such as Candy Land or Chutes and Ladders, and to explain the rules to each other. Then, give them a variety of materials—spinners, dice, playing cards, large pieces of cardboard or posterboard, stickers, rulers, game pieces, small figures, toy cars, markers—and encourage them to create a game of their own. Ask them to be sure to include a number maker (e.g., spinner, dice, cards). When the games are ready, students can gather in small groups to explain the rules to each other and play the games.

   For a more structured activity, you may want to specify a mathematical concept for the children to use in their game, such as addition, subtraction, or direction of play (forward, backward). Or, you might specify a theme for the game (e.g., animals, pollution) to tie it into other curricular areas or interests of the class.

Notes to the Teacher:

1. As children play the Dinosaur Game for the first time, observe who remembers the rules and who needs to hear them again. To see if children understand the rules and logic of the game, ask them to explain the rules to each other.

2. If some children are having difficulty with the numbers, try to work with them on a one-on-one basis to gain a deeper understanding of what aspects of the game they do and do not understand.

☐ PIE GRAPH

Objective:	Show how graphs can be used to organize information
Core Components:	Sorting and classifying
	Making and comparing sets
Materials:	Chalk
	String
	Scissors

Procedures:

1. Have children separate themselves into groups according to eye color or another criteria (e.g., male and female, number of sisters and brothers).

2. If you are outside, draw a large circle on the ground with chalk; inside, use string. Ask children to join hands around the circle, with the members of each group standing next to each other.

3. Make an X in the center of the circle. Have children draw lines (with chalk or string) from the X to the edge of the circle at the points between the groups.

4. Tell children that they have just created a giant living pie graph. Which group makes up the biggest piece of pie? the smallest? Try making pie graphs for other characteristics, such as age, number of siblings, gender, hair color.

Variations:

1. Make a three-dimensional bar graph using building blocks. Have children group themselves into categories once again, but this time they can use one block to represent each child, and stack the blocks into columns representing the groups.

2. Brainstorm ways to present the same information using different kinds of graphs. Show children examples of bar graphs and picture graphs (see illustrations). Let children suggest other types of information that they can present using graphs (e.g., favorite foods, favorite TV shows, pets). Encourage them to use graphs to record the results of science experiments and other investigations.

What Month Is Your Birthday?

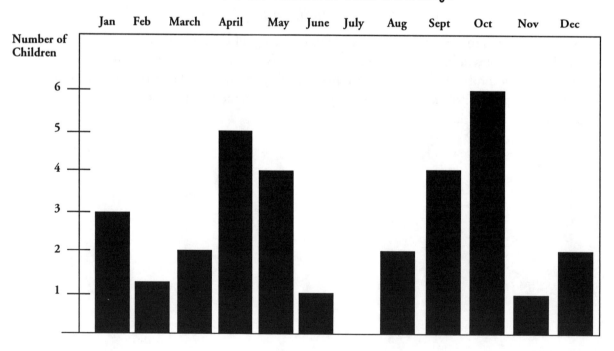

□ Relating Area to Volume

Objective:	Perform an experiment that relates area to volume
Core Components:	Problem solving
	Contrasting and comparing
	Drawing conclusions
Materials:	Chalkboard or chart paper
	Chalk or markers
	Heavy construction paper
	Scissors
	Tape
	Rice, beans, or dried pasta

Procedures:

1. Introduce the activity by asking children what they know about area and the relationship between area (two-dimensional measurement, or the amount of surface within a set of lines) and volume (three-dimensional measurement, or the amount of space occupied by an object). Write down children's responses on chart paper or a chalkboard.

2. Ask children to perform the following experiment: Cut a piece of paper (e.g., 9" x 12") in half. (Make sure that children know that the two pieces of paper are the same size.) Roll each piece of paper into a tube, but roll one piece the long way, so that the bottom is made of a small circle, and roll the other piece the short way, so that the bottom is made of a large circle. Tape the ends.

3. Ask children whether both tubes would hold the same amount of rice (or beans, pasta, etc.) If not, which would hold more—in other words, have a larger volume? Ask children to fill the tubes to find out.

Variations:

1. If your classroom has a carpet, ask children to estimate the length, width, and amount of surface (area) it covers. Then, let them measure it. Walk around the school and look for other spaces where the carpet might fit. Measure these spaces to make sure. Or, try to figure out where in the room you could move large pieces of furniture, such as desks and bookcases.

2. Do more activities with volume. Collect different-sized containers and see which box holds the most books or which can holds the most pencils.

This activity is adapted from M. Burns. (1975). *The I hate mathematics! book*. Boston: Little, Brown.

□ COPYCAT BLOCKS

Objective:	Give and interpret directions so that one child can recreate another child's design
Core Components:	Spatial reasoning Problem solving Use of visual imagery
Materials:	Blocks (2 of each size and color) Cardboard partitions

Procedures:

1. Two children each take the same number and kind of blocks; make sure that the two groups of blocks look alike. Put up a divider so that the children can't see each other's blocks.

2. One of the players makes a building or arrangement with the blocks. Then, she tries to explain to her partner how to make the same arrangement (e.g., put the small red block on top of the big blue block). The partner tries to build exactly the same block arrangement without peeking.

Variations:

1. If three children play the game, one can build the original arrangement, one can give directions, and one can try to recreate the arrangement.

2. To practice graphing, use two game boards that have a coordinate grid. One player can pile blocks on the grid and use coordinates to tell her partner how to make the same arrangement (e.g., put the blue block on A1 and the red block on B6).

□ COPYCAT GEOBOARDS

Objective:	Give and interpret directions so that one child can recreate another's design
Core Components:	Coordinate mapping skills Use of strategy Spatial reasoning
Materials:	Geoboards Rubber bands

Procedures:

1. Label the pins on the geoboards, using the letters *A* through *E* across the top and the numbers *1* through *5* down the side. Assign two children to each geoboard. Ask one player to create a very simple design using one rubber band, holding the geoboard so that the second player cannot see the design. The first player uses coordinates to tell the other player how to create exactly the same design on her geoboard. For example, the first player might say, "Start your rubber band at B2 and stretch it down to D2." She may not point to any pegs on the second player's geoboard.

2. The second player does her best to interpret the first player's directions. When the players are finished, let them compare geoboards. The results are often humorous!

3. Now the second player makes a design and gives directions to the first player.

Notes to Teachers:

It may be necessary to demonstrate at group time how to play the game and give directions by naming coordinates on the grid. Children can play alone once they understand the procedures.

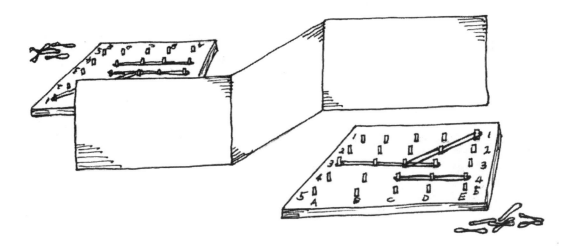

□ TREASURE HUNT

Objectives:	Use graphing skills to solve a puzzle
	Create a legend for a map
Core Components:	Use of strategy
	Creating effective notation
	Record keeping
Materials:	Treasure Map (see following page)
	Markers or crayons

Procedures:

1. Explain that this game is played by two players. Each player must "hide" four treasures on the Treasure Map grid and also guess where the partner has hidden his or her treasures. Give children the blank grids, or treasure maps, and have them practice using coordinates to identify the squares (e.g., C2, E5).

2. Let children think up four treasures and secretly create a legend, drawing a simple symbol to represent each of the four treasures. For example, they might draw a circle to stand for a gold coin, a diamond for a diamond ring, a triangle for a teddy bear, and a square for a present. Partners should tell each other the names of the four treasures they have selected. If any of the treasures are the same, one player needs to substitute a different treasure.

3. Children "hide" the four treasures on their maps. Without letting their partner see, they might draw one symbol in square C4, another symbol in E5, and so forth.

4. Children then take turns guessing the location of their partner's treasures. Children should record the results of their guesses on their own map using any system they please, so that the map records two things: their search for their partner's treasure, and the location of their own treasures. The better their record keeping, the better able they will be to find their partner's treasures. (If necessary, help children find a way to record their guesses. Encourage them to experiment with different methods.)

5. If a child finds a treasure then he or she gets another turn. The game is over when both children have found all the treasures.

□

Treasure Map

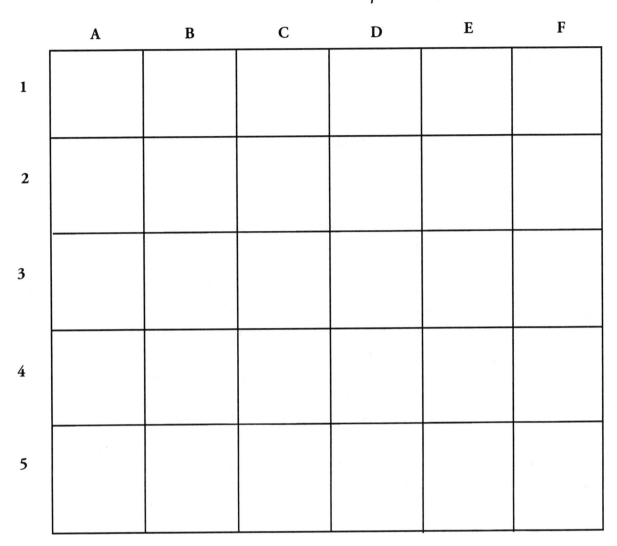

	A	B	C	D	E	F
1						
2						
3						
4						
5						

Legend:

1.	2.	3.	4.
=	=	=	=

☐ CREATE A QUILT

Objective:	Explore the concept of symmetry and create geometrical designs
Core Components:	Spatial reasoning Use of visual imagery
Materials:	Assortment of colored paper, cut into 3" squares, 3" right-angle triangles, and 1-1/2" by 3" rectangles 9" by 9" white paper, 1 piece per child Glue sticks Posterboard or oak tag

Procedure:

1. Explain to the children that they will be creating a paper quilt, using squares, rectangles, and triangles. Give each child a piece of white paper as a base. The paper should have a grid drawn on it that divides the square into nine smaller squares (three squares per side). Provide an assortment of bright-colored squares, triangles, and rectangles.

2. Ask the children to experiment with placing different shapes and colors on the grid. Explain that the grid can help them line up the pieces and explore their geometric relationship (it's OK, however, if a child can't manage to stick with the grid).

3. Next, ask children to create a design that has at least one line of symmetry—in other words, the pattern is the same on either side of the line. (If the children have not yet discussed symmetry, you may wish to have them do so before conducting this activity.) When the children have made a design they like, ask them to glue it onto the paper.

4. Let each child create at least three more quilt squares. Have children lay out their own four quilt squares on the floor or a table. Make sure that the edges of the quilt squares are flush with one another. Let the children move the squares around until they find an arrangement they like.

5. Let each child mount her squares on a piece of posterboard or oak tag and display in the classroom.

□ *NIM*

Objective:	Play a game to learn about numerical relationships and strategy
Core Components:	Seeing relationships
	Learning from trial and error
	Use of strategy
Materials:	Toothpicks

Procedures:

1. Give children 16 toothpicks each. Ask them how many different ways they can arrange the toothpicks in four rows (e.g., four rows of four, two rows of two and two rows of six, two rows of three and two rows of five). Ask children to write down the different arrangements.

2. To play the game, two children sit across from each other with the 16 toothpicks in between, arranged in four rows. Then they take turns; in each turn they can take away as many toothpicks as they wish, but from only one row at a time. The goal is to force the other player to take the last toothpick.

3. Once the children learn the game, you can ask them to reflect on their strategy. Is there a foolproof way to avoid taking the last toothpick? Does it matter how many toothpicks you leave in a row? Does it matter if you go first or second?

Variations:

1. This variation also calls for two players. Arrange 15 toothpicks in a pyramid, with one toothpick in the top row, two toothpicks in the second row, on down to five toothpicks in the fifth row. As in the game above, players can take away as many toothpicks as they wish in each turn, but from only one row at a time. They should try NOT to take the last toothpick.

2. Two players arrange 12 or more toothpicks in as many rows as they wish. They take turns removing toothpicks, taking either one or two toothpicks at a time. Whoever gets the last toothpick has to jump up twice. Ask children to reflect upon the strategy for playing this game. Is it different from the preceding games?

3. Make a grid eight squares long and four squares deep. Two or more players take turns putting markers on one or two squares at a time. The two squares must be connected on the top, bottom, or side, rather than diagonally. Players should try not to fill the last square.

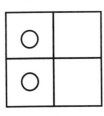
OK

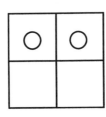
OK

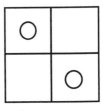
not OK

☐ BAKERY SHOP

Objective:	Learn the value of coins and explore different ways to add them up to a dollar
Core Components:	Planning and decision making Addition and subtraction
Materials:	Money (real or play) including dollar bills, quarters, nickels, and dimes Pretend doughnuts, cookies, cupcakes Pretend cash register Recording sheet (see following page)

Procedures:

1. Set up the pretend bakery. Work with children to decide the price of the food. For example, cupcakes might cost 15¢, doughnuts 10¢, and cookies 5¢.

2. Four children at a time can play the game, one as the storekeeper and three as shoppers. Each shopper begins with a dollar. The goal is to be the first shopper to spend exactly one dollar, but no more. Each shopper can spend up to 20¢ per turn.

3. As the shoppers place their orders, the storekeeper gives them the food and the appropriate change. All players should pay attention to the calculations to make sure that they are accurate. After every turn, shoppers should use the sheet below to record how much money they started with, how much they spent. and how much they have left.

Bakery Shop Tally

Name _____   **Date** _____

I bought	I started with	I spent	Now I have

□ BUS GAME

Objective:	Play a game to use numbers and record keeping
Core Components:	Counting skill Record keeping and creative use of notation Addition and subtraction Ability to handle more than one variable
Materials:	Bus Game (see Description of Materials, p. 141) Two dice (one with dots or numbers, the other with a plus sign on three sides and a minus sign on the other three sides) Paper and pencil Chips

Procedures:

1. Make the game board and materials according to the directions on p. 141. Then, introduce the game at a group meeting. Explain the rules, modeling whenever possible.

2. In this game, players take turns being the conductor and the bus driver. The bus driver moves the bus around the game board from one station to the next. At the first two stations, the bus driver rolls the number die to find out how many passengers should get on the bus. At the third and fourth stops, the bus driver rolls the plus-and-minus die as well, to find out whether to put passengers on the bus (+) or take passengers off the bus (-). At the end of the trip around the four stations, the conductor must tell how many passengers are on the bus without actually looking inside. The conductor can use paper and pencil to keep track.

3. Demonstrate a few rounds. Start simply by having only one or two passengers get on the bus at a time. Ask children to keep track of how many passengers get on and off *at each stop*. Encourage them to keep track using paper and pencil. If this is too difficult, they can use chips or other manipulatives. Let them compare the different notation systems they have devised for representing each stop and the number of people getting on and off the bus.

4. When the children have mastered the rules and a notation system, assign partners and let them play on their own.

Variations:

1. You might like to introduce this activity with just the number die and have children practice adding new passengers at each stop. Later, you can introduce the plus-and-minus die so that passengers can get off (as well as on) the bus and children can practice subtraction.

2. To make the game more difficult, designate some passengers as adults and some as children, and have players keep track of the two groups separately. They can also record other categories of passengers, such as women and men, or tall people and short people.

3. Introduce money. Have passengers pay a fare and ask the conductor to keep track of how much money is collected.

This activity, based on the work of Joseph Walters and Matthew Hodges,
is further explained in the *Project Spectrum: Preschool assessment handbook.*

□ How Many Minutes Until Dinner?

Objectives:	Use a clock or watch to tell time
	Learn the relationship between seconds, minutes, and hours
Materials:	A clock or watch with hands (preferably with a second hand and with minutes, as well as hours, marked off)

Note to Parents:

Clocks and watches are the most common ways to tell time. This exercise helps your child develop a sense of time (for example, understanding the difference between a minute and an hour) and practice telling time by reading the hands of a clock.

Procedures:

1. Have your child help you use the watch or clock to time a minute and a second. Show your child the second hand, the minute hand, and the hour hand and compare how fast and slow they move. Ask your child, "Which is longer—a second, a minute, or an hour?"

2. Help your child become more aware of his or her schedule. For example, the bus may come at 8:00 a.m. each day; school may be out at 2:30 p.m.; dinner time may be 6:00 p.m.; bedtime may be 8:00 p.m. Your child can learn to anticipate these events and perhaps get ready on his or her own.

3. Time several familiar events: a meal, a TV show, a commercial, a bath, reading a book, a day at school, fixing dinner. Encourage your child to suggest different activities to time. If you wish, your child can make a chart, with pictures, showing the length of these activities. For example:

Activity	Time of day	Hours	Minutes	Seconds

4. Your child can refer to the chart to answer questions such as these:
   - Which takes longer—a commercial or a TV show?
   - If you were hungry, would you want dinner to be ready in one second, one minute, or one hour?
   - Does it take hours or minutes to brush your teeth? watch a movie?

5. Ask your child to look around the house for other timepieces such as kitchen timers, a microwave timer, a stopwatch, and an alarm clock. How many can he or she find?

Sharing:

If your child made a chart, he or she can bring it to school to share with the teacher and classmates. Or, perhaps the teacher might ask your child to check the clock and announce recess or lunch time.

☐ HOW TALL ARE YOU?

Objectives: Measure and estimate length
                   Use chart to keep track of information

Materials: String
                   Ruler
                   Long sheet of paper or a wall you can write on

Note to Parents:

Children love to keep track of their height—they see the changes as a sign that they are getting bigger, and maybe more grown-up, too. In this activity, children practice measuring and estimating using different units of measurement.

Procedures:

1. Show your child the 1" mark on a ruler or give him or her a 1" piece of string. Show how to use the string to measure a book, a door, a table, your finger, a teddy bear, and other objects.

2. Give your child a sheet of paper and have him or her practice making lines of different lengths and labeling them (e.g., 1" long, 4" long, 6" long).

3. Now ask your child:
   - Which is longer—the door or the book? How do you know?
   - Which is longer—the 3" line or the 1" line? How do you know?
   - Can you tell me how much longer it is?

4. Have your child stand against the wall. Mark the wall (or a long sheet of paper you have attached to the wall) at the top of your child's head. Let him or her measure, with the 1" string or with the ruler, from the floor to the mark. Now your child knows his or her height in inches. You also can use a 12" ruler to help your child measure his or her height in feet. Save the chart so that your child can keep track of how big he or she is getting.

5. Your child may want to measure other family members, too. Ask questions such as, Who is taller? Who is shorter? How much have you grown since you measured last?

Sharing:

Your child can take the 1" string to school for measuring objects in the classroom. Or, your child might offer to make a growth chart for the class.

☐ COOKIE MATH

Objectives:	Learn about volume
	Learn about the relationship between different units of measurement
Materials:	Set of measuring spoons (1/4 teaspoon, 1/2 teaspoon, 1 teaspoon, 1 tablespoon)
	Clear containers with different shapes (e.g., glasses, bowls, bottles)
	Measuring cups
	Salt
	Water
	Cookie ingredients (listed below)
	Baking equipment (large mixing bowl, wooden spoon, 1 or 2 cookie sheets)

Note to Parents:

This activity will give you a chance to observe your child's ability to follow directions, to make accurate measurements, and to see the relationship between different measurements (e.g., a teaspoon and a tablespoon). The ability to use measuring tools is important not just in cooking and baking, but also in carpentry, art, science, and many other activities.

Procedures:

1. Ask your child to use each of the four measuring spoons to measure out the salt, and to place the salt in piles in a row. Ask your child to identify the largest pile and the spoon that made it. Have him or her match the other three piles with the correct spoon.

2. Ask your child to try to use the teaspoon to fill the tablespoon with salt. You might ask:
   - How many teaspoons does it take?
   - How many 1/2 teaspoons does it take?
   - If you lost your tablespoon, what could you use to measure the same amount?

3. Gather containers of different shapes; clear ones are best because the contents can be seen. Ask your child to use a measuring cup to put exactly one cup of water in each container. Ask your child questions such as:
   - Do all the containers hold the same amount of water? How do you know?
   - Why do some look very full and others only partly full?
   - If you didn't want a whole cup of water, what would you do?

4. As a special treat, make cookies with your child. You can use the recipe for chocolate chunk cookies that follows (donated by former Project Zero managing director Liz Rosenblatt), or try one of your own favorites. Baking cookies is a good math activity because most recipes require a lot of measuring. Be sure to let your child use all the measuring tools. It may be a little messy at first, but your child needs practice in order to learn.

Sharing:

Let your child take some cookies to class, along with the measuring spoons and the measuring cups. Or, eat the cookies for family dessert and let your child explain how he or she made them.

Liz's Chocolate Chunk Cookies

2 1/2 sticks butter, softened to room temperature
1/2 cup granulated sugar
1/2 cup packed brown sugar
1 1/2 tsp. vanilla extract
1/2 tsp. salt
2 eggs
2 1/2 cup flour
1 12-oz. package of chocolate chunks (Or, you can make your own by putting a 12-oz. bar of semisweet chocolate on a cutting board, still in its wrapper, and hitting it gently a few times with a hammer.)

• Preheat oven to 350°.

• Beat butter, sugar, brown sugar, vanilla, and salt in a large mixing bowl until smooth and creamy. Add eggs. Add flour in two portions. Stir in chocolate chunks.

• Scoop tablespoonfuls of dough onto an ungreased cookie sheet, leaving room for the batter to spread. Bake for 8–10 minutes (don't overcook).

• Let cool on a rack.

RESOURCES AND REFERENCES

The activities on the preceding pages are just an introduction to the teaching of mathematics. To help you explore further, we offer a brief list of resources that have proved valuable to us and to our colleagues. It is intended to provide inspiration rather than a review of the literature. Sources used in the preparation of this volume are marked with an asterisk.

Anno, M. (1992). *Anno's counting book.* NY: HarperCollins.

Anno, M. (1987). *Anno's counting games.* New York: Philomel.

Baker, A., & Baker, J. (1991). *Raps and rhymes in math.* Portsmouth, NH: Heinemann.

Baker, A., & Baker, J. (1993). *From puzzle to project: Solving problems all the way.* Portsmouth, NH: Heinemann.

* Baratta-Lorton, M. (1976). *Mathematics their way.* Reading, MA: Addison-Wesley.

Burk, D., Snider, A., & Symonds, P. (1988). *Box it or bag it mathematics.* Salem, OR: Math Learning Center.

Burk, D., Snider, A., & Symonds, P. (1992). *Math excursions 1: Project-based mathematics for first graders.* Portsmouth, NH: Heinemann.

* Burns, M., (1975). *The I hate mathematics! book.* Boston: Little, Brown.

Burns, M., & Tank, B. (1988). *A collection of math lessons.* White Plains, NY: Math Solution Publications.

Gonsalves, P., & Kopp, J. (1995). *Build it! festival.* A GEMS Teacher's Guide. Berkeley, CA: Lawrence Hall of Science, University of California.

Goodman, J. (1992). *Group solutions.* A GEMS Teacher's Guide. Berkeley, CA: Lawrence Hall of Science, University of California.

Hohmann, C. (1991). *High/Scope K–3 curriculum series: Mathematics.* Ypsilanti, MI: High/Scope Press.

* Kamii, C. (1982). *Number.* Washington, DC: National Association for the Education of Young Children.

Kamii, C. (1985). *Young children reinvent arithmetic: Implications of Piaget's theory.* New York: Teachers College Press.

National Council of Teachers of Mathematics. (1989). *Curriculum and evaluation standards for school mathematics.* Reston, VA.

National Council of Teachers of Mathematics. (1988, February). Early childhood mathematics. [Special issue]. *Arithmetic Teacher, 35.*

Russell, S., & Stone, A. (1990). *Counting: Ourselves and our families* [for grades K–1]. From the series *Used numbers: Real data in the classroom.* Palo Alto: Dale Seymour.

Stenmark, J. K., Thompson, V., & Cossey, R. (1986). *Family math.* Berkeley, CA: The Regents, University of California.

University of Chicago School Mathematics Project (1993). *Everyday mathematics.* Evanston, IL: Everyday Learning Corporation.

Welchman-Tischler, R. (1992). *How to use children's literature to teach mathematics.* Reston, VA: National Council of Teachers of Mathematics.

Whitin, D., & Wilde, S. (1992). *Read any good math lately?* Portsmouth, NH: Heinemann.

SOCIAL UNDERSTANDING ACTIVITIES

CONTENTS _____

Introduction

An Overview of the Social Understanding Activities 171

Description of Key Abilities 172

Description of Materials 173

Social Understanding Activities

Understanding of Self

Collage Resume 174

Treasure Chest 175

Fingerprints 176

Silhouettes 177

Wheel of Feelings 178

Understanding of Others

Face Recognition 179

Who Is Missing? 180

Telephone 181

Friends 182

Finger Puppets 183

Perspectives 184

Story Problems 185

Hospital 186

Assumption of Distinctive Social Roles

Class Census 187

Birthday Party 188

Visitors' Day 189

We Are a Team 190

Take-Home Activities

1 My Life Story 192

2 Feeling Faces 193

Resources and References 194

AN OVERVIEW OF THE SOCIAL UNDERSTANDING ACTIVITIES

The activities in this chapter are designed to promote children's social learning and to uncover their strengths in the area of social intelligence. We use the term *social intelligence* to include interpersonal and intrapersonal intelligences. The former builds on the capacity to notice distinctions between others, such as differences in their moods, temperaments, motivations, and intentions. The latter refers to self-knowledge: having a clear picture of one's own strengths, weaknesses, hopes, and emotions; the capacity to respond to situations based on this self-knowledge; and the capacity to draw upon emotions as a means of understanding and guiding one's actions. Whereas many efforts to examine children's social development focus on behavior (sharing, taking turns, expressing anger with words rather than blows), the Spectrum approach attempts to shed light on children's perceptions and understandings, on how they view the world of social relationships and their role within it.

We have targeted primarily three key abilities that indicate social intelligence in young children: understanding of self, understanding of others, and assumption of culturally valued social roles. These culturally valued social roles can be observed as children interact with their peers, acting as facilitators, leaders, and caregivers or friends. It is important to note that different cultures may value and therefore foster different social roles. Many of the social understanding activities encourage children to examine the ways in which they are both different from and similar to each other, and therefore lay the groundwork for the teacher's own activities or discussions addressing cultural diversity.

As in other guides, the social understanding activities are organized according to the key ability they foster (they may draw on other key abilities too, for children usually demonstrate their social competence through the interaction of all the key abilities). Many of the activities are group oriented and thus create an opportunity for children to develop reflective, observational, and communication skills as they interact with their peers. The children must work together to solve a problem, play a game, or fulfill their plans, such as celebrating birthdays with a small party.

You may wish to use the social understanding activities on an occasional basis throughout the year, or to present them in a unit called, for example, "All About Me" or "Friendship." In either case, an orientation session might help the children take a more thoughtful approach to the activities and to the materials you set up in a social understanding area. Many teachers choose to create a dramatic play space, stocked with furniture, clothes, and other accessories, that children can use to explore social roles and social situations. You can also use a small puppet theater with puppets, or the classroom model with toy figures or pictures representing the children in the class, to provide opportunities for dramatic play. In addition, you can "recyle" materials from other domains—math games and puzzles, art supplies, tape recorders, and the pretend "TV" and microphone used for reporting activities—to explore the ways in which children work and play with each other.

You might start the orientation session by asking children what the word *social* means to them. Does it mean getting together with friends? Does it have something to do with people's feelings, thoughts, and emotions? Does it involve the way people treat each other? After the children have shared their ideas, you might tell them that playing games such as Telephone and making up plays and stories with props and puppets are a few of the ways in which they will explore social understanding. You can discuss the dress-up clothes, classroom model, and other materials they can play with in the social understanding area. Encourage the children to talk about what they might learn from the activities.

Understanding of Self

- identifies own abilities, skills, interests, and areas of difficulty

- reflects upon own feelings, experiences, and accomplishments

- draws upon these reflections to understand and guide own behavior

- shows insight into the factors that cause an individual to do well or have difficulty in an area

Understanding of Others

- demonstrates knowledge of peers and their activities

- attends closely to others

- recognizes others' thoughts, feelings, and abilities

- draws conclusions about others based on their activities

Assumption of Distinctive Social Roles

Leader:

- often initiates and organizes activities

- organizes other children

- assigns roles to others

- explains how activity is carried out

- oversees and directs activities

Facilitator:

- often shares ideas, information, and skills with other children

- mediates conflict

- invites other children to play

- extends and elaborates other children's ideas

- provides help when others need attention

Caregiver/Friend:

- comforts other children when they are upset

- shows sensitivity to other children's feelings

- shows understanding of friends' likes and dislikes

Dramatic play clothes and accessories: a collection of clothing and accessories that children can adapt for use in role-playing activities. Children may bring items from home. Teachers can also use secondhand clothing. Include dramatic play clothing for boys as well as girls, such as jackets, belts, and vests. Accessories that suggest specific careers, such as stethoscopes, mail sacks, and conducting batons, are good additions.

For suggestions on setting up a dramatic play space, you might consult *Play and Early Childhood Development* by James Johnson, James Christie, and Thomas Yawkey. The authors suggest many ways to organize props and to make them accessible for playing different roles throughout the year.

Classroom model: a three-dimensional scale model of the classroom. The Spectrum classroom model was made out of a large cardboard box approximately 24" x 15" x 5", and decorated with furniture made of fabric scraps, wood, small boxes, and recycled items. Directions for making the classroom model are included in the Visual Arts guide (see p. 240). The classroom model also can be used for language activities.

"TV": a large cardboard box cut out and decorated to resemble a television set. The "TV" can be used for dramatic play as well as for the reporting activities in the Language guide.

☐ COLLAGE RESUME

Objective: Help children understand themselves and others by creating collage
                        resumes

Core Components: Reflective skills
                        Awareness of strengths of self and others

Materials: Paper
                        Glue
                        Scissors
                        Photos
                        Old magazines
                        Writing materials

Procedures:

1. Give brief introduction, showing a model of a collage resume to the class. You can say
    something like, "This is a poster about my child. It has pictures of books and pets and
    children swimming because those are some of the things she is interested in. We call this
    poster a 'picture resume' or a 'collage resume.' A resume can help other people know who we
    are and what we can do. Adults write their resumes and often use them to get jobs. You can
    use words, pictures, photos, or drawings to make a collage resume that tells about you."

2. Help children think of different ways to describe themselves. Encourage them to talk about
    their interests, their abilities, and favorite colors, foods, and pets.

3. Brainstorm with children ideas for items they might include in their collage resumes. Point
    out that along with photos and pictures, they can attach objects like a baseball card from a
    personal collection, a wrapper from a favorite candy bar, or tickets from a special
    performance.

4. Give children time to plan and collect their materials before they begin to arrange and attach
    items to the background. You might also send a note to parents explaining the project and
    asking them to help.

5. After the projects are complete, encourage the children to discuss their collage resumes with
    the class.

Notes to the Teacher:

1. The children's collage resumes can be revised throughout the year as they become more
    aware of their own strengths and interests.

2. Children's collage resumes can be displayed at an open house or parent conference night.

☐ TREASURE CHEST

Objective:	Explore thoughts, ideas, and feelings
Core Components:	Understanding of self
	Reflective skills
Materials:	Small boxes, 1 per child
	Stickers
	Glue
	Paper
	Markers

Procedures:

1. Introduce the project by telling children that their thoughts, ideas, and feelings are very special because they make each child a special person. Explain that they each will make a treasure chest for their special thoughts, ideas, or feelings.

2. Give the children boxes to make the treasure chests. Show them the materials they can use to decorate the chests in their own way. Afterward, they can write or draw their ideas and store the papers in their treasure chests.

3. Discuss privacy with the children. Explain that the treasure chests are private and challenge the children to share responsibility for insuring that no one goes into another person's box. However, set up a time for sharing so that, if children wish, they can choose to share their special thoughts and feelings with classmates.

Notes to the Teacher:

You can prepare for this activity by having a discussion about thinking. You might begin by telling children a story or posing a simple problem. Stop in the middle and ask children how thinking could help solve the problem. For example, what would you think about if:

- you and a friend wanted to play with the same toy at the same time?
- your mother said you couldn't watch television until you did your chores?
- you couldn't remember where you left your jacket?

Ask children how many different solutions they can think of. Point out how valuable it is to hear their different points of view.

☐ FINGERPRINTS

Objective:	Make a set of fingerprints to highlight each individual's uniqueness
Core Component:	Understanding of self
Materials:	Stamp pad Paper Magnifying glass Writing tools

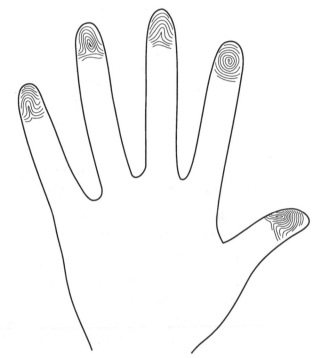

Procedures:

1. Introduce the project by explaining that fingerprints are one of the many things that make each person unique. No two fingerprints are alike. That's why fingerprints can be used to identify their owners—there's only one person in the world that a set of fingerprints can belong to!

2. Help children make prints. If you wish, you can give them each a sheet of paper with the outline of a hand, or show them how to make an outline of their own hand. Help children label the fingers.
    Then, they can touch each finger first on the stamp pad, next on the appropriate fingertip in the drawing. Encourage children to examine their prints with the magnifying glass. They also can compare their prints with a partner's to see how they are similar and how they are different.

3. Fingerprints come in different types (see the science activity What Tools Do Scientists Use? p. 53). Collect a clear fingerprint from each child and, if possible, enlarge on a copying machine. Make multiple copies and encourage children to categorize the fingerprints. Then, they can make a graph showing how many children have fingerprints with whorls, arches, or loops.

Variations:

1. Invite children to make a picture with their fingerprints. They can use their fingers like a stamp, and use markers or crayons to complete the picture.

2. Instead of making fingerprints, make handprints or footprints with paint across a long sheet of paper. This activity can be done inside or outside on a warm day—just be sure to have warm water and towels ready for cleaning up.

☐ SILHOUETTES

Objective:	Make a silhouette in order to see oneself in a new way
Core Components:	Understanding of self
Materials:	Paper
	Chalk
	Lamp
	Posterboard or
	colored paper
	Scissors
	Masking tape
	Glue or paste

Procedures:

1. Tape a piece of paper to a wall. Have a child sit in front of the wall and shine a light past her head so that her shadow is cast on the paper.

2. Outline the shadow with a piece of chalk. Cut out the silhouette and mount it on the posterboard or colored paper.

3. Create a display or gallery showing all the children in the class. As a game, you could have children try to identify the silhouettes, or match name tags with the silhouettes.

Variations:

1. Extend into other shadow activities. You might ask the children:

   - how can you make yourself look sad? happy? threatening?
   - how can you work with a friend to create a person with two heads? two noses? three hands?
   - how can you work with a friend to create an image that shows friendship? anger? fright?

   The children can show the silhouettes to their classmates and ask them to identify the different images and emotions they have tried to create.

2. You can turn the silhouettes into collages. Children can look through old magazines, cut out words or pictures that describe themselves, and glue them onto their silhouettes. Encourage children to think about their interests, relationships, and emotions as well as their physical characteristics. Invite them to explain their choices to the class.

□ WHEEL OF FEELINGS

Objective:	Help children identify and learn the words for the full range of their feelings
Core Components:	Reflective skills Understanding one's own feelings Understanding others' feelings
Materials:	Chart paper and markers or chalkboard and chalk Paper Crayons *Feelings* by Aliki, or other books about feelings

Procedures:

1. Read a book about feelings. Selections from the book *Feelings* by Aliki are particularly useful because they illustrate a wide range of feelings, from guilty, humiliated, jealous, and lonely to proud, generous, brave, and excited.

2. Draw a large circle on the chart paper or chalkboard and divide it into six or eight equal wedges. Tell children that it is a "Wheel of Feelings." Ask children to name some of the different feelings they just read about. You or the children can write the name of one feeling in each wedge. If prompting would be helpful, you might ask the children how they would feel in situations such as the following:

   - A friend says, "Go away!"
   - Someone helps them get up when they fall down.
   - Their sister or brother gets a present.
   - It's the first day of school.

2. If appropriate for your class, tell children that, during the next few weeks, they will have the chance to act out the feelings displayed on their wheel. Pick one of the emotions and encourage the children to share examples of times they have felt that way, or situations that could make someone feel that way. (For example, what would make them angry? what if a friend accidentally broke a favorite toy?) Ask for volunteers to act out the situation.

3. Discuss the skit. Would all the children feel the same (in this case, angry) in that situation? How else might they feel? Sad? Forgiving?

4. Invite a volunteer to color in the wedge with a color that might represent the emotion.

5. Another day, repeat the activity with a different emotion.

Variations:

1. Follow up the role-playing by making an "I Feel Sad" book (or, "I Feel Angry," "I Feel Happy," "I Feel Lonely," etc.). Give each child a piece of paper that says across the bottom, "I feel sad when _____." Ask them to draw a picture and write a few words about the situation. If necessary, help them with the writing. Put the pictures together into a book and laminate it if possible. Encourage the children to take turns taking the book home to read to their parents.

2. Encourage children to make their own wheel of feelings.

☐ FACE RECOGNITION

Objective:	Encourage children to learn about each other
Core Component:	Visual memory
	Recognition of classmates
	Understanding similarities and differences
Materials:	Two snapshots of each student in the class

Procedures:

Explain the game, which is played like Concentration. Children place the snapshots face down in rows on the floor, table or desk. Each player chooses two photos and turns them face up. If the player gets a match, she keeps the snapshots and takes one more turn. If she does not get a match, she turns the cards back over and the player to her right gets a turn. The person with the most pictures at the end of the game is the winner. The games works best with two to four players. You can try to select photos that will make the game more challenging—for example, the same child can be shown engaged in different activities, at different ages, front and back, or with and without a hat.

Variations:

Make face puzzles with the children. Take a close-up picture from the same distance for each child in the classroom. Enlarge all the pictures on a copying machine to the same size. You can make the puzzles in two different ways:

- Paste the enlarged pictures onto cardboard or posterboard. Invite children to cut up their own picture into four or five pieces, whatever shapes they please. Then, they can practice assembling the face. Small groups of children also can use the face puzzles to play the following game. Players take four or more puzzles and put all the pieces face down in a pile. Each player chooses one piece from the pile at a time, and tries to complete a puzzle. Players cannot put pieces back into the pile, but can trade pieces with each other. At the end of the game, players see who has assembled the most face puzzles.

- Or, let children cut puzzles so the faces have interchangeable parts. To do this, fold each copy in half lengthwise (producing two identical halves), and then widthwise in thirds. Let children cut along the folds. See what interesting faces emerge when children "mix and match" their own features with those of a friend. Finish the activity by having children reassemble their own faces and those of their classmates.

☐ WHO IS MISSING?

Objective:	Play a game to learn about classmates
Core Components:	Understanding of others Observational skills
Materials:	Egg timer Blindfold Blanket (optional)

Procedures:

1. Ask children to sit in a circle on the floor. Select one player to be the detective and another player to be the chooser (and timekeeper).

2. Cover the detective's eyes. Ask the chooser to select one child to leave the room or hide under a blanket. The other players should change places as quickly as possible.

3. The detective then faces the group and tries to identify the missing person in one minute while the chooser keeps time. The detective can ask yes-or-no questions about the missing group member.

4. The detective chooses the next detective.

Variations:

1. Play the same game using the classroom model (see Description of Materials on p. 173) for information about making the model). Remove one child's marker and ask children to guess whose marker is missing.

2. Gather children into a circle and ask a volunteer to stand in the middle. Encourage the group to study how she looks for about 30 seconds. Then tell the children to close their eyes while the child in the center quickly changes one thing about her appearance (e.g., switches watch from one wrist to the other; removes hair ribbon; tucks in shirt). Ask the group to identify what's different.

3. Tape the voices of the children in the class. Play the tape during circle time and ask children to guess who is talking.

☐ *TELEPHONE*

Objective:	Understand the complexity of communication
Core Component:	Communicating with peers
Materials:	Paper cups
	String
	Large cardboard boxes
	Plastic tubing
	Funnels
	Cans
	Chart paper and markers or chalkboard and chalk

Procedures:

1. Ask children to sit in a circle or row. Ask one child to make up a sentence and whisper it in the next person's ear. This person whispers to the next person and so on around the circle. Finally, the last person says the sentence aloud. Compare the last sentence with the first sentence. Ask children what they might do to make the message clearer, and list their responses on chart paper or a chalkboard. Talk about rumors and how stories can change and get distorted when passed among friends.

2. Instead of whispering a sentence, ask children to softly make a special sound (e.g., a cat's meow, a baby's cry, a doorbell's ring) into their neighbor's ear. Instead of passing the sound to one neighbor, the first person should send the sound around the circle in both directions. The child who receives a sound from both sides tells the group whether they are the same or different.

3. This time, pass a facial expression around the circle. One child makes a facial expression that her neighbor imitates and passes on to her neighbor on the other side. (You might ask children to keep their eyes closed until their neighbor taps them on the shoulder.) The last and first child make the expression for each other while the group looks for similarities and differences. [This and other getting-to-know-you games can be found in *The Responsive Classroom: Guidelines* by Ruth Charney, Marlynn Clayton, and Chip Wood.]

Variations:

1. Help children make paper-cup-to-tin-can telephones (make sure the tin cans do not have sharp edges). Ask children to take turns calling each other to chat, to invite someone to a party, or to give a message.

2. Set up different opportunities for independent play. Attach more than one cup or tin can to the same "phone," so several children can hear the same message. Or, make "phone booths" out of two cardboard boxes, each large enough for a child to sit or stand in, and a long length of plastic tubing or garden hose. Connect the two boxes with the pipe and attach a funnel to each end. Let children use the boxes to chat with each other quietly using the pipe as a telephone.

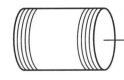

☐ FRIENDS

Objectives:	Explore the concept and scope of friendship; learn about classmates' physical, social, and intellectual attributes
Core Components:	Understanding of others Identifying others' interests and strengths
Materials:	Classroom model Small dolls or figures *The Giving Tree* by Shel Silverstein

Procedures:

1. Read aloud *The Giving Tree* by Shel Silverstein. Discuss with children the friendship between the tree and the boy. Have a discussion about different aspects of friendship:

   - What is a friend?
   - What makes somebody a best friend?
   - How do you make a friend?
   - What is nice about having friends?
   - When you are mad at somebody, is she still your friend?
   - Why do friends fight?
   - How do friends make up?

2. Use the classroom model to play a game called Friends. Ask children to think of one of their friends in the class. Invite them, one at a time, to get in front of the group or class and describe the friend's attributes as clearly as possible without telling that friend's name. They can move a doll or figure through the classroom model to show where their friend likes to play. Ask the other children to guess who the friend is.

3. You can adapt this exercise to increase children's awareness of others' special needs. For example, you could ask children to fix the classroom model to accommodate a blind child or a child in a wheelchair.

Variations:

The following activities build on the concept of friendship and help children recognize each other's individual strengths. They can be used individually or as part of a unit on friendship that includes reading books and singing songs about friendship, planning a party, cooking (measuring), writing letters or invitations, and playing movement games that require cooperation. Because the following exercises reinforce thoughtful behavior, they also help create a positive environment in the classroom.

- Make a friendship chain. Connect paper rings until they stretch from one side of the classroom to the other. Each time you notice a child doing something nice for others, write it down on a piece of paper and attach it to one ring in the chain. (Other teachers in the classroom should do the same thing.) When all the rings are full, have a classroom celebration.

- Play a friendship game. Ask children to sit in a circle and pair off. Now children should think of one nice thing about their partners. Beat a drum as children pass a ball around the circle. Stop beating the drum. The child who is holding the ball must tell the group one nice thing about her partner.

□ FINGER PUPPETS

Objective: Make simple puppets to reenact social situations

Core components: Understanding of others
Social problem solving
Ability to mediate

Materials: Old gloves
Felt scraps
Markers
Glue
Scissors

Procedures:

1. Cut the fingers off an old glove. Ask children to make finger puppets, representing either imaginary characters or real people — themselves, their parents, siblings, and friends. Children can create faces and clothes with markers and felt scraps.

2. Encourage children to use puppets to reenact general classroom situations, such as taking turns on the swings, sharing a toy, or planning a project together. Have the class work on solutions. You can prompt, "If you wanted to use the swings, what would you do?" This is a good opportunity to address, in a nonthreatening way, issues or problems that have you noticed in the classroom.

3. Once the children are familiar with the activity, they may wish to generate ideas themselves. Or, set up a "Problem Box" in the classroom. Children can write down (with a teacher's help, if necessary) situations they think need attention. Explain that by acting out different situations—without naming names or hurting feelings—the group can work together to come up with solutions.

4. Keep the finger puppets and other puppets available for children to use for independent play.

Variations:

1. Make different kinds of puppets. You might consider using paper sandwich bags (attach hair, eyes, and nose to the part of the bag that usually forms the bottom, and the mouth on or just below the fold so that it opens and closes); popsicle sticks (attach a face or even a whole body made out of felt scraps or construction paper); or small strips of paper (to wrap around a finger and attach like a ring). You can find more ideas in the Puppets activity in the Visual Arts guide on p. 246.

2. Challenge a small group of children to turn a large, sturdy cardboard box into a puppet stage. Help children with any cutting. You might provide fabric to attach as curtains, or paint for decorating the box. Place the stage on a bookcase or on a table with a tablecloth that reaches to the floor, so that puppeteers can crouch down and hide.

☐ PERSPECTIVES

Objective:	Understand different ways in which individuals can view the same situation Exchange ideas in a discussion
Core Components:	Understanding of others Reflective skills
Materials:	Pictures of people expressing different emotions Chart paper and markers or chalkboard and chalk

Procedures:

1. Show a picture of a person whose face expresses a recognizable emotion (you can use snapshots or pictures cut out of old magazines or newspapers). Discuss with students what they think the person is feeling and why the person might feel that way. Discuss pictures showing various emotional expressions.

2. Compare different pictures and ask children to categorize them. Encourage children to interpret, and categorize, the pictures in different ways.

Variations:

1. Find pictures in magazines that have two people involved in an emotional situation, such as a mother hugging a crying child or a parent looking angrily at a child's messy room. Do the parent and the child have the same feelings about the messiness of the room? Ask the students to role-play the people in the pictures and pretend to have a conversation. What might these people be saying to each other?

2. Ask children to name a number of things that look big and look small to them. Write down the two lists on a board. Ask children to look at both lists from the point of view of an airplane pilot and a baby.

□ Story Problems

Objective:	Listen to a story and discuss possible solutions to the central problem
Core Components:	Understanding of self and others Reasoning about sharing and fairness
Materials:	Pictures of children and a teacher

Procedures:

1. Tell children a story such as the following one, which is reprinted from *The Moral Child: Nurturing Children's Natural Growth* by William Damon (1988).

   "All these boys and girls are in the same class (show pictures of the children and their teacher). One day their teacher let them spend the whole afternoon making paintings and crayon drawings. The teacher thought that these pictures were so good that the class could sell them at the school fair. The pictures were all sold, and together the class made a lot of money. The children gathered the next day and tried to decide how to give out the money." (pp. 40-41)

2. Ask children questions about the story, such as the following ones adapted from the same book:

   - What do you think the class should do with the money?
   - There were some kids who spent their time fooling around while the others were drawing pictures. Should they get any money?
   - Someone said that the kids from poor families should get more. What do you think?
   - Do you think the kids in the class who made the best pictures should get the most money?
   - Someone said the teacher should get a lot because it was her idea to make the pictures in the first place. Should she?
   - Someone said that everyone should get the same amount, no matter what. Do you agree?

3. Have a bake sale in your classroom and talk with the children about how to spend the bake sale money.

❑ *Hospital*

Objective: Explore the community by role-playing various occupations

Core Components: Understanding of others
                               Planning and organizing
                               Working together

Materials: Dramatic play clothes and accessories, such as
                                   Bandages and BandAids
                                   Stethoscope, flashlight, blood pressure cuff (real or pretend)
                                   Crutches
                                   Empty medicine bottles
                                   Scrub suit, face mask, rubber gloves
                                   Cot, mat, or stretcher

Procedures:

1. Tell children that they are going to set up a corner of the classroom to serve as a pretend
    hospital room or emergency room, where for a few weeks they can pretend to be patients
    and their caregivers. (If you have a dramatic play area, you may wish to dedicate it to this
    project for a short time.) Discuss what a hospital is and the different reasons people go there.
    If possible, take a field trip to a hospital, or read books about hospitals.

2. Ask children to think about all the different occupations associated with a hospital. List the
    occupations on chart paper. Ask children to describe these jobs, and the qualities of the
    people who might be interested in them. Can women be doctors? Can men be nurses?
    Reinforce the idea that gender should not limit people's choice of career. If any parents work
    in a hospital, invite them to come and talk with the class.

3. Gather together any hospital-related dress-ups, clothes, toys, or equipment you have in the
    classroom. Talk with children about items they might have at home, such as an old crutch or
    a toy medical set, that they might be willing to loan to the class hospital for a short time.
    Brainstorm a list. If you wish, you might send the list to parents with a note explaining the
    project.

4. Once items have been collected, talk with the children about how they would like to set up
    their hospital. You might ask for a small group of volunteers to help you arrange the play
    area.

5. Designate a period of time each day for a few weeks in which small groups of children can
    play in the hospital area.

Notes to the Teacher:

This activity uses the hospital as a vehicle for exploring different occupations and ways to
participate in community life. You may wish to pick a different theme geared to the interests
of the children in your class or to a particular curricular unit. For example, you might set up
a restaurant with play food, table settings, and menus during a unit on food or nutrition; or
a gift shop selling jewelry and arts and crafts items made by the children during a unit on
tools or on the art of another culture.

☐ CLASS CENSUS

Objective:	Learn about classmates and how to work together by conducting a class census
Core Components:	Developing communication skills Learning about others Learning about social roles
Materials:	Paper Pencil Tape recorder Chalkboard and chalk or chart paper and markers

Procedures:

1. Introduce the concept of a census and the role of census takers. Discuss the census process with students and ask them to take a census in the classroom.

2. Have children generate a list of questions, such as, How many boys are there in the class? How many girls? How many students walk to school? How many ride a bus? How many have sisters and brothers? How many have pets? How many have birthdays in each month? How many are interested in playing baseball, swimming, reading, solving a math problem? How many were born in your city or town, and how many moved from someplace else?

3. Use the information to make graphs (see the Pie Graph activity in the Math guide, pp. 153–154). Collect the graphs into a book or a display.

Notes to the Teacher:

1. This project can be conducted over several days. The census taking can be organized into sessions for planning and decision making, assigning roles, collecting data, and finally displaying and evaluating data.

2. Children can use the "TV" to report their census results.

☐ BIRTHDAY PARTY

Objective:	Practice different social roles through planning birthday parties for classmates
Core Components:	Assumption of distinctive social roles, including
	Organizing an activity
	Planning and setting goals
	Exchanging ideas
	Working together toward a goal
	Identification of strengths of self and others
Materials:	Chalk and chalkboard or chart paper and markers

Procedures:

1. Plan a monthly birthday party for classmates whose birthdays fall within that month. Ask the children to consider the following questions:

   - Why will there be a party?
   - When is it the best time during the school day for a party?
   - What kind of food should be served?
   - Who will prepare it?
   - What else will we need for the party?
   - Who will bring it?
   - Who will clean up?
   - Do we want a theme for each party?
   - What should we do about birthdays that occur over the summer?

2. After children have made their decisions, help them list on the board the different jobs and who will do them.

Notes to the Teacher:

1. The Birthday Party activity can be an ongoing project throughout the school year (thus ensuring that all birthdays are recognized equally). Encourage children to become involved in the process of planning, organizing, assigning roles, decision making, preparing, executing, and clean-up. Allow children to switch roles for different parties.

2. During the planning process, offer several alternatives and let children decide which one to choose. Sort out the issues and structure the activity so that children can make appropriate choices within limits. For example, tell children that the parties will occur on either the first or the last day of the month, during either morning recess or afternoon recess. Which combination would be best and why?

□ VISITORS' DAY

Objective:	Evaluate possibilities and alternatives through group discussion
Core Components:	Assumption of distinctive social roles, including

        Decision making
        Negotiating and consensus building
        Communicating ideas to others
        Working together toward a goal
        Understanding of others

Materials:	Chalk and chalkboard or chart paper and markers

Procedures:

1. Invite children from another grade to visit your classroom. Your class must plan how to "orient" the visitors to your classroom, for instance, explain to them the things they would need to know in order to function as members of the class. For example, a first grade class might want to invite kindergartners to visit near the end of the year, to learn what it will be like to move up a grade.

2. Brainstorm with children what the visitors should know about your classroom. List all ideas on the board. Divide the class into several committees. Each committee has to select the three most important items and defend their choices.

3. Encourage children to choose special social roles during the Visitor's Day, such as facilitator, reporter, and organizer.

Variations:

Have children pretend that a visitor from outer space has landed on the playground. Ask children to consider the three most important things to tell about themselves, their class, their families, and so on. (This is a good opportunity to observe how children are able to work in a group to exchange ideas and reach a consensus.)

☐ We Are a Team

Objective:	Learn to work together to solve a problem or attain a goal
Core Components:	Assumption of distinctive social roles, including:

> Cooperating
> Social problem solving
> Communicating ideas to others
> Identifying strengths of self and of others

Materials:	Clear bottles with a narrow neck
	Small animal-shaped erasers
	Thread
	Hula hoops
	Floor puzzles
	Building blocks
	Calendar
	Ropes
	Blindfolds

Procedures:

Tell children that you will be presenting a series of challenges—such as putting puzzles together without talking, or passing a hula hoop around a circle without using their hands. To be successful, they will have to work together.

Rescue the Animals

Take four small animal-shaped erasers and tie each to a piece of thread. Drop them into a bottle with a narrow neck, so that one end of each string hangs out of the bottle. Give the bottle to a group of four children. Ask them to pretend that the four animals have fallen into a deep well. When you say "start," the children should try to rescue the drowning animals as fast as they can. Count aloud to see how long it takes.

Note: The bottle neck should be too narrow to allow all the erasers out at the same time. That way, the children have to work together to remove one eraser at a time.

Hula Hoop Hop

Ask children to join hands in a circle. Put a hula hoop on one child's shoulder and ask her to pass it to the child next to her without letting go of either neighbor's hand. The children on either side can help, as long as they don't break the circle. Tell children to pass the hula hoop all the way around the circle without letting go of their neighbors' hands. [This game is adapted from *The Responsive Classroom* by Ruth Charney, Marlynn Clayton, and Chip Wood.]

Pretend Present

Divide the class into groups of four to six children. Have each group form a circle. One child pretends to give a present to the child on her left by making gestures without talking. The child who receives the pretend present must guess and name what the present is. If the recipient has trouble guessing the present, other children can help—without talking. After the child has guessed the identity of the pretend present, she must give a different pretend present to the next child in the circle.

Puzzle Challenge

Divide the class into small groups (three or four children) and give each group an age-appropriate floor puzzle, just difficult enough to be interesting. Ask the children to put the puzzle together without talking. Assign one child to make sure that no one in the group speaks.

Block Challenge

Divide a collection of building blocks among the small groups of children. Ask them to see how tall a building they can build—without talking. Measure and record the heights of the buildings. Now let the children repeat the activity once or twice. Do they learn from their mistakes and get better at building tall buildings?

When Is Your Birthday?

Ask children to line up. Challenge them to rearrange the line—without talking—so that they are standing in order based on their birth month, with January birthdays in the front of the line and December birthdays at the end. Children with birthdays in the same month should stand together, but do not need to get in order by day. Post a year-long calendar so that children can consult it easily; if necessary, number the months.

Can We Make a Shape Together?

Organize groups of three to five children, and give each group a rope. Blindfold the children. Ask them to try as a group to form different shapes, such as a square, a triangle, or the letter *L*. Tell them not to let go of the rope or take off their blindfolds until they have agreed that they have achieved the desired shape. [This activity is adapted from "Move the Fence," in *Cooperative Learning in the Early Childhood Classroom* by Harvey Foyle, Lawrence Lyman, and Sandra Alexander Thies.]

Notes to the Teacher:

1. Notice the strategies that different groups use to solve the same problem. After each challenge, one child in the group can act as the speaker and explain the group's strategy to the whole class.

2. Take note of the roles that children assume in solving these problems. Does their role change depending on the activity, or on the other children in the group? As a result of your observations, you may feel that it is necessary to assign roles for the following reasons: to observe particular children in certain roles more closely, to nurture an identified strength in a child by giving her more experience in that role, to give children experience in roles they do not assume very often (e.g., giving a shy child a leadership role).

☐ MY LIFE STORY

Objective: Help children understand their physical, cognitive, and social growth

Materials: Photos of your child
Pictures drawn by your child
Documents and other materials related to your child's life
Posterboard, heavy construction paper, or paper folded into a book
Glue
Markers

Note to Parents:

This activity is designed to help your child see the different ways that he or she has developed over the past few years. Your child is now capable of doing many things that he or she was not capable of doing only a few months ago.

Procedures:

1. Collect materials and information that represent, in a visual way, your child's abilities at different ages. These might include:

    *   copy of birth certificate
    *   footprint at birth
    *   birth weight and height
    *   pictures of the child's physical growth (e.g., crawling, walking, running, playing outside, dressing self, riding a bike, tying shoes)
    *   pictures of the child's cognitive growth (e.g., talking, reading with a parent, playing with different toys, using a computer)
    *   pictures of the child's social growth (e.g., family, friends, holiday celebrations, preschool or elementary school experiences)
    *   samples of the child's drawing and writing

2. Discuss the idea of a "life story" with your child and ask him or her to choose the pictures or other materials that best represent different stages of growth. Try also to include information about the culture of your family or community.

3. Arrange the pictures and materials in chronological order. Ask your child to glue them onto the posterboard, or into a booklet made of folded sheets of paper. Encourage your child to draw on or decorate his or her life story.

4. When the life story is done, review it with your child, talking about the milestones in his or her development.

Sharing:

Let your child take the life story to class.

☐ FEELING FACES

Objective: To help your child learn that you can tell how people feel by looking at their facial expressions.

Materials: Colored paper
Scissors
Small paper plates (optional)
Glue or paste

Note to Parents:

Your child will identify familiar feelings, reflect on what makes him or her feel certain ways, and recognize that other people have the same feelings, too.

Procedures:

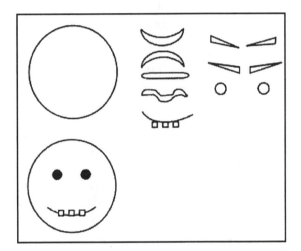

1. Cut shapes out of construction paper to represent the eyes (happy and sad), mouth (smiling and frowning), and other facial features. Let your child arrange the pieces on paper plates or paper circles to create the following emotions: happy, sad, mad, scared, bored, sleepy. Your child may want to add other features to the faces by drawing them in.

2. What other emotions are there? Ask your child to name some other ways people feel and make faces to match.

3. Your child can make up a simple story that he or she can illustrate with these faces.

4. Discuss situations in which people experience some type of emotion (such as joy, loneliness, anger, pride). Ask your child:
    - When do you feel proud? (Substitute different emotions, such as happy, sad, bored, lonely, excited, angry, or embarrassed.)
    - How do you feel at a birthday party? (Substitute different situations, such as entering the classroom, watching TV, winning a game.)
    - How can you tell when another person is feeling sad? (Substitute different emotions, such as proud, excited, lonely, or embarrassed.)

Sharing:

1. Your child can take to school the story that he or she has written and illustrated.

2. Ask your child to make a chart of emotions, illustrated with faces. Your child can bring this chart to school and share it with classmates as a guessing game by leaving off either the words or the faces.

RESOURCES AND REFERENCES _____

The activities on the preceding pages are just an introduction to the teaching of social understanding. To help you explore further, we offer a brief list of resources that have proved valuable to us and to our colleagues. It is intended to provide inspiration rather than a review of the literature. Sources used in the preparation of this volume are marked with an asterisk.

* Aliki. (1984). *Feelings.* New York: Green Willow Press.

* Barry, C. F., & Mindes, G. (1993). *Planning a theme-based curriculum: Goals, themes, activities, and planning guides for 4's and 5's.* Glenview, IL: Good Year Books.

* Borba, M., & Borba, C. (1982). *Self-esteem: A classroom affair* (Vol. 2). San Francisco: Harper & Row.

Carlsson-Paige, N., & Levin, D. E. (1987). *The war play dilemma: Balancing needs and values in the early childhood classroom.* New York: Teachers College Press.

Carlsson-Paige, N., & Levin, D. E. (1985). *Helping young children understand peace, war, and the nuclear threat.* Washington, DC: National Association for the Education of Young Children.

* Charney, R., Clayton, M., & Wood, C. (1995). *The responsive classroom: Guidelines.* Greenfield, MA: Northeast Foundation for Children.

Crary, E. (1984). *Kids can cooperate: A practical guide to teaching problem solving.* Seattle: Parenting Press.

* Damon, W. (1988). *The moral child: Nurturing children's natural moral growth.* New York: Free Press.

Derman-Sparks, L., & The A.B.C. Task Force. (1989). *Anti-bias curriculum: Tools for empowering young children.* Washington, DC: National Association for the Education of Young Children.

DeVries, R., & Zan, B. (1994). *Moral classrooms, moral children: Creating a constructivist atmosphere in early education.* New York: Teachers College Press.

* Foyle, H., Lyman, L., & Thies, S. A. (1991). *Cooperative learning in the early childhood classroom.* Washington, DC: National Education Association.

* Johnson, J., Christie, J., & Yawkey, T. (1987). *Play and early childhood development.* Glenview, IL: Scott Foresman.

Mallory, B., & New, R. (1994). *Diversity and developmentally appropriate practices.* New York: Teachers College Press.

McCracken, J. B. (Ed.). (1986). *Reducing stress in young children's lives.* Washington, DC: National Association for the Education of Young Children.

Neugebauer, B. (Ed.). (1992). *Alike and different: Exploring our humanity with young children* (rev. ed.). Washington, DC: National Association for the Education of Young Children.

Saracho, O. (Ed.). (1983). *Understanding the multicultural experience in early childhood education.* Washington, DC: National Association for the Education of Young Children.

* Silverstein, S. (1964) *The giving tree.* New York: Harper & Row.

Slaby, R. G., Roedell, W. C., Arezzo, D., & Hendrix, K. (1995). *Early violence prevention: Tools for teachers of young children.* Washington, DC: National Association for the Education of Young Children.

York, S. (1991). *Roots and wings: Affirming culture in early childhood programs.* St. Paul, MN: Redleaf Press.

LANGUAGE ACTIVITIES

CONTENTS

Introduction

An Overview of the Language Activities 197
Description of Key Abilities 198
Description of Materials 199

Language Activities

Storytelling

Group Storytelling 200
Storytelling with Storyboards 201
Making Our Own Storyboards 202
Classroom Model Storytelling 203
Storytelling with Sound Effects 204

Reporting

Interviewing a Friend 205
Reporting the News 206
Movie Review 207

Poetic Language

Poetry in Your Classroom 208
"Happy is . . ." 210
Our Own Song 212
Moving to Poems, Stories, & Songs 213

Reading and Writing

Letter Boxes 216
Reading to Each Other 217
Introduction to Journals 218
What Am I? Book 219
The Classroom Mailbox 220
"A House is a House for. . ." 221

Take-Home Activities

1 Make Your Own Book 222
2 Color Rhymes 223

Resources and References 224

AN OVERVIEW OF THE LANGUAGE ACTIVITIES

Learning how to read and write is a major focus of the early elementary years. Literacy, however, is more than just discrete skills—it is the ability to communicate and express oneself in a variety of contexts. In addition to being a good reader and writer, it is important to be a good speaker and, above all, a good listener.

The language activities are designed to foster children's listening, speaking, reading, and writing skills through meaningful, real-world experiences. For example, children practice writing by composing letters to friends and mailing them in a classroom mailbox, and practice speaking by interviewing classmates on a handmade "TV." Many of the activities, such as putting together a news report and writing a poem, introduce children to language-related careers. Thus, children can see the relevance of classroom activities to their lives outside of school. Please remember that the activities collected here are not intended to serve as a curriculum, but as examples of the many different contexts in which children can demonstrate and develop their language abilities. We hope they will give you some ideas for designing language projects that address the range of interests, tastes, and concerns that children bring to your class.

The language activities fall into four categories: storytelling, reporting, poetry, and reading and writing. Although there is some overlap among the four, in general *storytelling* focuses on expressive and aesthetic use of language, *reporting* on factual accounts and explanations, *poetry* on wordplay, and *reading and writing* on the written word. Some of the activities reinforce reading readiness skills, such as letter recognition, whereas others are designed for children who are working on more advanced reading skills.

A formal introduction to the language activities can help children understand what they should be learning, as well as prepare them to use the materials independently. You might hold a group discussion in which you describe the various language materials, then ask children their ideas for using them. By writing down the children's responses and suggestions, you can validate their ideas and give them a sense of ownership of the learning activities. For instance, when you introduce storyboards, encourage the children to talk about how the storyboard can be used and in which ways the storyboard activity might be different from reading books or storytelling. You may also introduce the handmade "TV" and ask the children how news reporting might be different from storytelling. Tell them that they will be able to use the "TV" to report their weekend news and other interesting things in their lives.

If you wish, you can also show children how to use a Koosh, or any other "talking stone," to designate the speaker. Explain that whoever is holding the talking stone gets to speak, while the rest of the class remains quiet. When the child is finished, she can hand or gently toss the talking stone to the next speaker.

Invented narrative/storytelling

- uses imagination and originality in storytelling

- enjoys listening to or reading stories

- exhibits interest and ability in plot design and development, character elaboration and motivation, descriptions of settings, scenes or moods, use of dialogue, and so on.

- shows performing ability or dramatic flair, including a distinctive style, expressiveness, or an ability to play a variety of roles

Descriptive language/reporting

- provides accurate and coherent accounts of events, feelings, and experiences (e.g., uses correct sequence and appropriate level of detail; distinguishes fact from fantasy)

- provides accurate labels and descriptions for things

- shows interest in explaining how things work, or describing a procedure

- engages in logical argument or inquiry

Poetic use of language/wordplay

- enjoys and is adept at wordplay such as puns, rhymes, and metaphors

- plays with word meanings and sounds

- demonstrates interest in learning new words

- uses words in a humorous fashion

Storyboard: a board, box top, or piece of felt outfitted with figures and a setting. Children manipulate the figures as they tell a familiar story or create a story of their own. You can make scenery and props from modeling clay, or assemble them from Playmobile and other commercial sets. These props can correspond to a particular book or story, or can be generic ones (ponds, trees, treasures, kings and queens, etc.) designed to prompt imaginative tales.

Storyboard block figures: photocopies of characters from books that are cut out, colored in and covered with clear contact paper. You can paste these figures onto blocks to give children a concrete, three-dimensional representation of characters for storytelling. You can add new block figures to the collection periodically, based on student suggestions and the stories you are reading in class. You also can make characters using pipe cleaners or other materials. Each story-related set can be kept in its own labeled container, with a name and photocopied page from the book that children can recognize easily.

Letter/word boxes and cards: boxes labeled with a single letter or word, in which children place objects or cards that match the label; these labels can be changed periodically. You can make your own word and letter cards or buy flash cards.

What Am I? book: a homemade book, made with sturdy paper and ribbons. To prepare the book, cut out magazine pictures or photos of objects that are hard to identify, and paste them onto the right-hand pages. Let children use the opposite pages to write down their guesses about what the objects might be. Later, children can cut out "mystery" pictures and paste them into the book.

"TV": a large cardboard box cut out and decorated to resemble a television set. The "TV" is used for special reporting activities and for several activities in the Social Understanding guide.

Classroom mailbox: a cardboard box construction that is decorated, by the teacher or the children, to resemble a mailbox. It can be used for special letter-writing activities or for communication within the classroom.

Classroom model: a three-dimensional scale model of the classroom. You can make the model out of a cardboard box and make furniture and other decorations out of fabric scraps, wood, small boxes, and recycled items. Add small figures, or make your own by gluing photographs of the children in the class onto small wooden blocks. Directions for making a classroom model are included in the Visual Arts guide (see p. 240).

Koosh or talking stone: a toy or stone used to manage group discussions. A Koosh is a commercially available ball that can be passed from child to child to designate the speaker. Large stones, shells, and many other familiar objects can be used instead.

□ GROUP STORYTELLING

Objective:	Use a storyboard and props to introduce children to storytelling
Core Components:	Storytelling, with emphasis on
	Imagination and originality
	Thematic coherence
	Sense of plot
	Dramatic flair
Materials:	Large piece of felt
	Generic props and figures
	Tape recorder (optional)

Procedures:

1. Gather the children on the floor. Explain that they will do a lot of storytelling during the year using a storyboard, and that they will start by telling a story all together.

2. Take out the large piece of felt and lay it on the floor. Select several props and figures, indicating to the children that you don't have one particular story in mind and that there are many different ways to tell a story. You might say, "I think I'd like to use this little person to tell my story, and maybe this will be his house. I'll put it right there." Ask children for suggestions about additional characters and props to choose for the story.

3. Tell a short story, using several components of storytelling (e.g., descriptions, dialogue, expressive voices).

4. Tell the children that they will tell the next story together, adding a new part to the story one at a time. As a group, plan what the story will be about, what types of things might happen, what the setting will be like, and where to place items on the storyboard.

5. Ask for a volunteer to start the story. Go around the group, giving each child an opportunity to add to the story and manipulate the materials. Remind children to pay close attention to what the other children say.

6. After everyone has had a turn (or two), you might want to add an ending or suggest that a child do so, to give the story some closure and a sense of coherence.

7. Discuss your story. What happened to the character(s)? What could have happened differently? Would anyone have liked it to end differently? How? Point out and reinforce examples in which children used dramatic flair, imagination, dialogue, or expressive voice.

Notes to the Teacher:

1. If you wish, use the Koosh to designate whose turn it is to add a part.

2. You can make all the storyboard materials available during activity times for children to tell their own stories.

3. You can use a tape recorder during the group storytelling and replay part of the story at the end of the activity. If possible, make the recorder available for children to tape their own stories independently.

□

□ STORYTELLING WITH STORYBOARDS

Objective:	Use storyboards based on familiar books to help develop storytelling skills
Core Components:	Storytelling, with emphasis on Character elaboration Plot development Performing ability or dramatic flair Story comprehension and retelling Use of dialogue Expressive language
Materials:	Books Figures and props that can be used to represent these books

Procedures:

1. Read a short story, using an expressive style. Briefly discuss the book with the children. Make sure you discuss the setting, main characters, plot, and ending.

2. Retell the story using the storyboard, changing some of the language and details to encourage children to tell stories in their own way. Ask for children's additions and suggestions.

3. Time permitting, allow one or more children to give individual versions of the story.

Notes to the Teacher:

1. When you prepare your storyboards, select books that are familiar to most children, such as those that you have read frequently to the class. This will be especially helpful for children who cannot yet read. Then, trace or copy pictures of the main characters, cut out the figures, and glue them to blocks or pieces of Styrofoam.

2. Over time introduce children to new books and storyboards. Leave these out for children to use. Encourage children to work together and to tell stories to each other.

☐ MAKING OUR OWN STORYBOARDS

Objective:	Make storyboards to learn about components of storytelling
Core Components:	Storytelling, with emphasis on
	Imagination and originality
	Dramatic flair
	Plot design and development
Materials:	Shoe boxes (ask children to bring them in)
	Crayons or markers
	Clay
	Various props and characters brought from home

Procedures:

1. Tell children that they will be making their own storyboards. Give them plenty of advance notice. Ask children to think about what kind of story they would like to create and what kind of materials (box, props, small characters) they might need. Help children make a list of these materials. Next, give the children a note to take home requesting the materials.

2. After all the children have a shoe box and whatever recycled items they need, give them each clay, crayons or markers, and other art materials. Ask them to make characters and props for their storyboards. Emphasize that they should think about the story they would like to tell before they make characters. Circulate around the room as the children work, helping with story and construction ideas.

3. Encourage children to use their storyboards to tell a story, either to the whole group or to a few classmates. Display the storyboards around the room and suggest that children continue to use them to tell stories.

4. After a while, send the storyboards home with a note to parents, suggesting that they use them with their children. Explain to children that they can show their parents how to use the storyboard.

☐ CLASSROOM MODEL STORYTELLING

Objective:	Tell stories based on classroom life
Core Components:	Storytelling, with emphasis on
	Plot design and development
	Character elaboration
	Use of dialogue
	Social Understanding
Materials:	Classroom model (see Description of Materials, p. 199)
	Tape recorder (optional)

Procedures:

1. Tell children that the classroom model will be available for storytelling. Encourage children to explore and play with the model during a free choice or learning center time. If you wish, you can set up a tape recorder so they can record their stories and play them back for themselves or classmates.

2. When the children are ready, encourage them each to take a short turn—use a timer if necessary—using the model to tell a story to the whole class or a small group. Emphasize that they can base their stories on real classroom events or imaginary ones. Intervene if the subject matter is sensitive or needs mediation.

Variations:

1. Encourage children to create and share their own stories using whatever materials you have in the classroom. Puppets are a good way to provide inspiration for storytelling; see the Visual Arts and Social Understanding guides for a few puppet-making suggestions.

2. Or, suggest that children use rubber stamps to create a story. They can stamp a series of characters or scenes onto a piece of paper, and then tell the story to a classmate. To use this as a writing activity, ask the children to write down as best they can what is happening in each scene. If you wish, they can use their own spelling to get their thoughts down on paper, and you can show them the correct spelling later.

☐ STORYTELLING WITH SOUND EFFECTS

Objective:	Develop expressiveness by creating sound effects for a story
Core Components:	Storytelling, with emphasis on expressiveness and originality
Materials:	Short story or book
	Instruments (e.g., bells, kazoos, wood blocks)
	Other sound effect materials appropriate to the story

Procedures:

1. Read a short book or story and ask children to come up with sound effects to accompany the action. Children could select a rhythm instrument, bell, or other object in the room to help produce sound effects.

2. Read the story again with appropriate pauses or places for children to add sound effects. Ask each child to be in charge of one specific sound effect.

Notes to the Teacher:

Almost any action story can be adapted for sound effects. For example:

One day long ago, in the forest near a waterfall [*pour water from a pitcher into a basin*], a king and queen [*play four short notes on toy trumpet or kazoo*] lived quietly with their new baby girl [*shake a baby rattle*] who slept most of the time [*open a music box*]. As the child grew older she often wondered what was on the other side of the waterfall [*pour water*]. One sunny day she got on her horse [*drum fingers on the table to sound like galloping*] and headed toward the horizon.

Variations:

1. Let children practice dialogue by changing their voices to represent different characters (e.g., low voice for a bear, high voice for a mouse). You can read the story, pausing to let children read or recite certain parts.

2. Emphasize the musical dimension of this activity by letting children play musical instruments to represent the characters in a story, just as a musical theme introduces each character in *Peter and the Wolf.* As the character enters the scene have a child play his or her instrument.

☐ INTERVIEWING A FRIEND

Objective:	Take turns interviewing a partner
Core Components:	Descriptive language, with emphasis on
	Skill of inquiry
	Accurate and coherent description
Materials:	None

Procedures:

1. Tell children that they will be interviewing each other to get to know one another better. Pair children or have them select partners. Demonstrate by interviewing a child yourself.

2. Explain that interviewing is a way of finding out what other people think, know, or feel about a topic. Give children a list of suggested questions to ask each other. Go over these questions as a group and ask children to generate additional ones. You might start with the following questions:

   > What is your name?
   > Where do you live?
   > Do you have sisters or brothers?
   > What's your favorite food?
   > What's your favorite thing to do?

3. As the first child of each pair interviews the other, circulate around the classroom, helping children conduct the interviews.

4. Have interviewers report on their interviews with their partners.

5. Repeat the interviewing process, having partners switch roles.

Notes to the Teacher:

1. This is a good introduction to other reporting activities that call for children to interview each other. Interview topics can include holidays, current events, and projects that children have completed in art, science, and other domains.

2. If appropriate for your class, you can pattern the interview after a television talk show. First, discuss any talk shows the children have seen. Then, encourage children to take turns acting as host and guest on their own talk show. If they wish, they can sit behind the "TV" or invite their classmates to watch.

☐ REPORTING THE NEWS

Objective:	Use "TV" to learn about and practice reporting
Core Components:	Descriptive language, with emphasis on:
	Accurate and coherent account of events
	Explaining how things work
Materials:	"TV"
	Play microphone

Procedures:

1. Introduce the "TV" and brainstorm with children about "TV" activities they could do.

2. Explain that the "TV" can be used just like a real one: for reporting the news. Suggest that the children present a show in which they report on their own news, such as a trip they have taken, something they did that was fun, something funny their pet did, or a sports event.

3. Model using the "TV." Sit behind it, pick up the play microphone, and tell a relatively mundane piece of family news, such as: "Yesterday afternoon my family went to the park. Katie fed the ducks. And now a word from our sponsors, Crest toothpaste. . . ."

4. Have children think of one or two things they would like to tell the class. Then, let them take turns sitting behind the "TV" and reporting their news. If children need help getting started, ask questions such as, Would you like to tell us about your dog? Did she do something special? What does she look like? Encourage children to applaud at the end of each news clip.

Variations:

1. Write different categories of news on slips of paper (sports, entertainment, local news, commercials, weather) and put them in a hat. Have children choose a category to report on the following day.

2. Make reporting the news part of your weekly routine. For example, each Monday children could use the "TV" to talk about what happened over the weekend. They could report to the whole group, or work in pairs.

☐ MOVIE REVIEW

Objective:	Develop reporting skills by reviewing a movie
Core Components:	Descriptive language, with emphasis on

        Coherent account of events

        Accurate reporting of sequence

        Choice of detail

        Critical TV- and movie-viewing skills

Materials:	Movie
	Movie tickets (optional)

Procedures:

1. Tell children that they will be viewing a movie. Ask them to watch carefully because they will discuss the movie afterwards.

2. Use a puppet theater or the "TV" as a box office, and ask one child to be the box office person who "sells" tickets. Children can line up to get their tickets and proceed to the "theater."

3. After the viewing, ask children for general comments about the movie. Did they like it or dislike it, and why? How did the movie make them feel? Did they think the events could really happen? Why or why not?

4. In small groups, lead a discussion regarding the sequence, plot, theme, and characters of the movie. Ask children, "What happened first in the movie? What happened next? And then what? What was the most important thing that happened in the movie?"

Notes to the Teacher:

1. Try to choose a movie that is unfamiliar to the children. Select one that runs for 15 minutes or less, and contains a clearly defined sequence of events.

2. If possible, do this activity regularly so children can practice watching a movie and recalling details of sequence, plot, theme, and characters.

3. You might suggest that the children watch the PBS television show *Reading Rainbow*, which includes book reviews by elementary students on each program.

☐ Poetry in Your Classroom

Objective: Introducing children to the reading and writing of poetry

Core Components: Enjoyment of poetry
                            Wordplay
                            Expressiveness

Materials: Poems

Procedures:

1. Including poetry—both reading and writing—as an important part of the classroom language experience encourages children to play with words and their nuances and gives them tools for rich expression. Reading and writing poetry are two sides of the same coin: If children are surrounded by poetry, they become familiar with the sound of its rhymes and rhythms; if they write poetry, they grow to see themselves as part of a great literary tradition.

   When you read poems to the children, emphasize words that are particularly vibrant, colorful, or animated. Encourage the children to talk about the poet's choice of words— words that rhyme or start with the same sound; words that paint a picture in the listener's mind. (This will help children when they write poetry of their own.) Read poetry often throughout the year. Try to follow up on the interests of the class, be it pets, monsters, holidays, seasons, or sports and games. Young children also respond to repetitions and silly, obvious humor. For example, here is a popular choice:

   Animal Fair

   I went to the animal fair,
   The birds and the beasts were there.
   The big baboon, by the light of the moon,
   Was combing his auburn hair.
   The funniest was the monk.
   He sat on the elephant's trunk.
   The elephant sneezed and fell on his knees,
   And what became of the monk, the monk?

   Read poetry often throughout the year, progressing to new themes and more subtle humor when you feel the children are ready.

2. In their article "Let's Talk a Poem," Theresa Brown and Lester Laminack suggest introducing children to poetry writing by "talking" them through the process. The poem can be written by the entire class or a small group with the teacher acting as coach, asking the group questions that stir children's imaginations and elicit specific, concrete imagery.

3. Suppose you decide to write about a shared experience, such as a field trip to the aquarium. Ask children to describe the aquarium so that people who have not been there will know what it feels like and looks like. Start by asking children for their reactions. You might hear a comment such as:

   "Cool fish at the aquarium."

Write the statement down on chart paper. As you proceed, ask children questions that will elicit a vivid description of the event. Remind them to think of all five senses. You might ask, "What did you see at the aquarium?"

"Big huge fish and tiny little fishies."

Write it down, then ask, "Can you tell me what the fish were doing?"

"They were swimming around and around, eating, and resting."

Write the comment and ask, "What did you do?"

"I said, 'Hello, fish.' "

"I smiled."

"I watched."

The finished product, written on chart paper, might look like this:

> Cool fish at the aquarium.
> Big huge fish, tiny little fishies
> Swimming around and around,
> Eating and resting.
> I said, "Hello, fish."
> I smiled. I watched.

4. Brown and Laminack suggest ways to help children find fresh, descriptive words. For example, if a child writes or states, "The dog walked away," you might ask, "Is there another word that helps me see how it walked away?" More specific scaffolding, if necessary, might involve making suggestions: "Did it sneak away, prance away, dash away, shuffle away?" The child can then choose a word and still feel like the author.

5. Writing poetry should be a joyous experience. In *Wishes, Lies, and Dreams: Teaching Poetry to Children,* poet Kenneth Koch says that a key element is finding the right topic, one that is familiar to children but exciting enough to prompt fresh ideas. Do not impose constraints that might limit children's imagination, such as asking them to rhyme or try a specific meter. Instead, present them with an idea that can encourage creativity and provide a unifying force for the poem. For example, he suggests a poem about wishing; each child in the class can contribute a line that starts with "I wish." Or, they might each try a line about a color (either the same color or all different colors); a line about a dream they have had, or a line about growing up (I used to_____ but now I _____). Other topics, such as asking children to describe a noise or make an offbeat comparison, can encourage young writers to take risks and use original, unconventional language.

6. Encourage and help children to write their own individual poetry describing events or personal experiences. Give children an opportunity to dictate poetry and to share poetry with classmates. The metaphor activity, "Happy Is. . ." (on the following page), offers a good transition between writing a poem as a group and on one's own.

□ *"HAPPY IS . . ."*

Objective:	Explore poetry through metaphor
Core Components:	Imagination and originality
	Wordplay
	Adeptness with metaphors
Materials:	Poems
	Chalkboard and chalk or chart paper and marker

Procedures:

1. Start with a movement activity. Ask students to act out what it's like to feel good, and to show their happiness with their whole bodies.

2. React to children's movements. For example, "I see lots of happy people now. Olga, you seem to be flying. Juan, you look like a puppy wagging its tail." Encourage children to describe what they did. For example, "I was a mommy, rocking a baby." "I was a clown making people laugh."

3. Ask the children, "Is it easier to act out feeling happy by being something other than yourself? Why?" Help children consider whether pretending to be something else is similar to using a comparison, and whether comparisons can help them express their feelings.

4. Read "Swing Song" (reprinted on the next page). Discuss what the poem has to say about feeling happy.

5. If you wish, read other poems about being happy. Ask children, "What makes you happy? What does it feel like to be happy?" Write their ideas on the board or chart paper and shape them into a poem, asking children to add a beginning (for example, "Happy is. . .") and an ending if necessary. Read the poem aloud with the children.

Variations:

Develop the idea of metaphor to identify things other than emotions, such as colors. Start by reading a poem that explores the subject and then brainstorm with children. Create metaphor sheets (for example, write across the top of a page, *What is white?* or *Red is _____*) and make the pages available for children to work on individually, in pairs, or in groups.

This activity is adapted from G. D. Sloan (1984). *The child as critic: Teaching literature in elementary and middle school* (2nd ed.). New York: Teachers College Press.

Swing Song

Oh, I've discovered
A happy thing!
For every game
There's a song to sing,
Sometimes with words
Sometimes without,
It's easy to tell
What a song's about
From only a humming
Like wind at noon,
It needn't be even
Half a tune
If only it goes
With what you do,
If what you do
Is exactly true,
Or anyway if
It seems to you.

The time I discovered
This wonderful thing
I really was swinging
In a swing.
And the song I was singing
Was just as true
For all the flying
Sky-things too,
For seagulls and eagulls
And bees and bugs
And arrows and sparrows
Enchanted rugs,
Clouds and balloons,
Balloons and bees —
A backward humming
A forward breeze,
Swinging without
Any tune you please.

—Harry Behn

☐ OUR OWN SONG

Objective:	Create new lyrics for songs
Core Components:	Poetic language, with emphasis on
	Play with word sounds, meanings
	Using words in humorous fashion
Materials:	Songbook, if needed
	Chalkboard and chalk or chart paper and marker

Procedures:

1. Tell children that they will be making up their own words for one of their favorite songs. Pick a song with a lot of repetition, such as "She'll Be Comin' Round the Mountain" or "The Wheels on the Bus." Sing the song with the children.

2. Ask children to sing the song again and to think (silently) what verses or lines they might like to add. Write the first lines of the song on the chalkboard or chart paper, leaving a blank where you want children to provide new words. For example, you might ask them to replace the words underlined below:

   She'll be comin' round the mountain when she comes,
   She'll be comin' round the mountain when she comes,
   She'll be comin' round the mountain, she'll be comin' round the mountain,
   She'll be comin' round the mountain when she comes.

3. Guide the children in their discussion of new ideas. Write down their suggestions and sing the new version together.

Variations:

If children are ready for a challenge, you might ask them to write new words for the lullaby "Hush, Little Baby," which requires them to think in rhymes. (For example, "Hush, little baby, don't you scream, Mama's going to buy you some chocolate ice cream. If that chocolate ice cream melts, Mommy's going to buy you a beaded belt.) The traditional words are given below. Children may either make up their own conclusion or try to rhyme their way into the last verse.

Hush, Little Baby

Hush, little baby, don't say a word,
Mama's going to buy you a mockingbird.
And if that mockingbird don't sing,
Mama's going to buy you a diamond ring.

And if that diamond ring turns brass,
Mama's going to buy you a looking glass.
And if that looking glass gets broke,
Mama's going to buy you a billy goat.

And if that billy goat won't pull,
Mama's going to buy you a cart and bull.
And if that cart and bull turn over,
Mama's going to buy you a dog named Rover.

And if that dog named Rover won't bark,
Mama's going to buy you a horse and cart.
And if that horse and cart fall down,
You'll still be the sweetest little baby in town.

□ MOVING TO POEMS, STORIES, & SONGS

Objective:	Create actions for poems, stories, and songs
Core Components:	Expressiveness Associating physical play with word sounds Enjoyment of poetry
Materials:	Poems Dramatic play clothes and props, if desired

Procedures:

1. Tell the children that they will be acting out a poem. Read them the poem slowly, so that they can understand all the words. Read the rhyme again, encouraging children to join in reciting it. (For this activity select poems that are humorous, familiar, and have repetitive phrases, such as nursery rhymes like "Simple Simon" or "Jack and Jill," or poems by Shel Silverstein, Ogden Nash, or Edward Lear.)

2. Ask children to stand in a semicircle so that they all can see you. Recite the poem, making gestures that illustrate the words. Encourage children to join you. Repeat until children have caught on.

3. Select another poem and invite the children to make up appropriate movements.

Variations:

1. Select a favorite poem, short story, or song. Explain to children that, once again, they will be creating movements to go with the words. This time, however, they will act out different roles, or parts.

   Read the poem or story aloud until the children are quite familiar with it. Brainstorm movement ideas; try out different suggestions and see what works best. (A few poems and stories, with accompanying actions, are included on the following pages to serve as a guide.) Encourage the children to take on different roles, either individually, in pairs, or in small groups. After the children have selected parts and gestures, practice the piece as much as children want or time allows.

2. Children can prepare a piece to perform for their families or other classes. Preparing the "play" can span several days and encompass different domains. Children might make props and costumes as an art project, or practice singing a song as a music activity. As an additional language activity, you might encourage children to write their own stories to be acted out. Children will be highly motivated to write stories if they know that their work will be performed and shared with others (see Vivian Paley's book, *Wally's Stories*).

Suggestions for Dramatization

Reprinted from R. Pangrazi and V. Dauer. (1981). *Movement in early childhood and primary education.* ©1981 by Allyn & Bacon. Reprinted/adapted by permission.

Jack the Giant Killer

Once upon a time, a giant called Caramaran lived on top of a mountain in a cave. He was a very wicked giant, so the kings of the country offered a large reward to the person who would kill him. Jack, a country boy, decided to try his luck.

Words	*Suggested Action*
One morning, Jack took a shovel and pick and started toward the mountain. He hurried as he wished to climb the mountain before dark.	Picking up pick and shovel and running around in a circle.
Jack finally reached the foot of the mountain and started to climb up.	Walking around in a circle with high knee movements.
He came to a place where he had to use his hands to help him climb.	Making climbing movements, using hands and arms.
Just as it grew dark, Jack reached the top of the mountain. When he was sure the giant was asleep in bed, he took his pick and began to dig a hole outside the cave entrance.	Vigorous digging, with trunk twisting, standing with feet apart.
After he had loosened the dirt with his pick, Jack took the shovel and threw the dirt up on all sides of the hole.	Vigorous shoveling, first right, then left, throwing the dirt in various directions.
Then Jack covered up the hole with some long straws and sticks he had picked up.	Bending down, picking up straws, twisting alternately left and right.

After this was done, Jack waited until morning, when he called loudly and wakened the giant, who strode angrily out of the cave. Because he was very tall, he took big steps.	With arms overhead, stretching up tall, walking around in a circle on tiptoes.
The giant was so very angry that he didn't look where he was going and walked right into the hole Jack had made. Down he fell and was killed.	Stooping quickly as if falling.
Then Jack filled up the hole with the dirt he had taken out.	Making forward, downward movements, pushing dirt into the hole, moving around in a circle, and doing the same thing over again.
Jack went into the cave, got the giant's treasure and ran home to tell his mother about it.	Running around in a circle in the opposite direction, carrying the treasure.
When he got home he was so excited and tired that he was all out of breath. Ever after this, Jack was called Giant Killer.	Deep breathing.

Wallaby Kangaroo

Words	*Suggested Action*
Wallaby, wallaby, kangaroo,	Holding hands in front of the shoulders, to represent the paws of a kangaroo.
How do you jump the way you do?	Looking around from right to left, but not moving.
I'm sure if I tried for a year and a day,	Jumping around like a kangaroo.
I'd never be able to jump that way.	Continuing to jump like a kangaroo.

□ LETTER BOXES

Objective:	Learn phonics by matching letters and blends with objects and pictures
Core Components:	Phonics skills Sound-letter matching
Materials:	Letter or word boxes (see Description of Materials, p. 199) Various objects and pictures

Procedures:

1. Introduce children to the letter or word box. Explain that each box will have a letter attached to it. Children can put word cards, small objects, and pictures that start with that letter in the box. For example, announce, "Today the *G* box is out (show the box with a large *G* on the front). I'd like you to put things in this box — words and pictures cut out from magazines, little objects, a word card — that start with the letter *G*."

2. Model the activity for children, cutting out a *G*-word from a magazine and putting it in the box, along with a small object that starts with *G*. Ask children for suggestions to ensure they understand the activity.

3. Tell children that the letter box will be available throughout the day or week. Ask children to check with you before they put in objects like class materials or toys that someone might want to use.

4. Check the contents of the box at the end of the day or week. Ask the group, "What is this? Does it start with a *G*?" If an incorrect object or letter is placed in the box, discuss how that mistake could have been made. For instance, "This doesn't start with *G*, but it's a dog, and the word dog ends with *G*."

Notes to the Teacher:

1. Make various objects, pictures, and letter cards available for children to put in the boxes.

2. Two or more boxes may be left out for children's use at the same time.

☐ READING TO EACH OTHER

Objective:	Read with a partner
Core Components:	Enjoyment of listening to or reading stories
	Reading in a compelling style, expressiveness
	Cooperation
Materials:	Books

Procedures:

1. Group the children into pairs. Have each child choose a book she would like to read to her partner.

2. Allow children to go to various corners of the room with their partners. Each takes a turn reading her book.

3. Gather together as a group. To help children develop both listening and speaking skills, ask them to describe the books that were read to them.

Variations:

1. Help children to see that reading can be a social as well as an individual activity, in which people share ideas and experiences with each other. Encourage children to read a story to the entire class. Children can bring in a favorite book or story from home or choose among the books in the classroom. Children who are not reading yet can be encouraged to tell, rather than read, a favorite story, using the pictures as a guide.

2. Read a poem or song all together, as a class. Distribute copies of the song or poem, or write it on the board or chart paper. Start by reading the piece with an expressive voice, then ask the children to read along with you. You may wish to point to the words as you go along. Next, ask the children to take turns reading one line at a time. End by reciting the poem or singing the song in unison.

☐ INTRODUCTION TO JOURNALS

Objective:	Use a journal to practice putting thoughts into words
Core Components:	Writing, with emphasis on
	Imagination and originality
	Expressiveness
	Accurate and coherent description
	Explaining how things work
	Wordplay, such as rhymes and metaphors
Materials:	Journal for each child
	Writing and drawing tools
	Decorations (optional)

Procedures:

1. Describe journals to the children. Explain that you will give them each a special book in which they can write and draw whatever they want. Tell them that grown-ups often use journals to reflect upon, or think about, events in their lives. The children can use them in the same way—to write their private thoughts, poems, stories, things they don't want to forget, whatever comes into their mind. They also can use their journals to draw pictures, by themselves or with stories to go with them. Discuss with children the types of things that they might like to write or draw in a journal, and list their ideas on chart paper or a chalkboard.

2. Pass out journals along with crayons or markers, and stickers or whatever other art supplies you feel are appropriate. Suggest to the children that they decorate their journals with pictures or designs, to make these books special and also easy to recognize as their own.

3. Describe to children how they can make entries in their journal. You might suggest a specific exercise, just to help them get started. For example, you could try a warm-up such as this: Ask the children to open their journals and on the first page scribble or doodle anything they want. Next, ask children to look at their doodles carefully and label what they see. Do they see a shape? A familiar object like a tree, a face, or an animal? Circulate around the room, helping children label their first entry.

4. Tell children that the journals will always be available for their use. Every so often, have children go back through their journals to review previous entries. Discuss entries with individual children or with the entire class.

Notes to the Teacher:

Encourage children to use their journals for private reflection—to express their feelings, voice ideas when no one is available to listen, or record events that they want to remember. Children can write in their journals during free time, when they are waiting for a turn at other activities, or when they have completed a project early. You also can set aside a few minutes for journal writing each day. Or, you can use the journals in a more structured fashion, giving the children specific topics to write about. In *The Creative Journal for Children: A Guide for Parents, Teachers and Counselors,* Lucia Capacchione makes these (and many more) suggestions: Draw and write about one of your dreams; describe one of your heroes; pretend you are granted a wish; draw a self-portrait and complete the phrase, "I am _____."

□ WHAT AM I? BOOK

Objective: Use What Am I? book to practice writing and self-expression

Core Components: Writing/invented narrative/descriptive language, with emphasis on
                       Imagination and originality
                       Accurate labeling and description
                       Interest in explaining how things work

Materials: Magazines
                       What Am I? book
                       Scissors
                       Glue or tape

Procedures:

1. To prepare for this activity, choose two photographs or illustrations from magazines that you would like to use as a model for the What Am I? book. The photos can be of anything that you cannot identify or that you think would be a challenge for children to identify and describe (for example, unfamiliar animals, foods, or machines).

2. Show children the What Am I? book. Model how children can make their own entries. Look through the magazines, explaining that you are looking for pictures of things that you don't know the name of or that you're not sure quite what they are used for.

3. Cut out and glue one picture into the What Am I? book. Lift the book up so that the children can see the picture, and ask, What am I? (Or, What do you think this is? What do you think this might be used for?) Write children's suggestions on the opposite page and display their comments.

4. Repeat the picture search, cutting, pasting and identifying another picture. Make some imaginative suggestions about what it might be, such as, "This is a pizza from Mars!" Then, let children look through the magazines and cut out their own mystery items.

5. Pass the What Am I? book around and help children paste their entries into the book, leaving room for comments. Tell children that they can also write down guesses about their own and others' mystery objects. Circulate around the room, continuing the discussion. Keep the book available for children to use throughout the year.

☐ THE CLASSROOM MAILBOX

Objective:	Develop communication skills by writing and mailing letters to classmates

Core Components:	Writing, with emphasis on
	    Imaginative or original writing
	    Use of wordplay or poetry

Materials:	Classroom mailbox Writing materials (paper, markers, pencils) Decorative items (rubber stamps, stickers) Magazines Scissors Glue or tape

Procedures:

1. Tell children that you are setting up a classroom mailbox so that they can send mail to each other and to you. They can decorate the box so that it looks like a mailbox.

2. Pair the children and have them each prepare a "letter" to the other (or, let children pick names out of a hat). Emphasize that the letter can be made from drawings, words, magazine pictures, or rubber stamps. Join in the activity, either writing a letter to an unpaired child or to the whole class.

3. Circulate around the classroom and help the children fold their letters, write the recipient's name on the outside, and "mail" them in the classroom mailbox.

4. Choose letter carriers. Help them deliver letters. The children will read their mail with great enjoyment, especially if they have not seen it already.

5. Leave the mailbox in the room so that children can send each other letters anytime.

Variations:

1. Write a letter as a group. Let children write or draw their own versions of the letter and mail them to classmates. Possible topics include class announcements, birthday wishes, and holiday greetings (be sure to present holidays from different cultures).

2. As children become more comfortable with letter writing, encourage them to work on specific themes on their own (such as get well, birthday, or holiday cards). Children can write to classmates and mail the letters in the classroom mailbox, or take letters home to family members. You may wish to encourage children to spell words their own way, then ask an adult to help "edit" their work.

3. At different times throughout the year, suggest that children write a letter, either as a group or independently, to an individual outside the classroom. You might suggest that they write:
   - to a child in another country
   - to a sick friend
   - to thank a class visitor
   - to invite someone to your classroom
   - to current heroes or favorite TV characters
   - to the president about an important issue.

☐ "A House is a House for . . ."

Objective: Practice writing descriptively and imaginatively

Core Components: Writing/invented narrative, with emphasis on:
Imagination and originality
Elaborate description
Word invention

Materials: "A _____ is a house for _____" sheets
Writing and drawing materials"

Procedures:

1. If available, read children the book *A House is a House for Me* by Mary Ann Hoberman. Discuss different types of homes for different types of creatures. Give each child a sheet of paper for drawing, with the words "A _____ is a house for _____" written across the bottom.

2. Explain to children that they should use their imagination to fill in the blanks. Give examples: "Let's say I filled in the first blank space with the word *house*. A house is a house for. . . ." Wait for children's responses. "That's right. A house is a house for people. In this space I would draw a house, and maybe a person or family in the window or standing next to the house." Encourage children to suggest other examples and ways to make the drawing complete.

3. Finally, suggest a nonsense creature. "Now what I think is fun about this activity is that I can make up an animal and its home. Let's say I fill in the blank with the word *slump*. A [*blank*] is a house for a slump. Do you know what a slump is? It's my pretend animal. And I'm going to say that my slump lives in a . . . tweezle! So in this space I'm going to draw a slump, which is a big huge bug, in its tweezle, its house made out of bits of grass and gummy bears."

4. Encourage children to fill in their own sheets, using either a real or pretend person or animal. Circulate around the room to help children get started. Later, you can collect the finished drawings into a book and give each child a chance to take the book home.

Variations:

1. Extend the activity by replacing *house* with other things. For example:

   A _____ is food for _____

   _____ is clothing for _____

2. Make up creative writing sheets with lots of different sentences for children to complete. You can focus the sentences around a theme, such as favorite things, trips, family members, hobbies, or pets.

☐ MAKE YOUR OWN BOOK

Objective: Make a picture book, complete with original drawings and captions

Materials: Five or more blank sheets of paper
                     Tape or stapler
                     Crayons or markers
                     Pen or pencil

Notes to Parents:

Seeing your work in print can be quite a thrill! This activity gives your child the chance to publish a story, and to see that he or she can be an author just as many adults are authors. It also will give you a chance to see how your child organizes and tells a story. Once complete, the book can become part of a library of homemade books that your child shares with friends, brothers, and sisters. It can go to school, too.

Procedures:

1. Give your child at least five sheets of paper, and help attach the sheets with tape or staples so that they form a book.

2. Ask your child to think up a topic for a story. Recall favorite stories or events if he or she is stuck. Next, ask your child to tell the story by drawing pictures on the pages of the book with crayons or markers.

3. When your child is finished, ask him or her to tell you what each picture is about. As your child tells the story, write the sentences, one or two to a page, underneath each picture. Use your child's words only, if you can.

4. When all the pictures have captions, read the story back to your child, allowing him or her to correct you if necessary.

5. Have your child title the book and make a cover. You can help think up ideas by asking, "What would be a good title for the story? What would be a good picture on the front to make people want to read it?"

Sharing:

Have your child "read" the book to family members or friends, or take it to school if he or she wishes. It is not necessary for the words your child reads aloud to be the exact ones written on the page. The idea of organizing a story is the important part of this activity.

☐ COLOR RHYMES

Objective: Use color words to learn about rhyme

Materials: Paper
                              Pencil
                              Colored pens, markers, or crayons

Note to Parents:

Children like to play with words, and sometimes invent their own. This activity encourages children to listen closely to the sound of words, an important step in enjoying and creating poems. It uses familiar words—the names of colors—that your child may be able to read. Color rhymes allow your child to use humor and learn new words at the same time.

Procedures:

1. Ask your child to name five colors. Write the words across a page, using the appropriate color if you wish. (Colors such as purple and orange can be hard to rhyme; try starting with easy ones such as red, blue, and green.)

2. Choose a color that is easy to rhyme and ask your child, "Tell me as many words as you can think of that rhyme with the color _____." Write down the words your child says. If he or she seems stuck, pick another color (such as black) and find rhyming words together (tack, rack, pack, sack, and so forth). It's OK for your child to invent words. Ask what they mean.

3. Now read back one of the lists and ask, "Can we put some of these words together? How about a red bed? Can you put that in a sentence?" Write down your child's sentences, so that the two of you can "read" them later. Repeat the exercise with the next color.

4. If you want a little more challenge, you can see how many rhyming words you can put into a single sentence. For example, "Ted in the red bed has a cold in the head." Or, you can put rhymes together into a poem like this:

> In the red bed
> Was a man named Ted.
> He had a cold in the head.
> His brother was Fred.

Sharing:

Colors, color words, and rhyming fit very well into your child's schoolwork. Ask your child if he or she would like to bring any color rhymes to school.

RESOURCES AND REFERENCES _____

The activities on the preceding pages are just an introduction to the teaching of language. To help you explore further, we offer a brief list of resources that have proved valuable to us or to our colleagues. It is intended to provide inspiration rather than a review of the literature. Sources used in the preparation of this volume are marked with an asterisk.

* Brown, T. M., & Laminack, L. L. (1989). Let's talk a poem. *Young Children, 9,* 49–52.

* Capacchione, L. (1989). *The creative journal for children: A guide for parents, teachers, and counselors.* Boston: Shambhala.

Cazden, C. (Ed.). (1981). *Language in early childhood education.* Washington, DC: National Association for the Education of Young Children.

Cole, J.(Ed.). (1994). *A new treasury of children's poetry.* New York: Doubleday.

* DeVries, R., & Kohlberg, L. (1987). *Constructivist early education: Overview and comparison with other programs.* Washington, DC: National Association for the Education of Young Children.

Fox, M. (1984). *Teaching drama to young children.* Portsmouth, NH: Heineman.

Graves, D. (1992). *Explore poetry.* Portsmouth, NH: Heineman.

Harper, B. (Ed.).(1993). *Bringing children to literacy: Classrooms that work.* Norwood, MA: Christopher-Gordon.

Heard, G. (1989). *For the good of the earth and sun.* Portsmouth, NH: Heineman.

Heinig, R. (1992). *Improvisation with favorite tales: Integrating drama into the reading and writing classroom.* Portsmouth, NH: Heineman.

* Hohmann, M., Banet, B., & Weikert, D. (1979). *Young children in action.* Ypsilanti, MI: High/Scope Press.

Holdaway, D. (1979). *The foundations of literacy.* New York: Ashton Scholastic.

* Hopkins, L. (1987). *Pass the poetry please!* New York: Harper & Row.

Koch, K. (1970) *Wishes, lies, and dreams.* New York: Chelsea House.

Maehr, J. (1991). *High/Scope K–3 curriculum series: Language and literacy.* Ypsilanti, MI: High/Scope Press.

Mallan, K. (1992). *Children as storytellers.* Portsmouth, NH: Heineman.

McClure, A., with Harrison, P., & Reed, S. (1990). *Sunrises and songs: Reading and writing in an elementary classroom.* Portsmouth, NH: Heineman.

* Paley, V. G. (1981). *Wally's stories.* Cambridge, MA: Harvard University Press.

* Pangrazi, R., & Dauer, V. (1981). *Movement in early childhood and primary education.* Minneapolis, MN: Burgess.

Raines, S. C. & Canady, R. J. (1989) *Story s-t-r-e-t-c-h-e-r-s: Activities to expand children's favorite books.* Mount Rainier, MD: Gryphon House.

Schickedanz, J. (1986). *More than the ABCs: The early stages of reading and writing.* Washington, DC: National Association for the Education of Young Children.

* Sloan, G. D. (1984). *The child as critic: Teaching literature in elementary and middle school* (2nd ed.). New York: Teachers College Press.

Strickland, D. & Morrow, L. (1989). *Emerging literacy: Young children learn to read and write.* Newark, DE: International Reading Association.

VISUAL ARTS ACTIVITIES

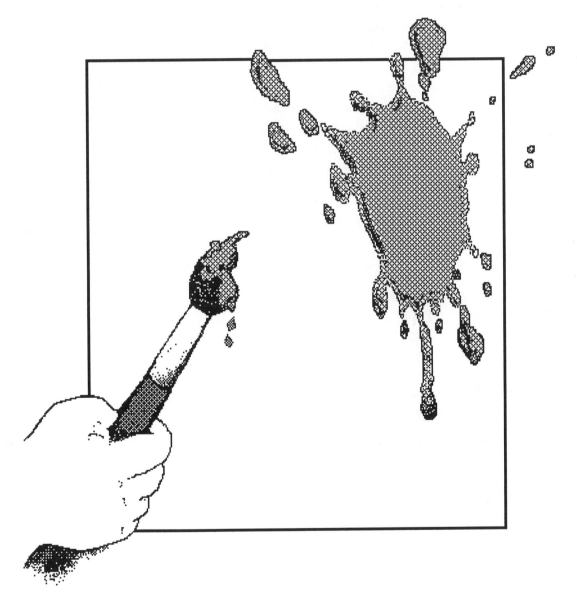

TABLE OF CONTENTS

Introduction

An Overview of the Visual Arts Activities 227

Description of Key Abilities 229

Visual Arts Activities

Art Perception Activities

Shape Search 230

Texture Rubbing 231

Sensory Learning 232

Black-and-White Photo Exhibit 233

Looking at Nature Up Close 234

Sorting Art Reproduction Cards 235

Exploration of Style and Technique 236

Art Production Activities

Representation

Drawing without and with a Model 237

Looking and Drawing 238

Drawing from Different Viewpoints 239

Making a Classroom Model 240

Artistry

Constructing an Art Portfolio 241

Color Mixing with Different Media 242

Tissue Paper Collage 243

Let's Print Greeting Cards 244

Exploration

Assembling a Nature Scene 245

Puppets 246

Straw Blowing with Paint 247

String Painting 248

Take-Home Activities

1 Shapes All Around 249

2 Textures All Around 250

3 Texture Art 251

Resources and References 252

An Overview of the Visual Arts Activities

The artist views the world with trained eyes, sensitive to nuances of line, color, texture, composition. This guide is designed to help children begin to develop the artist's powers of observation and creation. The activities included in the first section, Art Perception, are intended to help children become more sensitive observers of the visual world and of work by practicing artists.

The second section of this guide, Art Production, offers a variety of activities to help children use their growing knowledge of pattern, color, and other visual characteristics to create their own work. The activities help children develop the skills they need to translate their ideas into physical form with a feeling of success: representational ability; artistry, or imagination; and a willingness to explore and take risks. Generally, these categories begin with two or three "dry and tidy" activities involving few liquids, followed by activities that might be called "wet and messy." However, this sequence can easily be adapted to meet your own interests and needs as well as those of your students.

In addition to participating in structured activities, children need the chance to experiment with art materials in their own way and at their own pace. This type of free play gives children a chance for self-expression, a sense of the variety of effects that can be achieved with different media, and the opportunity to develop the experience and skills necessary to manipulate art materials and tools with ease.

Materials can be made available to children in an art area or learning center after you have explained or modeled some basic techniques, such as how to wipe a brush on a sponge to remove excess water, how to mix colors, how to rinse a brush so as not to contaminate new colors, and how to attach two pieces of clay by wetting and scraping together the surfaces to be joined. Once they master these how-to skills, children will be better able to represent their ideas successfully and creatively.

You can expand children's sensory experience by offering as wide a variety of materials as possible. Help children discover the difference between painting with tempera paints and watercolors, on a flat surface and at an easel, with a brush and with their fingers. Finger painting is great—it not only encourages children to use their large and small muscles to explore lines and shapes, but also helps them release emotional tension.

You also can show children how to use familiar materials in new ways. They might use glue to draw a picture, holding the container like a pencil. Then they could shake sand, salt, glitter, or chalk flakes over their glue drawing. Encourage them to experiment with different ways to use chalk: rubbing it over sand to make the sand different colors; dipping the end into a mixture of sugar and water or milk to produce an effect like paint; or simply using the long side, rather than the pointed end, to apply a broad swath of color.

Be sure to supply materials that children can use to work in three, as well as two, dimensions. Block building is a good way to start; children must think about balance as well as composition. Encourage them to walk around any structure they have built, to see it from different angles. You can also gather a group of children in a circle around the structure and encourage them to say what it looks like from different viewpoints. Next, children can create sculptures by stacking or gluing together a variety of boxes, tubes, straws, berry baskets, and other recyclables. Or, they can push pipe cleaners, bottle caps, paper clips, and other items into a ball of clay or a piece of Styrofoam. Encourage children to build things both from the real world and from their imaginations.

In the Spectrum classrooms, we collected children's artwork throughout the year and reviewed it periodically, to enable both the child and the teacher to see the child's artistic development over time and to note any strong preferences of subject matter or media. If you would like try this approach, you can show children how to make and decorate their own portfolios early in the year (see Constructing an Art Portfolio, p. 241) and then use the portfolios for saving work.

Since most children start drawing and scribbling as soon as they can hold a crayon, they enter school with a range of experiences and opinions about art. One way of introducing the art area is to discuss these experiences.

For example, you might ask the children to talk about the kinds of artwork they have done before, their favorite art media or tools, and any other ideas they have about art. Also ask them whether they have been to a fine arts museum, what they thought about the museum, and what impressed them most.

If possible, invite the school art specialist or local artists to the classroom. They could show their artwork, including unfinished work and scribbles. They could also tell children how they started working in art, how they was trained, and how their style and interests developed, perhaps sharing their own childhood artwork. Personal stories will help children understand that in creating artwork, the process can be as important as the product—and that art is fun as well as hard work.

You can also show children some materials you have for art activities, such as different brushes, papers of different textures and colors, and recycled items. Ask children for their ideas on how to use the recycled items. Write down these ideas and tell the children that they will be able to try them out later.

Next, you can introduce the art portfolio. Explain that it will help children to collect samples of their work, so that they can compare the work they do now with the work they will do over the next few months. They will be amazed at the progress they make. Tell children that if they wish, they can bring the portfolio home to show their parents, or have a classroom art exhibit at the end of year.

Visual Arts: Perception

- aware of visual elements in the environment and in artwork (e.g., color, lines, shapes, patterns, detail)

- sensitive to different artistic styles (e.g., can distinguish abstract art from realism, impressionism, etc.)

Visual Arts: Production

Representation

- able to represent visual world accurately in two or three dimensions

- able to create recognizable symbols for common objects (e.g., people, vegetation, houses, animals) and coordinate elements spatially into unified whole

- uses realistic proportions, detailed features, deliberate choice of color

Artistry

- able to use various elements of art (e.g., line, color, shape) to depict emotions, produce certain effects, and embellish drawings or three-dimensional work

- conveys strong mood through literal representation (e.g., smiling sun, crying face) and abstract features (e.g., dark colors or drooping lines to express sadness); produces drawings or sculptures that appear "lively," "sad," or "powerful"

- shows concern with decoration and embellishment

- produces drawings that are colorful, balanced, rhythmic, or all of these

Exploration

- flexible and inventive in use of art materials (e.g., experiments with paint, chalk, clay)

- uses lines and shapes to generate a wide variety of forms (e.g., open and closed, explosive and controlled) in two-dimensional or three-dimensional work

- able to execute a range of subjects or themes (e.g., people, animals, buildings, landscapes)

□ SHAPE SEARCH

Objective:	Identify specific shapes used in artwork
Core Components:	Art perception Awareness of shape as element of design
Materials:	Black, gray, or white construction paper Art reproductions (books, postcards, or posters)

Procedures:

1. Give children black, gray, or white construction paper and encourage them to cut out a variety of shapes, such as circles, ovals, rectangles, triangles, and half-circles.

2. Hold up the shapes and ask children to identify them. Have children look for examples of these geometric shapes in the classroom. Or, if they close their eyes, can they think of any classroom items of the same shape?

3. Give children two or three shapes and ask them to find similar shapes in reproductions of paintings, sculptures, and other works.

4. Encourage children to look for patterns in the paintings and for the different ways that artists use and create geometric shapes. Ask children questions such as, What shapes do you see in this artist's work? Do artists group items in their paintings to make shapes? (For example, do they cluster people, trees, or other objects to form a triangle?) How does the artist use the same shape to form different objects?

5. Provide tempera painting materials. Let children explore the use of shapes in their own art work.

Variations:

1. Ask children to use their bodies to make different shapes. For instance, they can use their fingers, mouth, arms, and whole body to make a circle. Ask children to find a partner and make a circle with him or her. Have the class together make a giant circle, small circle, and medium-sized circle. How can they change the circle into a triangle or a square?

2. Give each child a paper towel or toilet paper tube; colored, transparent paper; and a rubber band. By covering one end of the tube with the paper and fastening it with the rubber band, children can make a play telescope. Children may look around the classroom through their "telescopes." Ask children the shapes and colors of the things they see.

☐ TEXTURE RUBBING

Objective:	Learn about texture through texture study and crayon rubbings
Core Components:	Art perception Sensitivity to texture
Materials:	Large crayons with paper peeled off Newsprint, thin drawing paper, or typing paper Posterboard Masking tape Bag of textured items, such as

              Wire screen   Leaves
              Sandpaper   Plastic bubble wrap
              Velcro

Procedures:

1. Prepare a sample sheet by attaching samples of textured items to a piece of posterboard, and labelling the samples. Show the class the sample sheet and ask each child to choose and identify one item.

2. Have children reach into the bag without looking and, by using their sense of touch, find the same type of item that they selected from the sample sheet. After children find the item, have them place it on the table and examine its texture using their eyes as well as hands.

3. Show children how to make a texture rubbing by placing a piece of paper over the textured item and rubbing across it several times with the long side of a peeled crayon. Their rubbings will look best if they keep the pressure even and rub over as much of the area as possible. It sometimes helps to tape the textured items to the table.

4. Ask children to compare the texture rubbing to the actual item. Collect all the texture rubbings and ask children to match the rubbings with the items they came from.

Variations:

1. Let children cut out their texture rubbings and glue them on a background sheet to make an individual or group collage. Or, make booklets (cut typing or copying paper in half, put several pieces in a stack, fold the stack in half, and staple on the crease) and glue the texture rubbings onto the pages.

2. Encourage children to bring in textured objects from home. The class can then make its own bag of textured items and sample sheet, and repeat the activity with the new items.

3. Ask children to collect textured items in the environment during a nature walk or outdoor playtime. They can sort the items according to their own categories, then create bags of items and sample sheets with themes like "Natural Textures" or "Artificial Textures."

4. Look at reproductions of different drawings and paintings with the class and discuss the use of texture. You might include the following questions:
    *   What different textures can you find in these paintings?
    *   How did the artist use lines to show these textures?
    *   Can you use a pencil and paper to show how a line would look if it were smooth? bumpy? rough? jagged? wiggly? sharp? a little bumpy? very bumpy?

□ SENSORY LEARNING

Objective:	Explore the notion that using the senses helps you better understand objects
Core Components:	Awareness of different features of objects
Materials:	Objects that can be looked at, touched, listened to, smelled, or tasted

Procedures:

1. Present the objects and ask children to sort them. Ask children to tell the group the categories they used for sorting.

2. Acknowledge children's way of sorting. If the way that we sense the objects has not been used, tell children that you have another set of categories—our five senses: touch, hearing, sight, smell, and taste.

3. Ask children how our senses might help us better know or understand an object. Explain that the more we know about the things we are drawing or sculpting, the better the picture or sculpture we can make. For example, we might draw a better apple if we could see, feel, smell, and taste the apple. If possible, show artwork that illustrates this point (e.g., work by Henri Matisse, John James Audubon, Georgia O'Keeffe).

4. Ask children to draw an apple without a model. Next, let children look at, touch, smell, and taste an apple, then ask them to draw the apple again. Encourage children to talk about the differences they saw and felt when they drew the second picture.

Variation:

Many different places or objects can be used to create a "before-and-after" type of experience. Children begin by drawing, then "experience" the object through the senses, then draw again. For example, they might taste a hot pepper and find out how spicy it is, or ring a bell and figure out how it works.

☐ BLACK-AND-WHITE PHOTO EXHIBIT

Objective:	Increase sensitivity to black-and-white representations
Core Components:	Sensitivity to artistic styles
	Sensitivity to shapes, shadows, lines, and other aspects of black-and-white photographs.
Materials:	Magazines (preferably photo or art magazines with black-and-white photos)
	Scissors
	Black posterboard or a large piece of black paper
	White paper
	Black pen
	Glue

Procedures:

1. Ask children to look through the magazines and cut out black-and-white photos that they like. Remind them to look only for black-and-white photos.

2. Study the photos with children and explain that when photography was first invented all photographs were black and white; there were no color photos. At present, we still enjoy black and white photography for several reasons. For instance, our eyes are more likely to focus on the shapes and shadows in a photograph when it has no colors. We often can see people's facial expressions more clearly. And there is more left to the viewer's imagination.

3. Let children make additional comments on the pros and cons of color versus black and white photographs.

4. Encourage students to work in small groups to make an exhibit of black-and-white photographs. First, each group should select four or five photographs that relate to each other. Children can arrange them on the background paper and imagine a story tying them together. Ask questions such as, If there are people in your photos, who are they? How do they know each other, if they do? What is happening now? What happens next? How do the photos make you feel?

5. Encourage children to use white paper and a black pen to write a short caption for each photo, or a story explaining how the photos relate to each other. Glue the photos and captions to the black background. Put the posters on the wall and have a photo exhibit.

Variations:

1. You can use real photos instead of magazines for this activity. Most antique and consignment stores have collections of old black-and-white photos. Parents also might be able to provide some photos of themselves or ancestors.

2. If you or any parents are willing to lend a camera for a day, you can show children how to take their own photographs. Children can take some pictures of classroom objects with black- and-white film and then with color film. Later, ask them to examine the black-and-white photographs and guess what colors the different objects are, based on the quality of tone in the photo. For instance, a dark color would appear black. Next, ask children to compare the black-and-white pictures with the color photographs of the same objects. How do the photos compare to each other? to the real object?

☐ LOOKING AT NATURE UP CLOSE

Objective: Explore differences in the way objects look close up and from a distance

Core Components: Art perception
Attention to detail
Sensitivity to different art styles

Materials: Reproductions of paintings by Georgia O'Keeffe
Nature items (flowers, leaves, etc.)
Magnifying glass
Oak tag
Paint and brushes, markers or colored pencils

Procedures:

1. Show children a reproduction of an O'Keeffe painting (one of her magnified flowers would be best). See if the students can describe what it represents.

2. Discuss O'Keeffe's painting style. Ask children what they think is the purpose of magnifying an object or part of an object in painting.

3. Divide the class into small groups and give each group a leaf, flower, or other nature item (or, if supplies allow, give each child her own item). Ask the children to make a drawing or painting of their entire nature item.

4. Ask children to make a representation of just one part of the nature item, such as a flower petal. Children can use an oak tag "window" to help choose which part to draw. (A window is a piece of oak tag with the center cut out to a desired size, like a picture frame.)

5. Have children look at their nature item through a magnifying glass. Ask children to observe carefully the part they just drew, then draw the part over again based on the magnified view.

6. Encourage children to draw the whole item again and compare their four drawings. Discuss with children the differences between their two drawings of the item as a whole, as well as between their two close-up drawings.

Notes to the Teacher:

Like the next two activities, this exercise explores the different ways artists see and interpret the visual world—and how works of art can introduce us to new ways of thinking about objects that surround us every day. We used reproductions of paintings by Georgia O'Keeffe, but we hope you will select any artist whose work you enjoy and feel comfortable working with.

☐ SORTING ART REPRODUCTION CARDS

Objective: Increase awareness of different artistic styles

Core Components: Sensitivity to different artistic styles
Ability to recognize specific artwork/artists

Materials: Postcards of paintings by different artists representing a range of styles.

Procedures:

1. Have children sort postcards of paintings into categories that they think are meaningful. Encourage children to sort the paintings in more than one way.

2. Discuss with children the categories they selected, such as subject, shape, color, mood, artist, or styles of art. If children need prompting, suggest these or other categories.

3. Ask children to identify their favorite paintings and to give reasons why. Share information about the different artists, including the subjects they painted most often, their most famous paintings, and particular styles they used.

Variation:

Play recordings of various styles of music and ask children to select a painting or two that best suits the music. Discuss similarities and differences in the paintings that the children selected.

Notes to the Teacher:

1. When showing paintings to the groups as a whole, you may wish to use slides rather than postcards because of their greater accuracy and larger size.

2. Postcards of paintings can be kept in a box or other accessible location for children to use independently at other times during the day.

3. Postcard and poster-size reproductions generally are available through art stores or art museum shops; calendars and notecards are other sources of fine art from different cultures. Other resources include *Mommy, It's a Renoir!* by Aline Wolf, an art appreciation curriculum that can be ordered, along with various sets of art postcards, through the publisher.

☐ EXPLORATION OF STYLE AND TECHNIQUE

Objective:	Explore and experiment with different artistic techniques
Core Components:	Art perception
	Sensitivity to different artistic styles
Materials:	Reproductions of work by Seurat, Mondrian, Homer, or other artists (see previous page)

Procedures:

1. Show children reproductions of work by Seurat, Mondrian, and Homer (or other artists you have selected). Ask if anyone sees differences in the way each artist paints. Discuss these differences.

2. Discuss the reasons that artists paint in different styles. You might explain that in the field of art, there is no one right way to paint, draw, or depict the world. Each artist sees the world in a personal, individual way that he or she is sharing with the viewer. Some artists may be most interested in color; others, in how objects look from different angles; still others, in creating an emotional response or communicating an idea.

3. Talk with the children about the different techniques and styles used in the paintings you selected. For example, introduce the concept of pointillism through Seurat (*Sunday Afternoon on the Island of La Grand Jatte* is a good example), cubism through Mondrian (*Composition in Red, Yellow, and Blue*), and American realism through Homer (*Boys in a Pasture*). (See Notes to the Teacher.)

4. Show the children other paintings by the same artists, but let them figure out which artist painted each one.

5. If you do this activity in the winter or spring, children will have had a chance to collect artwork in their portfolios. Let them review their work, trying to identify something special about their own styles (such as favorite subjects, favorite colors, use of particular details).

Notes to the Teacher:

In this activity, Seurat, Mondrian, and Homer are used as examples of particular artistic styles. Please feel free to substitute other styles, eras, or individual artists. A school art specialist may even be able to demonstrate different styles for the children, for example, showing how different-colored dots can form a face (pointillism). Then, children can experiment with painting in the technique (or techniques) themselves.

Sample definitions follow:

- Pointillism: A painting technique characterized by the application of paint in small dots that blend together when seen from a distance.
- Cubism: An early 20th-century school of painting and sculpture in which the subject matter is portrayed by geometric forms without realistic detail.
- American Realism: A painting technique that attempts to be visually accurate.

☐ DRAWING WITHOUT AND WITH A MODEL

Objective:	Compare drawing with and without a model
Core Components:	Representational ability Attention to detail
Materials:	Carton of small labeled boxes, each containing a three-dimensional object (e.g., leaf, paper clip, and pencil)

Procedures:

1. Choose one box from the carton and read the contents listed on the box. Do not open the box.

2. Ask children to draw this item from their memory or imaginations.

3. Ask children to label the drawings with their names, with the item's name, and the words *from memory*. Collect the drawings.

4. Open the box, and place the item on a table in front of children. Encourage children to take a moment to observe and study the item. Elicit children's comments on the shape, color, and texture of the item.

5. Now ask children to make another drawing of the object. Place the item in front of the children so that they can observe it carefully while drawing. Encourage children to put as much detail into the drawing as possible in terms of color, line, texture, and shape.

6. Ask children to label this drawing with the name of the item and the words from *observation*, and to sign their names.

7. Return the first drawings to the children and have them compare their two versions. Ask children questions such as:

    - What did you rely on when you drew something without looking at it?
    - Did the drawing improve after you observed the item?
    - Why might that be?
    - Do we usually draw better and with more detail after we take time to observe an item closely?

Notes to the Teacher:

Try to choose objects that are relatively familiar to the children and not too difficult to draw. During other classroom times, encourage children to work individually or in small groups on drawing other objects. Suggest that they draw the item first without a model, then with a model, and finally compare the two.

☐ Looking and Drawing

Objective:	Draw an object while looking only at the object
Core Components:	Representational ability
	Composition
	Attention to detail
Materials:	Drawing paper
	Marker or pencil
	Blinder box

Procedures:

1. Introduce the activity by asking children to think about the previous activity, Representational Drawing Without and With a Model. Emphasize the importance of studying carefully the lines and shape of the objects they want to draw.

2. Tell children that sometimes they might get a better idea of how to draw something by looking less at their paper and more at the object they are drawing. Ask children if they agree, and why or why not.

3. Let children experiment (this technique requires practice). Hold up a drawing of a circle, square, or triangle. Ask children to draw the model without looking at the paper or their hands.

3. Ask children to select any small or medium-sized object in the classroom that they would like to draw. Place the object in front of the children, or let the children sit in front of the object.

4. Ask children to study the object carefully and notice the lines and shape before they start to draw. Also ask children to keep their eyes on the object as they draw.

5. Suggest to children that they try putting their pencils on the paper, making the first line and then continuing on with the entire drawing without ever lifting the pencil from the paper. Some children may wish to use a "blinder box" to keep themselves from looking at their work in progress; however, they do not need to use it if they find it too frustrating. A blinder box is a box about 12" square, open on the bottom and front, which can be placed over a child's drawing to allow freedom of movement but to prevent the child from seeing her hands or work.

6. Guide children's reflections on the activity. You might discuss why knowing the details of objects is important for representational drawing; how drawing without looking at the paper can help people notice more detail; and how that in turn helps the artist make a drawing that looks more like the object.

Notes to the Teacher:

Encourage children by explaining that at first it can be hard to draw an object without looking down at their hands, but that as they practice it will get easier and easier. This message is important to give from the beginning so that children do not give up out of an initial sense of frustration.

☐

☐ DRAWING FROM DIFFERENT VIEWPOINTS

Objective:	Become aware that objects look different from different perspectives
Core Components:	Representational ability Awareness of different perspectives
Materials:	Drawing paper Crayons A box that is a different color on each side

Procedures:

1. Arrange the desks in a circle around the multicolored box so that each child sees the box from a different angle.

2. Ask children to use the crayons to draw a picture of the box, using only the colors that they can see from where they are sitting.

3. When all the drawings are complete, display and compare them. Ask children questions such as:

   - What colors could you see from where you were sitting?
   - Why is your drawing different from those of the other children, both in color and in the way the box looks?
   - When you look at a particular drawing, do you know where the child who drew it was sitting?

Variations:

1. You can prepare a special introduction for this activity by shooting a series of photographs of one object from different angles. Show children the photos and discuss how the outline, shape, and colors change depending on the angle.

2. For a more challenging activity, ask children to choose an object in the classroom and draw it from different perspectives.

☐ Making a Classroom Model

Objective:	Construct a scaled-down model of the classroom
Core Components:	Representational ability in three dimensions
	Awareness of spatial relations

Materials:

Small boxes	Markers or crayons
Cardboard	Recycled items
Fabric scraps	Scissors
Wood scraps	Tape
Glue	
Sturdy cardboard box	

Procedures:

1. Work with a small group of volunteers to draw a map of the classroom. Guide children in identifying the key features of the room (doors, windows, desks, blackboard, teacher's desk, etc.). When the map is complete, let these children describe their work to the class.

2. Cut the top half off the sturdy cardboard box to make the classroom model. Divide the class into several small groups, giving each group responsibility for making certain objects to go inside. One group, for example, could decorate the box itself (e.g., cut out doors and windows, paste on felt for blackboards). Another group could make tables and chairs. (See drawing on p. 203.) Another group could make figures by cutting up photos of the teachers and students and pasting individual pictures onto wooden blocks.

3. Lead a short discussion of scaled-down models, explaining that although the model is much smaller than the original, the features retain the same size in relation to each other. For example, the chair is still smaller than the desk, and the door is still taller than the window. If you feel your class is ready, describe the concept of proportion by relating it to real objects in the classroom. For example, if the cabinet is six feet tall and the puzzle box is one foot tall, then this six-to-one relationship can be transferred to the classroom model by using a box that is six times taller than another.

4. Encourage each group to take time to plan the model and develop ideas. Ask them to consider which construction materials are best suited for different features of the room. Work with each group to make sure the proportions are appropriate and offer suggestions when needed.

5. Have each group select one representative to put its objects into the model.

Variations:

1. Let each small group make its own classroom model.

2. Let each child make a scaled-down version of her own desk and one other item in the classroom.

3. Give each child a sticker (or a small piece of colored paper). Ask her to decorate the sticker so it can be identified, then hide it someplace in the classroom. Next, give each child a piece of paper with just an outline of the room. Ask the children to turn this outline into a map that would help a friend find the sticker, showing the path from the friend's desk to the hiding place. Finally, let the friend use the map to find the sticker. This variation can be used either to introduce or to supplement construction of the classroom model.

☐ CONSTRUCTING AN ART PORTFOLIO

Objective: Make and decorate a large portfolio for collecting original artwork

Core Components: Concern for decoration and embellishment
Use of imagination
Reflection

Materials: Large sheets of oak tag
Masking tape
Scissors
Markers and crayons

Procedures:

1. Talk with children about portfolios. Why do artists keep portfolios? Why might children want to save their work? Invite the children to make and decorate personal portfolios in which they can save all their paintings and drawings. If they wish, at the end of the year they can display the work they have collected in a classroom art exhibit.

2. You can help children make the portfolios by putting together two large sheets of oak tag and taping three sides. Leave one long side (the top) open to form a large envelope.

3. Children can write their names in large letters on the front of the portfolios; help them if necessary. Explain that they can decorate their portfolios in any way that they like with the crayons and markers. If they need ideas, you might suggest drawing a self portrait, their family, their house, or a favorite real or imaginary animal.

4. From time to time ask children to reflect on the work collected in their art portfolios. Suggested topics for reflection include:

   • Which were their most favorite and least favorite art projects? Why did they like or dislike those projects?
   • Which two pieces of their artwork are the most different from each other? Why are they different? Are there any similarities?
   • How has their artwork changed over time?
   • What have they learned about themselves as artists?

☐ COLOR MIXING WITH DIFFERENT MEDIA

Objective: Experiment with mixing colors

Core Components: Sensitivity to color

Materials: Overhead projector
                        Flat, clear glass plate or transparencies
                        Eyedroppers
                        A variety of dyes

Procedures:

1. Have children experiment with color mixing during finger-painting activities. Discuss how all the wonderful colors around them can be made from the three "primary" colors: red, yellow, and blue. Ask them to create new colors — such as orange, green, and purple — by mixing together two primary colors. Encourage children to describe how they made their colors. List all the colors they combined and the new colors that resulted.

2. To show children another way of mixing colors, focus an overhead projector on a screen or white wall. Place a flat, clear glass plate or transparency on the projector. Use an eyedropper to mix drops of dye on the plate. Start with a drop of red dye and then add yellow. Add a drop of water at a time to make the colors swirl around each other in new and exciting combinations, or gently nudge the plate.

3. Children can take turns adding colors with the dropper. Between mixings, you can blot the dye from the plate with a white paper towel and display the towel as an art print.

4. Children can make a chart to show what colors appear when certain colors are mixed. Compare this chart with their finger-painting list. Repeat the experiments to verify the information on the chart.

Variations:

1. Help the class develop a color chart for tempera paints. Give each child a small empty cup, two small cups each containing a primary color, a paint brush, a piece of paper, and a pencil. Ask children to paint swatches of color on the far left and right of a piece of paper, and label each swatch with the color name. Ask children to put equal amounts of each paint into the third cup and mix. What *secondary* colors did each child make? Let them show their results on a chart for the whole class.

   Next, ask children to make *tertiary* colors by mixing together their two primary colors, but using twice as much of one color as the other. For example, they can add two spoonfuls of red to one spoonful of yellow to make the tertiary color red-orange, or add two spoonfuls of blue to one spoonful of yellow to make the tertiary color blue-green. The children can show these proportions by drawing the appropriate number of spoonfuls (or measuring cups) under each color sample on the class chart.

2. Place a large, clear plastic container filled with warm water next to a window or under a desk lamp and let it settle. Children, either by themselves or in small groups, can use an eyedropper to add food coloring to the water, then watch color drops fall gracefully down and slowly mix together. This activity is easy to clean up and set up for the next child or group.

☐ Tissue Paper Collage

Objective:	Explore the use of color to express feelings
Core Components:	Composition
	Use of color
	Expressiveness
Materials:	Tissue paper in several colors
	8 1/2" by 11" paper
	Glue (mixed with water)
	Scissors
	Brushes

Procedures:

1. Lead the group in a discussion about feelings and emotions and how they can sometimes be related to certain colors. You might mention that in our culture the word *blue* is sometimes used to describe a feeling of sadness; people traditionally wear black to funerals; and bright colors are used for happy celebrations like birthdays.

2. Divide the class into small groups and give each group a box of colored tissue paper. Ask children to select colors of tissue paper that best express how they feel today.

3. Ask children to cut or tear the tissue paper into pieces of many different sizes and shapes. Suggest they experiment with designs on the desktop. Point out the shapes that children create in the spaces that are formed between the pieces of paper.

4. Tell children that once they are satisfied with their arrangement, they can wet the background paper with the glue and water mixture, and then place the pieces of tissue on the background. They can brush more glue over the tissue if necessary to keep it attached.

5. Ask children to notice how the tissue paper changes when it is wet.
   - Does the tissue paper become more transparent when it is wet? How can you tell?
   - What happens when you overlap yellow and blue tissue paper? Does it create a new color? How about overlapping red and blue? Yellow and red?
   - Can you use these new colors to show how you feel?

6. When children finish their work and their collages are dry, hang the collages around the room and ask questions such as:
   - What feeling does this collage suggest? Can you tell how someone was feeling by looking at her collage?
   - What colors were created from other colors in this collage?
   - Do the lines in this picture make it look busy? peaceful? nervous? messy? tidy?

Variations:

This activity can be modified for multicultural education. Explain that different cultures have different associations with colors. If the class includes children from different cultures, ask them to ask their parents which colors are used in their culture to represent joy, sadness, fear, death, and so on. Or, you can ask all of the children to do a home survey and then compare and graph the results. Save the scraps of tissue paper—you can make dye by adding them to a few drops of water.

☐ Let's Print Greeting Cards

Objective:	Design and print greeting cards to explore design in functional art
Core Components:	Sense of decoration and design
	Composition
	Color exploration
Materials:	Tempera paint
	4" printing roller
	Butter knives as carving tools
	Construction paper
	Wax paper
	Scrap paper for print design drafts
	Standard envelopes
	Templates the size of greeting cards (optional)

Procedures:

1. Discuss with children the tradition of sending greeting cards for special occasions. You can ask questions such as, When do people send cards to each other? Have you ever sent a card to someone for a special occasion? Tell children that they will be making a *print,* a picture that they can use over and over again like a rubber stamp to make many cards. Emphasize that children will make their own designs to print onto cards, and that they may wish to work carefully because they will use their design many times.

2. Model the following steps for the children. First, give the children pieces of scrap paper small enough to fit into a standard envelope. Show them how to draw a greeting card design on the scrap paper. Explain that relatively simple designs will print more clearly than complex ones. Let the children practice until they are satisfied with their designs.

3. Next, help the children tape a piece of wax paper over their designs. Use the butter knife to trace the design, removing the waxy layer from the wax paper so that paint can seep through. The wax paper will now serve as the print.

4. Show the children how to make the cards by trimming construction paper down to a size which, when folded once, will fit into an envelope. You may want to make templates available, along with different-colored construction paper.

5. Each child should place the wax paper on one of the cards. Help children to roll the roller in the paint and then roll over the wax paper evenly. Lift the wax paper. The print should leave a design on the card. Children can repeat this process with several cards.

Notes to the Teacher:

1. If a clear imprint is not left on the card, the lines on the print may need to be deepened more with the knife. If necessary, you can even cut clear through the wax paper.

2. This activity can be used for holidays or seasonal greetings. If appropriate, use cardmaking as an introduction to multicultural holidays.

3. This activity can extend over two sessions or days. Create the prints and size the cards on the first day; do the actual printing on the second.

☐ ASSEMBLING A NATURE SCENE

Objective: Explore how to use natural objects to mimic real nature scenes through careful arrangement and design

Core Components: Inventive use of materials
Composition and design

Materials: Lunch bag for each child
Shallow box with clear lid (or plastic wrap) for each child
Masking tape
Construction paper
Scissors

Procedures:

1. Take a nature walk, outfitting each child with a bag. As you observe and discuss seasonal aspects of the environment (color of leaves, height of grass, etc.), ask children to collect small natural objects (small twigs, leaves, stones, weeds). Have a discussion with children after the walk about what they observed and collected.

2. Give each child a box. Ask the children to arrange the natural objects they collected in a way that represents the season or a particular site outdoors (such as a forest or meadow). Have on hand additional items that they can use for their scenes (e.g., beans and grains). Let them use construction paper, if they wish, to make the sun, birds, or other objects they could not collect.

   Point out to the children that the color and shape of natural objects are often affected by the forces of wind, rain, and sun. So, the grasses in a scene may look more natural if they all lean gently the same way as if they have been blown by the wind. The leaves and flowers might have their brightest sides facing the sun. What other types of scenes can the children create? How can they get a desired effect with their materials?

3. After children have formed their nature scenes, ask them to tape the lid over the box. Or, they can cover the entire box with plastic wrap, pull it tight, and then secure it in the back with masking tape. Encourage children to name their nature scenes.

4. Ask children how they would like to display their scenes.

☐ PUPPETS

Objective: Explore the use of different materials to make a wide array of
                         puppets

Core Components: Inventive use of materials
                         Sense of design

Materials: Styrofoam
                         Tongue depressors
                         Potatoes (for puppet heads)
                         Paper bags
                         Stuffing materials (e.g. tissue paper or Styrofoam bits)
                         Fabric
                         Buttons
                         Socks
                         Recycled materials
                         Paint
                         Paper

Procedures:

1. Brainstorm with children about ways to create a puppet. If they can read, ask the children to look in the library for different puppet-making ideas. Next, they can make a list of materials they need. Help them figure out which materials are available in the classroom and whether they need to bring supplies from home.

2. Point out during the discussion that children will need to make decisions concerning colors, media, clothing, and the features and facial expression of their puppets. Encourage children to use various materials and to make unusual choices for hair, clothes, and other parts of puppets. Suggest that the children make preliminary sketches to help them decide on the design of their puppets.

3. Give children plenty of time to make their puppets.

4. When the puppets are complete, ask children to describe them in two ways: how they made them and who or what the puppets are (e.g., their names).

5. On the next day, ask children to make a completely different puppet, using the same or different materials. Discuss their efforts once again.

Notes to the Teacher:

We suggest extending this activity over two or three sessions.

☐ STRAW BLOWING WITH PAINT

Objective:	Explore the role of the medium—straw blowing—in creating artistic effects
Core Components:	Inventive use of materials Composition Expressiveness
Materials:	Tempera paint diluted with water Soda straws Glossy paper Water basin for rinsing straws

Procedures:

1. You can start this activity with a demonstration of straw blowing, in which paint is blown onto a background so that it creates a design. Give each child a piece of glossy paper and a straw. Show the class how to pick up a drop of paint by dipping the straw into the paint, then holding a finger over the top of the straw to keep the paint in the straw.

2. Next, show the class how to blow paint through the straw onto the paper. Ask the children to try doing it themselves. Show them how air stream can control the paint movement to create free-form abstract art.

3. Tell the children that they can move the paper to create different effects such as swirls and shapes, but that they should not touch the straw to the paper or paint. They should use air alone to direct the paint. Demonstrate how to change the direction of the paint by moving the paper.

4. After rinsing the straw or getting a second one, children can drop another color of paint onto the paper. Ask children to blow on the new color so that it merges with the first in some areas. What new colors are created? What new art forms are created?

5. Discuss the project with children as they work. Encourage children to come up with their own questions and responses to other children's art work. Some possible questions or topics of discussion include:

   - What shapes and lines did you create?
   - How does the artwork make you feel?
   - Does the action of the picture "move out" from the places where the paint first touched the paper? How? Why?
   - Do the shapes formed by your paint remind you of anything?
   - If the picture does not look like something you have seen before, what words would you use to describe it?
   - Can you use straw blowing to produce a painting that you've already designed?

Notes to the Teacher:

Take special care to warn children not to inhale while straw blowing.

☐ STRING PAINTING

Objective:	Explore the role of the medium—string painting—in creating artistic effects
Core Components:	Sensitivity to artistic elements (line, shape, color) Composition Expressiveness
Materials:	Manila paper Pieces of cotton string about 14" long Tempera paint (if necessary, thin with water) Shallow dish Toothpicks

Procedures:

1. Children can use the following procedure for string painting, but it works best if you model it for them. Children can start by holding both ends of a pieces of string with one hand and dipping it into the paint. If the string floats on the surface of the paint, they can use the other hand to push the string down into the paint with a toothpick.

2. Ask children to lift the string out of the paint and place it near the center of the paper.

3. Children then fold the paper over the string and press the paper gently with one hand as they pull the string out with the other hand.

4. Ask children to unfold the paper and see the double image. Encourage children to describe the artwork they created.

5. Encourage children to continue to work on the same painting if they wish, using the same or other colors.

6. After the pieces are complete, you can discuss topics such as these:
   - What shapes and forms do you see? How do they make you feel?
   - Do these shapes and lines make the painting look busy? quiet? peaceful? active? nervous? messy? tidy?
   - Do you think you might be able to make a string picture that looks like a volcano? a storm? anger? happiness?
   - What else might you be able to create with string art?

□ SHAPES ALL AROUND

Objective:	Discover and explore basic shapes among natural and fabricated objects
Materials:	Paper
	Crayons or markers

Note to Parents:

This activity will help sharpen your child's ability to look closely at his or her environment and to discover patterns and shapes. Your child also will practice making basic shapes.

Procedures:

1. Ask your child to find a square, rectangle, triangle, circle, oval, and semicircle around the neighborhood. These shapes may be disguised as a clock face, a window, or a mountain. See how many of each your child can find.

2. Ask your child to draw pictures of the objects and outline the shapes.

3. Next, you can ask your child to identify and cut out the shapes in magazine photos.

Sharing:

Bring the drawings to class to show classmates and to display on the bulletin board.

☐ TEXTURES ALL AROUND

Objective: Become aware of and copy textures in the environment

Materials: Paper
Crayons
Objects with different textures (e.g., bricks, sand, stones, bark)

Note to Parents:

Your child will see that everything has a "feel" to it and that you can recreate each feel through artwork.

Procedures:

1. Take your child on a walk through the house or through the neighborhood. From time to time, ask your child to close his or her eyes and touch different objects—rugs, tiles, bricks, grass, tree trunks—paying attention to how different they feel.

2. Place a sheet of paper over each of the objects. Ask your child to rub a crayon back and forth over the paper until a pattern shows up. Help label each rubbing so that your child can remember what it was.

3. Your child can make a chart by pasting the rubbings onto a piece of cardboard or posterboard. Or, your child can staple the rubbings together to make a booklet. Ask your child to explain how he or she has arranged the rubbings. Are they grouped by texture? by color? by size?

Sharing:

Your child can take the chart or booklet to school to share with classmates. Or, your child can make a game by leaving the labels off the chart or booklet and writing them on separate slips of paper instead. In class, the other children can match the labels to the rubbings.

☐ TEXTURE ART

Objective: Help your child use his or her knowledge of textures to make abstract or realistic drawings

Materials: Paper
Crayons or markers
Materials with different textures (e.g., cotton balls, string, bark, sandpaper)

Note to Parents:

Awareness of the "feel" of things and the way that textures make patterns can help children use textures in their own artwork. Watch how your child's ability to represent common objects and to create new shapes is developing.

Procedures:

1. Ask your child to collect objects outside and around the house that have different textures, such as leaves, sand, grass, sponges, or pieces of cloth.

2. Ask your child to figure out a way to use these items to make a picture that shows where the items came from. For example, your child could use bark and leaves to make a tree, or pebbles to make a mountain.

3. Let your child use the other items to create a make-believe picture. He or she could use a cotton ball for a cloud or sandpaper for a beach, or make a design out of torn-up bits of cloth and paper.

Sharing:

The pictures can be hung in the classroom, or shown to your child's teacher, classmates, or friends. Your child could bring to class a bag of items you've collected and let classmates try to make pictures with them.

RESOURCES AND REFERENCES

The activities on the preceding pages are just an introduction to the field. To help you conduct further explorations in the teaching of visual arts, we offer a brief list of resources that have proved valuable to us or to our colleagues. It is intended to offer inspiration rather than a review of the literature. Sources used in the preparation of this volume are marked with an asterisk.

Barnes, R. (1989). Current issues in art and design education: From entertainment to qualitative experience. *Journal of Art and Design Education, 8*(3), 247–55.

Cherry, C. (1972). *Creative art for the developing child.* Carthage, DE: Ferron Teacher's Aids.

* Cohen, E. P., & Gainer, S. R. (1984). *Art: Another language for learning.* New York: Schocken.

Engel, B. (1995). *Considering children's art: Why and how to value their works.* Washington, DC: National Association of Education for Young Children.

Gardner, H. (1980). *Artful scribbles: The significance of children's drawings.* New York: Basic Books.

Hart, K. (1988). *I can draw!* Portsmouth, NH: Heinemann.

Hart, K. (1994). *I can paint!* Portsmouth, NH: Heinemann.

* Haskell, L. L. (1979). *Art in the early childhood years.* Columbus, OH: Merrill.

* Herberholz, B. (1974). *Early childhood art.* Dubuque, IA: W. C. Brown.

* Ingram, B. K. (1975). *The workshop approach to classroom interest centers.* West Nyack, NY: Parker.

Kohl, M. (1989). *Mudworks: Creative clay, dough, and modeling experiences.* Bellingham, WA: Bright Ring.

Kohl, M., & Potter, J. (1993). *ScienceArts.* Bellingham, WA: Bright Ring.

Lasky, L. ,& Mukerji-Bergeson, R. (1980). *Art: Basic for young children.* Washington, DC: National Association of Education for Young Children.

* Linderman, E., & Herberholz, B. (1970). *Developing artistic and perceptual awareness: Art practice in the elementary classroom.* (2nd ed.) Dubuque, IA: W. C. Brown.

Rowe, G. (1987). *Guiding young artists: Curriculum ideas for teachers.* South Melbourne, Australia: Oxford University Press (distributed by Heinemann, Portsmouth, NH).

Schirrmacher, R. (1988). *Art and creative development for young children.* Albany: Delmar.

* Stephens, L. S. (1984). *The teacher's guide to open education.* New York: Holt, Reinhart, & Winston.

* Thomas, J. (1990). *Masterpiece of the month.* Huntington Beach, CA: Teacher Created Materials.

Venezia, M. (1993). *Getting to know the world's greatest artists: Georgia O'Keeffe.* Chicago: Children's Press.

Wilson, B., & Wilson, M. (1982). *Teaching children to draw: A guide for teachers and parents.* Englewood, NJ: Prentice Hall.

* Wolf, A. (1984). *Mommy, It's a Renoir!* Available from Parent Child Press, P. O. Box 675, Hollidaysburg, PA 16648 (814-696-5712).